ISAAC POLVI

The Autobiography of
a Finnish Immigrant

Edited by
Joseph Damrell

North Star Press of St. Cloud

Library of Congress Cataloging-in-Publication Data

Polvi, Isaac, 1878-1951.
      Isaac Polvi : the autobiography of a Finnish immigrant / edited by
Joseph Damrell ; [translated from the Finnish by Alex Sironen].
      208 p. 23 cm.
      ISBN: 0-87839-066-9 : $12.95
      1. Polvi, Isaac, 1878-1951.   2. Finnish Americans — Michigan —
Upper Peninsula — Biography.   3. Upper Peninsula (Mich.) — Biog-
raphy.   I. Damrell, Joseph.   II. Title.
      F572.N8P65   1991
      977.4'904945402—dc20   91-35581
      [B]   CIP

Cover Painting: Rick Kurki, *Kävelyllä*, *(Walking)* 1991.

Selection from *"The Ninth Elegy,"* (page xii) by Rainer Maria Rilke. *The Selected Poetry of Rainer Maria Rilke*, edited and translated by Stephen Mitchell.
New York: Vintage Books, Random House, Inc., 1989.

Design: Corinne A. Dwyer

Published by North Star Press of St. Cloud, Inc., P.O. Box 451, St. Cloud,
Minnesota 56302. Printed in the United States of America.

ISBN: 0-87839-066-9

Acknowledgements

Many people supported this project, and I am deeply indebted to them. Alex Sironen's translation efforts constituted a labor of love that made what followed possible. The late Kenneth Grant and Carl Bylkas told me about Isaac Polvi's writing of the manuscript, as did Ernie Bylkas and Lydia Grant. Lydia also showed me copies of excerpts that appeared in a Finnish language newspaper. The late Alex Kurki discussed the manuscript with me many times, and Bertha Kurki not only searched the records of Finnish organizations, but made herself available to me as my Finnish language consultant and translated a song that appears in the text. Rick Kurki's painting, which I commissioned for the book, derived from his study of the Tolstoy-influenced painters known as "The Itinerants" who, in the nineteenth century, wandered the country-side of Russia painting the peasantry. I am in awe of Rick's talent and greatly appreciative of his contribution to this project.

Colleagues and friends who encouraged me and thus helped me to maintain my enthusiasm for this project include: Bennett M. Berger, Lee Merrill, Patricia Shifferd, Larry Reynolds, Alice Littlefield, Albert and Irene Blakely, James and Cheryl Fisher, Rick Penn, Malcolm McLean, David Kurki, Don Albrecht, Al Subera, Bruce Hackett, and John Snider. Gerald and Senia Hendrickson and Mary Hokens of Ewen, Michigan, filled me in on a lot of detail about the Polvi family farm, and my brother, James Damrell, and sister, Judith Preble, shared their insights about and memories of our grandfather with me. My wife and partner, Doris Hendrickson Damrell, formerly of Ewen, saw me through this project's various stages and worked tirelessly on the page proofs. Finally, the Dwyers of North Star Press are to be thanked for their belief in this book's importance.

Whoever reads this book owes its discovery to Elma Damrell, who had the foresight to preserve it and the patience to promote its publication. I thank her for entrusting it to me and for allowing me to work on a project that has had many rewards.

I began this project while a member of the faculty of the Department of Sociology, Anthropology and Social Work at Central Michigan University. I received strong support from the intellectual community there, for which I am grateful. For the past nine years I have taught at Northland College in Ashland, Wisconsin, a liberal arts/environmental school where my friends, colleagues and students have inspired me to complete this work. I am fortunate to have found such a warm academic home in the north country.

J.D.D.

Photo: Cheryl Fisher

About the Editor

Joseph D. Damrell, a writer and ethnographer, earned a Ph.D. at the University of California, Davis, and is Professor of Sociology and Anthropology at Northland College, Ashland, Wisconsin. He lives with his wife and three children in the Chequamegon Bay area where he observes and writes about life in the north country.

This book is dedicated by the author's grandson
to the spirit of cooperation and community
that lives on in Ewen, Michigan.

Translated from the Finnish
by
Alex Sironen

Introduction

THE AUTHOR OF this book, Isaac Polvi, was born in 1878 in the village of Polvi in rural Vaasalani, Finland, and died in 1951 in Ewen, in the western end of the Upper Peninsula of Michigan. For the brief time that I knew him in my early childhood, my grandfather impressed me as a stern, yet beneficent, presence. Already an old man and showing signs of the disease that would ultimately take his life, I remember "Ikie," as everyone called him, as a lively, spirited fellow with a volcanic laugh and a temper to match. The biggest impression he made on me came during one of my family's visits to the Polvi farm the year before he passed away. I was doing what my grandmother Annu called "russing"— which is to say, snooping—when I felt his icy glare on the back of my head. "Look but don't touch!" he bellowed, as I turned to face him. Then, seeing that he had startled me, he drew me onto his lap and held me, telling me not to be afraid. "The only thing to fear is a mad bull or a strange dog—there is nothing else to fear in the whole world. But remember: look, but don't touch." It was an unforgettable lesson—made all the more poignant by what was to happen nearly forty years later.

In 1978, on the centennial of Isaac Polvi's birth and twenty-seven years after his death, I was invited to a family reunion held on his farm outside of Ewen. Amidst the heady reminiscing that inevitably occurs at such constitutional events, my mother, Elma Damrell—Isaac and Annu Polvi's only daughter—showed me a manuscript she had found while in the process of renovating the farmhouse. It was book-length and hand-written in pencil in Finnish. Isaac's signature appeared on the last page. No one in our immediate family had known of this book's existence, but later a cousin of my grandmother Annu showed me excerpts that had been printed in the Finnish language newspaper, *Työmies-Eteenpäin*, in 1951. I also learned from relatives and friends of the Polvis that Isaac had treated them to an oral account of his life story while the writing was in progress. Although no date appears on the manuscript, I have concluded that it must have been written in the months just prior to his death in November 1951. Who could have believed that the manuscript would lie undisturbed for over two decades among a pile of old newspapers and magazines before its accidental discovery?

Word of the manuscript traveled. Alex Sironen, a former resident of the area who had taken up the formal study of the Finnish language, heard about it and asked Elma Damrell for permission to attempt a translation. I suggested that he do a verbatim translation, and he agreed, vowing to stay as true to the original Finnish work as possible. I received Mr. Sironen's hand-written translation in April 1980, along with an explanation that Polvi had used no punctuation whatsoever in his writing, and that the language was a uniquely Americanized version of a distinctly Swedish-influenced Finnish dialect that had developed in the region around Kurikka in Vaasalani. Fortunately, Mr. Sironen's parents had come from a nearby village and spoke a similar dialect, thus, in a sense, making him ideally suited to undertake the task of translating something that might otherwise be virtually incomprehensible even to a native Finnish speaker.

On reading the English translation for the first time, I came to know my grandfather more fully. But more than that: I realized that his book made great reading—and its importance extended beyond the potential meaning that it held for me and for his other descendants. The story of Isaac Polvi's life was filled with memorable characters, dramatic events and vivid descriptions of rural Finland and the Upper Peninsula of Michigan in the late 1800s and early 1900s. Moreover, it had an internal structural integrity which seems intentional—as if the author were employing an almost novel-like form as a vehicle for his autobiography. Though an unlettered writer, Polvi's prose had beauty and power—and, I think, a purpose. Almost from the moment I finished reading it for the first time, I thought that the manuscript deserved to be published—this despite occasional grammatical and syntactical lapses, certain minor factual contradictions and a fair amount of word-for-word repetition.

Because of my own academic background in sociology and anthropology, I initially thought of this work as an artifact of ethno-history. Isaac Polvi's life story was something to be preserved and made available to Finnish historians or sociologists—or even to laypersons—who desired to uncover, understand or promote the unique experiences and cultural contributions of the Finnish people to American society. So, in preparing a draft for submission to a publisher, I limited myself to adding punctuation and correcting a few of the aforementioned errors, while leaving the text in the "original" condition of Alex Sironen's verbatim translation. I finished this draft in the fall of 1981 and immediately tried to find a publisher.

After a few near misses with university presses and publishers of Scandanavian folklore, I put the manuscript aside for quite a while, showing it on occasion to a friend or colleague, until I learned about North Star Press, which expressed great enthusiasm for the project. Following a great deal of discussion with Corinne Dwyer, North Star's editor, I was persuaded to take up the cause of my grandfather's book by actually rewriting it. I had considered doing just that from time to time over the preceding nine years, but I never began, mostly because I was still thinking of the story as an artifact and didn't want to diminish its authenticity—not to mention the fact that a few publishers had already accused me of personal bias: I was allegedly touting my grandfather's book under the guise of presenting something of academic importance to the Finnish-American heritage.

Fortunately, by the time I was in contact with Corinne Dwyer, I had already discovered that, indeed, the manuscript did have historical value. The Bentley Historical Library on the University of Michigan campus, where a microfilm of the original is kept for interested scholars, considers it one of their finest immigrant documents. In addition, the Emigration History Research Center at the University of Turku in Finland, found the descriptions of life on the rural estates in the late nineteenth century nonpareil. For me, then, all that was left was to "prove" that Isaac Polvi's life story was all that I believed it to be—a great story in its own right. Although I was afraid to try it, Corinne Dwyer convinced me that I was the one to do it. "Who loves this book more than you?" she asked, adding, "and isn't that the way it should be. . . ."

So, in May of 1990, I began. In the process of rewriting Isaac Polvi's book, I Anglicized and modernized the language somewhat, but tended to concentrate on clarifying ambiguous pronouns and modifiers, removing some repetitious dialogue (e.g. "He said," "I said," "She said"), and changing the order of some sentences. Here and there for continuity's sake, I added a short phrase of my own or changed a word to make the text more clear. While this might leave some readers wondering how much of this work is Isaac Polvi's and how much of it is mine, I want to state that the facts remain as Isaac Polvi presented them, and nothing pertinent to the story has been deleted or added. Furthermore, the reader will notice that some passages which are repeated word for word at various times in the text have been left intact. These stylized automisms are the stock-in-trade of the oral storyteller, and they serve as important vehicles for Polvi's central theme.

And just what is that theme? Is there a message here? Much of this story is set in Finland in the households of the author's childhood on the banks of the Kurikka River. The people are trapped in a system of tenant farming that guarantees only their poverty, not their livelihood. All-powerful ministers, officials and landlords rule the countryside. Superstition is widespread, as are misery and disease. Yet the system is eroding as the church and state lose their legitimacy, and the people, though oppressed, offer up their resistance in unique ways. In this setting a small boy is set adrift by the push and pull of forces that are disintegrating rural communal life. His own farm household is dispersed. Thus "marginalized," he wanders as a beggar, absorbing the lessons of his circumstances and applying his precocious wisdom in behalf of the common folk he meets.

In time, the boy is reunited with his family in America, but, now approaching manhood, he finds his ambitions thwarted and his youth foreshortened by labor conditions in the mining region of upper Michigan. Again, Isaac makes the most of his circumstances, retaining both his ideals and his energies. Moreover, he discovers his roots while undertaking to raise a family of his own. Ultimately, he takes his wife and children to a cabin in the woods, there to live the life of a farmer, close to the land and to nature.

True, on one level this book is simply a Finnish immigrant's autobiography, a tale told with humor and grace. Finnish people everywhere should find it fascinating and revealing. Yet, on another level, I think this book has a central theme around which all of the stories within stories, the anecdotes and descriptions of events and characters revolve. The theme is simple, yet it is profound. In my view, Isaac Polvi wrote his autobiography in order to put his life in order. His was a life, after all, that was uprooted—a dream deferred, to coin a phrase. Yet he believed that it had a purpose that was relevant to today's sojourners. He wrote, I believe, to discover and convey this purpose, not just to indulge in memories of his life. His book is significant in the way his writing allows his life to typify the immigration experience. It was, after all, the character of that experience which, in a sense, impelled him to retrace his footsteps in order to explore the sources of his identity. That he did so successfully gives us the opportunity to explore the interface between a man, his culture, and history.

Of course, readers are free to draw their own conclusions, but I think this book has to do with what oppression meant to my grandfather, and his unbending dedication to the principles of equality, the dignity of man, and to what novelist and poet Jim Harrison has called "the theory and practice of rivers." Here, then, is the autobiography of Isaac Polvi: Peasant, vagabond, woodsman, proletarian, temperance advocate, union man, husband, father, farmer, and—what allows us to know these facets of his life—a writer. In presenting his book I have tried to stay well within hearing range of Isaac Polvi's voice in order to allow his life story to come across as he might have told it in the English language. I only hope that I have followed the advice he gave me so long ago: "Look, but don't touch." Whether or not I have succeeded, I realize that there is nothing to fear and much to celebrate.

Joseph David Damrell
Washburn, Wisconsin
August 13, 1991

Isaac Nestor Polvi, 1898.

Why, if this interval of being can be spent serenely
in the form of a laurel, slightly darker than all
other green, with tiny waves on the edges
of every leaf (like the smile of a breeze)—; why then
have to be human—and, escaping fate,
keep longing for fate? . . .

Oh, *not* because happiness *exists*,
that too-hasty profit snatched from approaching loss.
Not out of curiosity, not as practice for the heart, which
would exist in the laurel too. . . .

But because *truly* being here is so much;
because everything here apparently needs us,
this fleeting world, which in some strange way
keeps calling to us.
Us, the most fleeting of all.
Once for each thing. Just once; no more. And we too,
just once. And never again. But to have been
this once, completely, even if only once:
to have been one with the earth, seems beyond undoing.

Rilke

By the Name of the Land

IN FINLAND WHEN one acquired owner's rights to a property, the place where one settled was given its own name, and the owner's surname changed to match it. In other words, the buyer's name always changed, but the name of the house never did. Whoever owned a property was known by the name of the house. Thus it was for my father's father and his wife. They once owned a tenant farm named Lahdesmaki, which means "Springhill." It was near Kurikka in Vaasalani Province. Eventually they sold the place, and my grandfather got permission to make a new home and fields for farming at the foot of a cliff on land called Hakuni land, which was a large estate. He built a small house that held a couple of beds, a small barn to accommodate a few cows, and a small storehouse for keeping food. After he was done, he said to the master of the Hakuni estate, "Now that I have sold my place at Lahdesmaki, I don't wish to carry on that name. You should notify the officials that I now have a new house, and I will honor the gentlemen if they would name my home."

My grandfather's name was Herman. He was a big man. Six-foot-six on a powerful frame; full of strength—but certainly no one had ever taken measure of it. It was said that he never fought, although I heard tell that at a wedding one time some men began to harass him, and as fast as you can count one-two-three, three men flew out the window. He was as cross as a bear if he wasn't obeyed. By contrast, Herman's wife Anna was an average-sized woman, and it was said of her that no mortal had ever seen her angry. She was known throughout the parish as honest, friendly and an example to others. She and Herman had four living children at the time. My father Isaac was the eldest, then Herman and Samuel. They had a girl, too—Fiia. She was born between Father and Herman; Samuel was the youngest, and two or three had died when the family still lived at Lahdesmaki.

Anyway, after a visit to the officials the master of the Hakuni estate returned and notified Herman Lahdesmaki that his place was now called Kallio, which means "cliff," and that, henceforth, he was to be known as Herman Kallio. "It is a strong and enduring name," the master added.

The old man sat down and thought awhile. Eventually he said, "The cliff is there behind me. I have built this farmyard below the cliff. Didn't those soup-headed officials from hell understand this? The place should be called *kartano*, after my farm. I would have listened gladly to Herman Kartano, Anna Kartano and all the Kartano brats. Kartano it should have been!"

Somewhat taken aback, the master of Hakuni quickly said, "The buildings you've built are so neat and well-arranged that one doesn't even have to stand on one's tiptoes to sweep snow off the roof with a broom. Within the village we can certainly call this place Kartano among ourselves, even though it will be Kallio in the records."

I guess this satisfied grandfather, and the place that he built, and he himself, were known in the village by the name of Kartano. He only used the name Kallio when he paid taxes, so I don't believe that even half of the villagers who knew him were ever aware of the name Kallio. Certainly none dared to mention it.

My father related to me a little of the life there, especially how the children all left home to work elsewhere when they were able, but some anecdotes besides. One time, as a boy hired to dig potatoes, he saw his sister Fiia and brother Samppa—a nickname for Samuel—walking along a riverbank. Fiia must have been around fourteen, but Samppa was just a child. They frequented the spot to wash the laundry. Suddenly, Fiia gave a cry of alarm. Father immediately guessed that his little brother had fallen into the river. He ran to the bank and saw that Samppa was being carried downstream by the strong current. He tore off his clothes and began swimming to the struggling boy. "If he goes down again, he won't rise any more," Fiia exclaimed, believing that if he sank three times he was finished. But Father said he managed to reach Samppa just as he was going under for the last time and brought the boy to shore. Some villagers had arrived on the riverbank and knew how to revive a drowned person. Father said it took several hours before they had Samppa breathing normally once again.

That was the Kurikka River. It was some six hundred feet across and fifteen deep—even deeper in spots; and the speed of the current was around a mile an hour, which made it very strong. The people living in the village of Laulaja on the other side collectively built a bridge across the water. Forest-length spruce trees were brought in from the deep woods. As many of these poles as were needed to reach across were attached end-to-end. Then a second string of poles was laid alongside about eight feet away. Now thick planks about fourteen feet long were laid down as a roadway on top of these parallel poles. The bridge lay virtually on top of the water, but during low water it was high up on the shore at both ends.

Heavy, horse-drawn loads frequently crossed the river on this bridge, including in winter when the river froze solid. But when the spring thaw started and the ice began to break up, all the men of the nearby villages came to chop the bridge free from the ice. They used manpower, horsepower and various devices to pull the bridge up onto one of the riverbanks before the ice could carry it away. When the ice was gone and the water had receded so that it was easy to get the bridge back in place, they again settled one end where it belonged. The other end was then hauled out into the current and allowed to float into place, so once again the people had a bridge with which to cross the river.

My mother was a servant-girl in Laulaja when she and my father married. For a time they lived near the Herman Kartano place on Kreivi hill. My brother Viktori was born there. Shortly thereafter my father left to find work near the Russian border—perhaps it was in Karelia—on the White Island Railroad. When he returned, he and my mother moved to Polvi, Mother's home in the village of the same name. Mother's mother—my grandmother—had died, and my grandfather remarried. My father then bought the Polvi farm from my mother's father, Isaac Polvi. A one-room house was built there for my mother's father and his wife. My mother's father and his first wife had several children—two boys, named Juko and Iisakka, and six girls. The girls were Soffia (my mother), Liisa (the mother of Isaac Hakala), Mari, Emma, Heta and Aliina. But soon after Aliina was born, my mother's mother died. Aliina was still a young girl when the new wife bore a son. His name was Jackob and he was around a year older than me. If memory serves, he was born before Father bought the Polvi farm.

Since there was not enough food produced on the farm to sustain everyone, all of the children went to work for strangers as soon as they were able to do some type of work and wherever work could be found. My mother's brother Juko went to work in a household named Antila, along with my mother's sister. The latter was but a child of fewer than ten years. She was small, yet handy and wise, and so she won everyone's favor and became a small sun in that household.

Thinking back as far as I can remember, I clearly recall when my sister Anna was born and she is two-and-a-half years younger than me. I remember Hilma's birth and how I rocked her in her cradle. Likewise do I remember our house in Polvi where, nearby, there was a small river. I guess it was more like a creek, but when it rained the water was high. My friend Jaako and I went to the river, and, I well remember, waded about until I stepped into deep water. The current immediately took me, and, as I tried to straighten my legs, I sank. So I stayed in a sitting position with the strong current taking me downstream at a bewildering speed.

A little ways downstream there was an overpass made of two hewn poles set side by side across the stream on posts high enough so that the flood waters couldn't take them, thus making it possible to cross even during a flood.

Well, my friend Jaako ran to the top of the riverbank and hollered, "Iikka's being taken by the current!"

Father was at work in an adjacent field. I saw him stop doing what he was doing when he heard Jaako's cry for help. He spotted me, ran to the little bridge, and, climbing atop one of the poles, he got down on his knees. With one hand holding onto the bridge, he grabbed my thick hair with the other as I sped by and lifted me out of the water. In a manner that was typical of him, he later said to me, "Good thing I didn't get around to cutting your hair yesterday. It made a good handle to lift you with."

Strangely, I hadn't been in any distress at all. My head and shoulders remained quite dry even though the current carried me at least a quarter of a mile.

I was to have many lessons on this river. I recall once when the water was high, and I was traipsing alone along the riverbank. Two large birds landed on the water. I ran to the house as fast as I could to tell my father. "They aren't merely wild ducks," I said, "they're three or four times as large."

Father accompanied me back to the river carrying his gun. On seeing the birds he lifted it and fired. One bird rose in flight but when its mate didn't move it came back down nearby.

Father's gun was a muzzle-loader, so first he had to put in the powder and then press the bullet on top of that and finally put in a percussion cap. While he reloaded the gun I inspected the bird. I remember its long, beautifully curved neck. Meanwhile, he shot the other bird. "What are they?" I asked him.

"A migratory bird," he answered, "preparing to migrate south. They are called swans."

I tried to lift one to take it in the house to show Mother but couldn't budge it as it was too heavy.

Father hunted occasionally and, like others, molded his own bullets of lead. People carried the bullets in a leather pouch. And a powder horn too, made from an animal horn. This was to keep the powder dry. And there was another small horn for the percussion caps. These two horns and the leather pouch were fastened to a leather thong around the hunter's neck, which made them readily accessible when needed.

On the gun there was a ramrod with a powder measure at one end. A small cork on the powder horn was removed and the powder measure held against the opening. The horn was tilted carefully up and down, and the cork was replaced. Then the gun itself was raised up with the muzzle placed over the powder measure and the ramrod pushed in all the way. Only then was the gun tilted so that the muzzle was up. Next the ramrod was raised a little bit and jiggled slightly so that the last bit of powder was left there at the bottom. One then took a bullet and pressed it into position with the ramrod. The gun was then pointed down as the hammer was raised. If the powder showed through the detonator opening, a percussion cap was put in place. A rabbit tail was generally put over the percussion cap and then held down by the hammer so that the detonator wouldn't by any chance get wet.

Everyone had a sauna and ours was built on the creek bank. It had a roof made of long rye straw which was laid about six inches thick bottom to top with poles set crosswise over that. The sparrows made nests there, and one day Father took a ladder and climbed the roof to destroy them.

Next to the sauna, the high water had formed a pool into which Father tossed a baby sparrow. No sooner did it hit the water than a fish took it. Seeing this, Father got a net and stretched it across the pool. Then he chased the fish into the net. He got one, but it hadn't swallowed the sparrow. Repeatedly he drove the fish into the net. Finally, on opening the fifth pike he found the sparrow.

From that creek we got a lot of fresh fish. There were turbot in it as well as what were called *taimen*, which is a kind of migratory sea-trout not unlike a steelhead. The latter resembled the speckled trout of America but were larger—twenty-four inches and longer. In reality, I guess they were some sort of salmon. They never came up river as far as Polvi village, but they were abundant below the village where the river flowed through a rocky narrows.

This small river—which I believe was known as the Lahiluoma—flowed into the large Kurikka River at the village of Mieta. Polvi village was located at the headwaters of the Lahiluoma, perhaps five miles from Mieta.

There must have been around thirty-five families in the village of Polvi, ours included.

Behind the village was a large bog, and the people had many fields crossed by a six-foot-deep ditch with another ditch some thirty-five feet away. The people burned the surface of their fields, and then in the winter hauled clay and put it atop the ashes. From this procedure came an excellent crop.

That entire bog at some point in time had been a large lake. A great carpet of moss had grown on top of the water. In fact it had grown and grown and sunk deeper and deeper into the water for hundreds and perhaps thousands of years. In any case it had to have been there for a long time for the moss to reach a depth of six feet. It was altogether like pine sap.

When that aforementioned six-foot ditch was dug, the people didn't reach earth, but only an occasional fallen tree. Nor had the tree rotted; it had remained preserved underwater for ages. There were places where there was open water, but one couldn't get to them easily, as the bog sunk under one's weight. When one went nearer to this open water the edge sank, and the water rose, yet the moss and roots had knitted together so tightly that even though it sank under one's weight, it didn't allow water to come through for many hours. I recall several of us boys made a hole in the moss to investigate the lake underneath. We caught a small fish but it was blind. Rather, I should say it had no eyes, but otherwise it was an ordinary fish.

Berries grew on the bog on four-inch plants. First a white flower appeared and then dropped off, and then the berry began to grow. It was exactly the same in appearance as a raspberry—light-colored and hard—but it grew until it was an inch to an inch and one-half thick. Then it began to turn yellowish, and, when it was ripe, it was like the flesh of an orange—very juicy—so that when picked and put in a dish, the bottom ones were squashed. They were that delicate! They were the best berries imaginable; the best I have ever eaten, and were called *hilla*, which I believe is the correct Finnish name, although in our region they were called *valokki*.

Hilla berries were the first berries of summer, which were ready to pick in June. We also used to pick them when they were turning red, and as red berries they were called *muurain*, or cloudberries. *Juomukoita*, or whortleberries, grew on the other side of the bog. They grew along the bog's edges on two foot high stems. These berries were altogether like blueberries only they were lighter in color and half again as large or larger, and, I believe, much sweeter.

Cranberries also grew on the bog, but they were so bitter that we didn't want any until spring, after they had been nipped by the frost in the fall and had been frozen a few times. Then in the spring as the snows retreated, the hummocks where the cranberries grew came into view and we went out early in the morning on the crusted snow to pick them.

Our only competition in picking cranberries came from the migratory cranes that arrived in Finland in the spring. These birds were so large that they could reach out to strike a man in the head with their beaks. They had long legs, too, and rather large bodies to go with their necks. They looked like sheep running around on the bogs. Needless to say they weren't eaten.

The adopted son of Juko Leppa had caught a baby crane there in the Polvi bog and had raised it. It traveled to the bog and back again on a regular basis. In the fall when it had reached its full growth it was hardly prudent for a stranger to visit Juko Leppa's home. The crane would attack, striking one about the head and face with its beak. Eventually it had to be killed.

Behind the bog there was a granite cliff. Here the people quarried stone two feet wide by two feet thick by ten feet long, and even longer. A row of holes two feet deep was made with a drill and hammer atop and below the stone. Two iron bars were placed into adjacent holes with a wedge fitted in between. The wedges were tapped in evenly in all the holes so that the slabs could be taken out whole. The slabs were used as the footings for houses built in the village.

I was still a small boy when my mother's half-brother Jaako Polvi, who was about a year younger than me, went with me to pick lingonberries at the bog. There we discovered a rock protruding above the surrounding ground. It wasn't granite but had the same light-grey color. Moss had grown on top of the rock in a large flat area, and when we pulled some loose to form a resting place, what a wonder we found! There, beneath the layer of moss we had removed was the clear imprint of a sheep's hoof in the rock. On investigating we uncovered some larger tracks as well, which we judged to be that of a cow, although, I now think it was something different. The impressions had been made by animals running before that rock was solid.

When I was small, all the fields were cleared with a mattock. But old fields were tilled with plows, most of which were made of wood. Once we were hoeing a new field when we uncovered an animal horn. I believe now it was possibly that of a Finnish reindeer, and most likely the hoof prints were also. They were not known here at all nor had they ever been seen in the district of Vaasa. Yet, later, in the year 1893-1894, elk appeared there and were often seen even in Kurikka.

Once my friend Jaako and I went to pick berries at the place where we had found the tracks. We filled our birch bark knapsacks (which are called *kontti*) with lingonberries, and, with our birch bark berry dishes in hand, had just begun to descend from a hill along a cow trail into the Polvi bog when we came upon a brown bear.

I was walking just ahead of Jaako. The bear was maybe thirty to forty feet away. It was large and stood up on its hind legs, raising its paws above its eyes as if to shade them from the sun and enable it to see us better. It clapped its paws together and made a loud grunt: "*Hei!*" Then it took off running along the edge of the bog.

It seemed quite comical to me the way it put its front paws on the ground, then its hind feet and then its front paws once again. Its belly was always visible, so it seemed like a furry wheel rolling along on its rim. I turned to look for Jaako, but he had already started running in the opposite direction. "Come back," I called, "we don't need to fear the bear; it's afraid of us."

The *rutas* was the first plant to appear on the bog after the snow was gone. It was only six or seven inches high and as thick as a pencil. This plant grew abundantly along the bog's edge. Generally the cows were turned out to pasture on the first of May, known as *Vappu*. The cattle were quite fond of the rutas but incurred some risk in eating it. The bog was quite treacherous. If a cow's legs went through the layer of moss, there the animal would remain until its owner helped it out. It was basically for this reason that the farms employed herd-boys. The herd-boys either prevented the cows from falling through or else showed the owner where stuck cows were to be found.

My mother's sister Aliina was a couple of years older than my brother Viktori, who was our herd-boy, and the two of them often went together with the cattle to the woods, taking the route leading behind the large bog. They were usually given a lunch to carry in the birch bark knapsack, and a flagon of clabbored milk besides.

One day when they arrived at the edge of the bog, Viktori said to Allina, "You can't walk behind my cows."

Allina was not one to be intimidated and answered, "I walk where I please."

Suddenly Viktori struck her in the face with the flagon; its edge made a bad cut under her eye. They both came home crying, Allina because Viktori had hit her with the flagon, and Viktori because he was sorry for his deed.

I saw my chance. I said to Mother, "I'll go with the cattle. I can manage."

She was against the idea of my going but Father intervened saying, "Let him. All he has to do is stay with the cows, and he won't get lost."

So he took me to the cows and admonished me not to leave them. "Always stay behind them."

Here I was about five or six—no older than that, at any rate—and toiling along behind the cows until evening began coming on. Yet the cows were going further into the woods. What should I do? I decided to wait, thinking that perhaps they'd soon turn for home. As the sun settled downward I thought that surely it was time for the cows to turn home, but try as I might I couldn't change their direction. Instead, they began running, and all I could do was run along behind them. When we came to a bog I thought I knew, I realized that I had never seen a large bog there in the past. Ultimately, I ran and ran, crying as I went, crossing the entire bog. To my great surprise, not to mention relief, I was home.

Allina had a scar under her eye, and old Mrs. Palo used to say, "Yes, this is where Viktori hit you with the flagon of clabbored milk." But, for me, Allina's scar marked the May day when I had my first experience of being lost.

Once Father obtained a young horse whose tail was constantly turning like a windmill's vane. Hardly any hair grew on this tail. Of course, it never had a chance to grow. Only when the horse was lying down was its tail still. Yet, it was one intelligent horse; among other things, it could open hooked gates. In the winter when it was out and wanted back into the stable, it would open and close the door with its teeth. This came in handy one time when Father was coming downhill along the road with a large load of hay behind the horse. I was at the foot of the hill and tripped as I tried to move aside. The horse, being unable to stop the load as it was pushed along at a fast trot, snatched me with his teeth and tossed me into a ditch as it went on by.

Fall came, and one night we had the season's first snow. Sleighing was good so Father got the sleigh ready to go for a short drive. "I want to go, too," I said, so Mother bundled me up. Father put hay in the sleigh box and soon I was sitting snugly in the sleigh, and we were off.

He took the road to the village of Virtainen. On the way we met a man who signaled for us to stop. I knew who he was; a thief, liar and wrongdoer who was not to be trusted, or so everyone said. At the time I believed even my father hated him. His name was Isaac Karsteen but he had acquired the nickname *Letku* because he was undependable. If he promised to do something for you today, he would either do the opposite of what he promised, or else nothing at all. Stopping the horse, Father said, "And where is Letku going?"

"I was on my way to your home to have a talk with you. I want permission to live in your cow barn."

"My cow barn?" Father was surprised. "But don't you live with Virtainen?" he asked.

"Indeed I do, but all of our children have smallpox so Virtainen threw us out. Our five children are sick and lying in the snow. All our worldly goods are likewise outside. So, will you agree to it? May we move into your cow barn?"

"No," my father said, and I was surprised he could be so unfeeling in the face of Letku's misery, even if Letku was a bad man. "No, the cow barn is for livestock. You and your family shall move in with us. Now, jump in the sleigh, and together we shall fetch your children from the snow."

Mr. Karsteen wept with joy. By and by the children were arranged to lie in the sleigh, and I sat among them, pleased at what Father had done, but perplexed about his feelings for Letku.

"We can't take the furniture now," said Father, "but I'll get it later."

Then he took a chair that looked like it was made for a child and told Isaac Karsteen's wife to sit on it. Mr. Karsteen hung on the runner and Father stood up in the sleigh. As he held the reins he muttered, "I hope that Virtainen will soon be shelling peas with the devil for having done such an ugly deed."

We got home amidst much clamor and commotion. A bustling seven-member family, including five sick children, moved in with us in our one-room farmhouse. I don't know to this day where the beds and other necessities came from. The Karsteens had no food, much less adequate clothing and furniture.

Later that same evening a man named Samuli Tilta arrived at the house. He was an odd-looking fellow, with a long back, rather short legs, powerful torso and long arms. He was slow-moving and taciturn, too, and always grinning, with tobacco juice spilling down his chin. He came into the house, padded up to Father, took his hand and said, "Everyone in the village is angry that you have taken this family into your home. But I am here to thank you for doing so. I know there is much more than warmth and shelter needed now, so if I can help out in any way, let me know. Remember the heartfelt thanks from the only friend you have left in the entire village."

He was almost a daily visitor in our home from that time on. And the smallpox spread like wildfire, sparing very few. Many people died in the two villages. More children than adults died, but you must consider that the majority were children. There were four children in our family and the illness never found us. Nor did my parents or Isaac Karsteen and his wife get sick, even though, as I said, all five of their children were down with the pox. Mother told me that when they were given milk in a cup, pus ran down the sides of the cup as they drank. I frequently took the remains of what was left in the cup. Samuli Tilta never became ill either, but two of the five Karsteen children died, while three recovered. All the Virtainens died, parents and children alike. Years later I heard it said that God had protected us from the smallpox.

After the snows receded and the ground thawed, the planting proceeded. Isaac Karsteen, no longer called Letku, helped Father all he could. Father went to the granary to get two barrels of seed grain he had stored there in the fall, but there was nothing there. Father puzzled over this, since the granary had a lock that could not be opened with any key but his own, and the granary had always been locked. Or so he thought. Meanwhile, he told Mother, "We mustn't breathe a word of this to anyone. The person who stole the seed will return it. Whoever took it was in need and only borrowed it from us."

Father hitched the horse to the wagon and went to get seed elsewhere. He didn't return until the following day. Nor did he tell Mr. Karsteen that the seed had disappeared. After the planting was done, Isaac Karsteen, his wife and their three surviving children moved away. Where I don't know, and I haven't seen or heard of them since.

Late one evening around Christmas of that same year, Samuli Tilta came to our house. Now it looked like he didn't have any legs at all. As it was his legs were short, but when his trousers slipped, it seemed as though his back reached the floor. He moved slowly as usual. "Sit down," Father said.

He answered in his typically soft voice, "I don't have time."

"Where's your hurry?" Father asked him.

Samuli stood in one place looking uncomfortable. Finally he said, "Isaac, I have come to confess to you. It was I who stole the two barrels of seed from you, and I've brought you three to replace them." He took Father's hand and said, "Can you forgive me? You see, I knew that I couldn't get credit anywhere, which would have left my fields unplanted. My family must live. God helps him who helps himself."

Father laughed. "I will forgive you just as soon as you tell me how you were able to get the seed out of my granary. It is always locked, and only my key will open it."

"It wasn't always locked," Samuli replied. "Remember last December when the Karsteen children died? We set a platform atop the seed barrels and laid the bodies side by side on it. They were there as long as it took me to make the coffins. You didn't lock the door again, so I came by night, lifted the bodies off the platform, emptied the barrels into sacks, placed the platform back on the barrels, and returned the bodies to the platform once again. I carried the sacks to a snowdrift beside the road, retrieving them some three weeks later. When I had finished the children's coffins, my wife and I wrapped the bodies, placed them in the coffins and added shrouds as is the custom. I'm certain that we are the only people who visited you all winter, because the entire village was angry with you. They were angry with us, too, because we were friendly with you. I tried to see to it that you had a helping hand. In the fall I even sent three boys by to see to it that you had help with the grain harvest and threshing and wouldn't need to hire extra help. We didn't get smallpox because God protected us. If we, too, had been angry because you took those unfortunate people into your home, I don't believe we would have been spared the ravages of that terrible disease. I knew that you could get more seed, but I couldn't. Do you forgive me?"

Father smiled broadly and said, "I forgive you everything from my heart. Nor have I uttered a word about this to anyone—not even to Karsteen who helped with the spring planting."

Then Samuli said in manly fashion, "Come, open the granary and put these three sacks of grain inside."

After the seed had been put in the granary, Samuli climbed into his sleigh and said, "Now I can lie down and go to sleep with a clear conscience. May our friendship continue!"

I guess I should say a bit more about my mother's father, Isaac Polvi, prior to his death in, I believe, the year 1884. He was a man who liked children, and I remember him as I was around him a good deal. He traveled around by horse selling stone crockery, lime, pitch oil, oil of wood, turpentine, sewing needles, cobbler's needles and all sorts of baubles. He got them from a factory, but how far away it was I never knew. He had pursued this occupation for many winters, but on one trip he became ill with what I believe was pneumonia. He returned home that time and, after a short illness, passed away. Shortly thereafter his wife and son moved back to where he had originally come from, which I believe was the village of Kangas in Kauhajoki Province. Their house at our place was then made into a storehouse.

I recall how my father used to saw planks from logs. A fine log was raised up to the top of a scaffold. Two men, one on top of the scaffold and one below, first hewed the log on two sides, marked it, and then sawed it along the mark. They took these planks to the city from where they were exported, mostly to England. Needless to say, they certainly didn't get much money for their efforts.

There was not much money among us rural folk, and everything was paid for with labor. For example, the landowners had large holdings which they would develop into tenant farms by giving young couples permission to go into the backwoods of their land to build homes and make fields. They made a fifty-year contract which stipulated that every fourth week the tenant would work for the estate. This varied more or less with the kind of place the tenant farmer had built. But, in general, the young couples built the buildings, cleared off the forests and raised their families, while working every fourth or fifth week for the estate, according to the contract. This was what was called "taxes." There were no other land taxes.

The minister, however, collected what was called a "head tax." This tax was paid by all adults whether or not they owned property. I believe at the time it was one Finnish mark. But say you had cattle. Then you had to provide butter and milk, make cheese, and one-tenth of everything you grew belonged to the minister. The minister himself traveled about collecting these taxes.

The story was often told about a certain farm wife who knew what day the minister was going to come around to get butter and cheese. She arranged to make her cheese on that very day. When she saw the minister and his assistant coming, she tossed the unfinished cheese on a bench. She was wearing only a chemise and she sat her bare backside on the cheese, proceeding to turn and twist her body briskly. "What are you doing performing in such a manner?" the minister asked her.

Very innocently the farm-wife replied, "Sir, I'm making a cheese, which will be quite ready for you when you return from your rounds in the village."

They say that the minister never wanted cheese from those tenant farmers again, and, if money was not available for paying the head tax in cash, then they had to go and work for the minister until every adult's tax was paid off.

It was told that when Isaac Kohtoola went to work to pay off his family's head taxes, the minister knew that he was someone with the skill to build a fish trap for use in the river. The fish swam into his traps and could be kept alive and free for weeks. When one wanted fresh fish, one simply took a hoop-net and scooped out whatever amount was needed.

Isaac was working on such a trap for the minister but hadn't completed it after two days. The minister told him to go ahead and finish the job. "Surely," he added, "we can settle up afterwards."

Isaac knew that he would have difficulty settling his account. He had a pair of gloves which were made of thick cloth and were quite worn. He put them in a tar pot and left them there until he finished the trap. Then he would see whether or not the minister would pay him his wages, which in turn he would use to pay his family's head taxes. So he finished the fish trap and then asked the minister to pay him his wages.

"Surely I can pay you later," said the minister while he greedily admired the splendid fish trap.

"Listen," said Isaac, "Let me tell you a thing or two. A devil-take-it bloodhead [a pike] won't enter that trap so long as you refuse to pay me my wages."

And with that Isaac collected his tools nearby, removed his old gloves from the tar pot, put one glove inside the other and placed them at the throat of the trap. Then, following the minister's orders, he put the trap in the river. Naturally, the fish directed the odor of tar in the trap and turned away. So, when the minister went to get some fish there weren't any, and he began to believe. "Not even a hell-bound bloodhead will enter the trap so long as I don't pay Isaac his wages."

The minister went to Isaac and asked him, "Will fish go into the trap if I pay you for the two day's work I owe you?"

"If you pay me right now," said Isaac confidently, "there will be fish in the trap tomorrow morning."

Well, the minister paid, and Isaac went at dusk to the river and removed the tarred gloves from the throat of the fish trap.

The tenant farmers of Finland made more fields each year according to their abilities. They reared their children and sent them off to work for strangers. By and by, the original tenants who had toiled on the farm grew old about the time the tenant farm began to attain the state where it could provide a better living. Usually one of the children would be capable of managing the farm, but if that fifty years stipulated in the original contract had passed, then the farm reverted back to the estate with the contract's expiration. Now one could buy the farm from the master of the estate, but the master was allowed to set his own price or even refuse to sell at any price.

In my opinion, the man who made the farm and for fifty years had worked every fourth or fifth week for the estate deserved to own it outright without any finagling. But the estate owners and the rich had no heart and no compassion. To those who have, more must be given, and from those who have little, even that must be taken away. Oh, the wrongs endured by the poor!

There was no doctor in our village, and no one in the rural areas even thought about getting a doctor when someone became ill. It cost too much, and, as I said, there was little money. People used liquor for medicine, as well as tar, pitch-oil and sauna steam. Those who weren't cured by these homemade remedies died.

Well, yes, there were masseuses and blood-letters, whom we called cuppers. Generally the masseuse or cupper was an older village wife or widow who kind of took on this role. She had a sack in which she carried the cupping horns. The large end of a cow's horn was made smooth and the tip of the horn cut off so that a small hole appeared. A fine membrane was then put over the hole. The cupper soaked these horns in warm water, so the entire process worked best in the sauna. The large end of the warmed horn was pressed against the skin in a place where the "bad blood," which was thought to be causing, say, an ache, could be removed. The cupper sucked on the horn's small end containing the membrane. The horn remained there, and, after a minute, she removed it leaving a mark on the skin. Now she took a knife and made some small incisions, and the horn was sucked back onto the mark. When the horn was full it fell off the body of its own accord. It was rinsed and washed in warm water and placed on the same place again. Fourteen or fifteen of these horns might be used at once during a session in the sauna.

In Finland the air was so light that talking could be heard for miles. I recall when the hired hands drove along in the winter singing their sleigh songs, one of which went:

> The cupper sits upon the crockpot
> a pipe fixed upon her lips.
> She asks the village crone,

is there heat in the sauna?
And the cupper has a strange nature,
stranger than the others.
She sucks the blood from people
with the bones of animals.
If my darling should die,
then the cupper I would wed;
and if the cupper should die,
then the horns and sack I would get.
Combs from the horns I would make,
and trousers from the sack.

There were no schools, and it's a wonder people learned to read. However, there were few who couldn't. I recall Mother making wool on her spinning wheel. I sat next to her with a book in my hands. She taught me first how to recognize the letters of the alphabet and then how to spell. Once I learned the alphabet, a book wasn't needed. She simply said, "Spell 'Anna,' now 'Manta,' now 'Antti.' "

Then I had to begin practicing reading directly from a book. She spun wool yarn, and there I sat. Whenever my mind wandered from the book, she would grab me by the hair and give me a good shake, saying, "Think about what you're reading." Then, again, after a short time, "What are you thinking?" I was wishing I was bald-headed.

We didn't have an *Aapinen*, an ABC primer, at first. Mother had an old hymnal from which she showed me characters and taught me how to spell. This book was old indeed. I believe it to have been from the seventeen-hundreds. Today's Finns would not be able to read it due to the strange characters. In the last section there was a Bible history. Parts of biblical history are written in a different way in today's Bibles. Every chapter has been worked over. The story of Christ's death in that old hymnal read: "He died on the cross and descended into the Kingdom of Death." Currently it reads, "He descended into Hell."

When we got an ABC primer we had to work at re-learning the characters, but it was that much easier once we knew how to spell. I have often thought of my mother's work. What cares and responsibilities she had with us. Then I didn't comprehend the enthusiasm with which she taught us and steered us in the right direction on this life's pathways.

I remember one event that I must relate. My father was working in the field with a harrow. Mother sat at the window watching Father work. Anni was on her lap. The implement Father was using was properly called a knife harrow. It was a three-cornered apparatus drawn by a horse, and it had sharp spikes very much like knives. He finished harrowing the field and had to drive across a ditch to another field. He turned the harrow upside down, and the horse and Father jumped over the ditch, but Father fell on top of the harrow, and one spike went into his neck, opening a blood vessel. Blood surged out as from a spigot.

Mother tossed Anni into the cradle and ran outside. Father said, "Quick! Go to the neighbor's and tell Matt that my blood is spilling out."

Matt Perapolvi had a gift that, if he was merely informed that a person was bleeding, the blood flow stopped immediately. He himself said that if he went into a cow barn while a cow was being milked the cow would not give any milk however much he would wish it to. Thus he could not be told when the milking was being done. This seemed crazy, but my father assured us that it was so. Father later said, "I lay alongside the harrow, holding my head up and watching. As Mother ran to the neighbor's, I thought, 'Is Matt in?' I saw her go around the house to go in. Now she was on the porch. She opened the door and the flow of blood immediately stopped."

Matt said to my mother, "It has already stopped, but perhaps he needs help. Go and tell him that I will come there to see what good I can do for him."

Father was deeply in debt for the Polvi farm. When he bought it he took the responsibility on his shoulders to work every fifth week for the estate. He tired of this, and things didn't seem to be improving, so he decided to sell his interest in the place and get rid of the debt in order to be a free man. A buyer named Jaska Jyra came along. This happened in 1887.

A new house was being constructed between our place and Matt Perapolvi's place. It had a good shingled roof and was well built out of hewn logs. It was a large L-shaped building that was left uncompleted. I don't know this building's history. It was brand new. Father made a fireplace, built a chimney, and put in a floor, ceiling, two windows and a door. And we moved in. Father also brought along a cow and a horse. At the other end of the "L" was a cow barn.

I remember my father telling visitors, "I am leaving for America, and would do so immediately, but . . ."

I didn't know what the "but" meant, but I guessed later.

Father worked at various small jobs and brought a lot of logs in from the forest, cutting them up into firewood ready for the burning. The morning of May 14, 1887, when we children—Viktori, Anni, Hilma and I—awakened, we didn't see Father or Mother in the house, but from the window we could see that they were coming across the field from the Saarenpaa farm. Mother was walking slightly ahead of Father, who was carrying a small basket made from shingles on his arm. In it was a small sister for us who was named Selma Aliina.

2

Freedom from All Fear

MOTHER WAS BACK on her feet in a couple of weeks. Father sold the house and the cow and then left for America. His traveling companion was Kalle Perakorpi. A few weeks later Mother received a letter that had been written at the Sampi Iron Mine in Michigan. Father had found work and was staying at a Finnish boarding house. Kalle was also working but was on a different shift.

Father sent money to Mother on several occasions. He often stated in his letters that he was upset with the fact that men died and others were injured in daily accidents. He also said that he wouldn't be staying long at the mine.

For a time Mother received his letters and the money, but then a letter came that told about an incident involving Kalle. Father was on the night shift and Kalle on the day shift. On this particular occasion Father was at the boarding house sleeping while Kalle was, as usual, at work. Father dreamed that over Kalle's bed there appeared a huge glass ball on which were printed the words *Kalle kuoli*, which means "Kalle died."

Father awoke with a start and couldn't get these words out of his mind. Nor was he able to get back to sleep. Finally he got dressed and went into the living room of the boarding house to await his work shift. Two hours later word came that Kalle was dead, crushed to death in the mine by a falling boulder. In the letter explaining this Father wrote, "I'm not going back into the mine again. I shall find work above ground."

In due time Maija Perakorpi, Kalle's wife, received notice of his death and burial in the Sampi cemetery. However, it was over a year before we heard a word from Father again, and it wasn't until much later that I learned what had befallen him in that lost period.

Mother had a most difficult time supporting the five children. She did it by raking hay and cutting grain. The older children took care of the younger ones. During the day Mother worked outdoors in the fields. Her nights were spent at home sewing clothing for the children, herself and for others. I know that this was an extremely lonely period for her.

Finally we received a letter from Father. In it he explained that he had been ill for many months. Intestinal fever had nearly killed him, but he was now well again and back at work. "Write soon. I hope to send you a little money," he wrote, "but my real wish is to hear how you have managed that flock of children alone without any help."

Mother wrote back that she had survived by working and sewing for a lot of people. Father then sent her some money for a sewing machine. This was purchased on her orders, and a man came to give her instructions on how to use it. Soon Mother could use it efficiently. She sewed men's clothing.

Tailors would take a man's measurements, cut the pattern from cloth and then send the cloth to Mother to sew. She was proud that she was able to manage much better than before.

Our nearest neighbor was Matt Perapolvi. The Perapolvis had three daughters, Estla, Maija and Sanna, who were coming of age. They had one son, Eeli. He was the youngest, around my age. Matt's mother and father were still living in a room in Matt's house, even though Matt's father, Mikko, had been bedridden for twenty years. He was not in any pain, however, and I have since thought that perhaps he had the same problem I have, in that the legs don't support the body. This condition is called Parkinson's disease. Mikko's wife used to pull him to the sauna on a sleigh.

I remember once when the old woman was pulling and tugging while Mikko just sat there in the sleigh. She was in a rebellious mood and grumbled, "Here I have to take care of you in bed; carrying food and drink to you, performing your bodily functions; even washing and drying you in bed. Plus I have to take you to the sauna and be your horse into the bargain."

"Shut your mouth this instant," Mikko snapped at her, "or I'll drive you at full speed around the village too!"

The old woman couldn't help but laugh at Mikko's joke. Indeed he was often able to get her into a better mood with his humor.

Eeli, Matt's young boy, and I were together a great deal and often whiled away our time at his grandfather's. Once it grew very late, and still I lingered.

"*Vai*," I exclaimed, "how am I going to get home now? It's dark and I'm afraid."

"Come here, dear child," Mikko said, "and listen to me. Believe everything I'm about to tell you."

I did as I was told, and he continued. "First, those tales you have heard about evil spirits and such are lies, pure and simple. Believe me, boy, there are no evil spirits. If there are any at all, they are merely people. All that is bad that is in us is of the devil, and all the good is of God. Understand that in each of us there exist two natures—one good and one bad. Because we are this way, we may take on the appearance of an evil spirit, or, by contrast, of a benevolent angel of good and God. Look here, I'm an old man, and I can say that I have met no evil spirit other than man. Dear child, you need not fear anything save an angry bull or a dog. Protect yourself from these and there is nothing here that can do you harm. My desire is to rid you of this fear. If you do as I say, you need never fear evil spirits. Keep in mind always that emptiness does not go 'bang.' Emptiness does not go any way. If you hear something, investigate to determine what made the sound. Every time you will find some natural cause. And when you think you have seen something supernatural, investigate this also, and you will find only an illusion, the cause of which is some natural object. If you follow my advice, all the fear that is in you will disappear like mud from your hands when you wash them in clear, warm water."

"Thank you," I said. "I intend to follow your advice now and always."

A full moon had risen in the sky by the time I left. To be sure I didn't have a long way to travel, but along the way there was a certain threshing barn where bodies were customarily kept until they were put into coffins and buried. Threshing barns such as these were places of horror to the children and even to adults.

As it happened, when I approached the barn I saw a man in a long white robe standing there under a roof that had been set on posts in front of the building. I even thought I saw a wide-blade scythe draped over his shoulder. I hesitated, but then the promise I had made to Mikko came to mind, so I decided to creep closer to determine just what this so-called specter might possibly be. And, as I did get closer to the barn, I realized that the moonlight had created the image. Then I took heart, whistling as I went even closer. Suddenly I heard something move, and, in the same instant, an awful shriek froze the blood in my veins, as though I had been doused with ice-cold water. In the wink of an eye, two cats raced past me and scrambled under the building. Now I felt satisfied that the specter had a natural source, just as Mikko had said. I went home to tell Mother my discovery.

"It was your baptism by fire," she said laughing.

"No, Mother," I corrected her, "my baptism was by ice. That's how cold I felt!"

Even after she had gone to bed I could hear Mother laughing to herself every now and then. Finally she said to me, "Everything Mikko said to you is true. There should be more Mikkos in this world."

The next day I sought out Mikko again and related my experience. He didn't laugh. Instead he became stern and said, "I wish to give you additional counsel. There are adults and elderly people who fear the dead though a corpse may be their own father and mother, or someone else who loved them and others when they were alive. There is nothing to fear from a corpse. If it should happen sometime that you are afraid of a dead body, feel its hands and face and you will be reassured that you have nothing to fear. What was good or bad in the living person is gone. Only the clay abode is left, and this is not different from a stick of wood."

Mikko often gave me this type of lecture, and I remain thankful to him for having removed all fear from my mind. Indeed I received many valuable teachings from him.

One day two of Mother's brothers, John and Isaac, came to visit. They said they came from Antila where John and his sister Heta had been servants, though they were now on their way to America. Later I learned that the master and mistress of Antila had not married out of love, but rather for the material rewards their union would bring, as each had an abundance of worldly goods. Yet the master was incapable of performing his manly function in the marriage and for this reason they had no children. After a number of years passed my uncle John and the mistress of Antila became aware that they had fallen in love with one another. Thus they began to avoid each other as much as possible, a situation that lasted many years. But everything must come to an end—if not one way then another. Under these circumstances life became unbearable for them. By nature John was a decent man. He gave the Antilas notice at mid-year that he was leaving and sought out his brother Isaac to explain matters to him.

"I've hired on at this estate for a year, which is over next fall," Isaac said. "As it is spring, I won't get paid if I leave now for America."

"Don't be concerned about that," John replied, "just come with me. Anyway, this love affair of mine is such a big deal that, when I went to bid my mistress farewell, she put her hand into my coat pocket and said, 'Use this as you need it.' I found a large wad of currency in my pocket. We have plenty of money for the journey."

And so the boys left for a strange land to seek their fortunes among a foreign people.

Some years later the master and mistress of Antila approached Heta. "Are you aware that twenty years ago today you came to our house?" the mistress asked her. "You were then a youngster, not quite ten years old. We've taught you to the best of our ability. We are satisfied with you in every way, but we're afraid that you'll become an old maid if you don't marry soon."

"I'm already an old maid," Heta replied, "Soon I'll be thirty years old."

"You are to us our very own child," continued the master. "We have changed your name in the records, and you are no longer a Polvi. You are now Heta Antila, just as people have known you in the village these many years. What we are saying is that you are our only heir, and if you ever go elsewhere, one-third of the estate belongs to you, as you have earned it with your work and skill. All the servants and the other workers honor you. Whatever the job may be they seek instructions from you. You handle all matters with skill and genius. And more than that, you have done more than your share of heavy physical labor, and we don't want you to have to do that any more. Take on another servant and have her do the heavy work. Teach her to prepare meals and to be as capable as you are so that you can take time off."

My mother's sister Heta stayed on at Antila for the rest of her life. I heard that she has died.

Samuli Tilta and his family lived nearby, and I occasionally visited them. They had a son named Kalle who was my age. He was a chap to my liking, and we became pals.

One day when I was there at the Tilta place, one of Kalle's brothers was cutting firewood for the sauna. His name was Samppa and he had a build like his father—a long back, long arms and short legs. But he moved faster than the old man and talked as fast as his mother. Mrs. Tilta came outdoors and called Samppa in for a cup of hot coffee and then went back inside the house. Kalle and I went in too, taking our place before the cookstove. It was plenty warm there, which was fine with us. Although the snow was all gone, it was a cold spring day.

Eventually Samppa came in, and his mother poured his coffee. Before he approached the table to drink it, he pried a large chew of tobacco from his cheek and set it on the window sill. Kalle sidled over to the window, a red pepper pod in his hand. He opened up Samppa's chew, stuck the pepper inside, and molded it into shape. He came back to his place next to me, and we sat and waited. Finally, Samppa finished his coffee. He got up, reached for his wad of tobacco, tossed it into his mouth, turned it over with his tongue, and bit into it.

He turned and, with hooded eyes, looked directly at Kalle, who was smiling innocently. "You devil," said Samppa.

Kalle bolted for the door with Samppa in hot pursuit. Once outside Kalle made for a ditch that was six feet wide when full of water. Kalle knew that with his short legs Samppa couldn't jump over it, so Kalle made it across to safety. Samppa lay down alongside the ditch and began splashing water into his mouth with his hand. Mrs. Tilta came to the steps to see what was going on but wasn't aware of what it was all about.

"Mother," Kalle called from the safety of the far side of the ditch, "bring Samppa a cup or ladle. You must have salted the coffee twice to make Samppa so thirsty."

His mother quizzed him, but Samppa only replied with curses and threats to do Kalle great bodily harm should he venture back to this side of the ditch.

Kalle laughed and said, "In a half-hour I won't have to fear Samppa as his mouth will have cooled off and his anger will have evaporated."

Indeed Samppa was already laughing. He told his mother what that rascal Kalle had done and said to Kalle, "Come on over. I won't hurt you. It was all in fun."

Kalle pulled this sort of trick quite often. And another sort as well. I recall one Sunday he came to me and said, "Everyone in the village knows that you are Mikko Perapolvi's apprentice and that you don't fear devils or sorcerers or anything. They are saying that he has trained you to be a sorcerer, and that you are so powerful that you can even cast a spell on other sorcerers so that they are powerless to harm you."

I was quite amused by this, so I said, "Yes, it's true that Mikko has taught me. I am most grateful for his teaching. He taught me that there are no real sorcerers if you believe there are none and have no fear of them. But if you believe that they exist, and you fear them, then you are a party to sorcery and conjuring. Therefore, you yourself are a sorcerer."

Kalle was disappointed. "Well," he asked, "don't you even believe that it's possible to cast a spell on anything, or to use magic?"

"No," I replied.

Now he was really disappointed. He then told me that Matt Pera-polvi had the only turnip field in the village, and when he discovered turnip peelings on the road he knew that the turnips had been stolen from his field. "Come one more time," Matt had said, "and you won't get out of my field again. I have taken the measure of the field with a body-measuring stick. Whoever goes into my field stays in until I come with my stick to open the road."

"He now sits at one end of the turnip field with that body measuring stick in his hand and reading the Book of Moses," Kalle said.

I said to Kalle, "Come on, don't believe it. What has a body-measuring stick to do with a turnip field? Just stay out of Matt's sight and there is nothing to fear."

"Five boys are waiting by the roadside. They sent me to see you. Come over with me," Kalle replied.

I went with him and learned that the boys wanted me to prove that they wouldn't be trapped in the turnip field even though it had been hexed and measured with a body-measuring stick. They wanted me to go into the field and dig some turnips for them.

"I'll do it on the condition that you not tell anyone that I got the tur-nips for you. Furthermore, you must take the turnip peelings to the road between Matt and his house and put the turnip greens next to his house. If you do that, I'll get a turnip for each of us."

The boys promised, and so I crouched down and moved along a ditch. When I arrived at the edge of the field, I raised my head and saw that Matt was quite close, although his back was to me. I climbed into the field, selected seven turnips and came back to the group. They began peeling the turnips, and, one by one, they wanted to know why the peel-ings had to be taken to the road between Matt and his house and why the greens had to be put near to the house.

"Is there some magic in it?" one asked.

"The magic," I said, "is that Matt will see that the body-measuring stick doesn't help any more than his reading the Book of Moses or his keeping watch. Matt is a poor watchdog." The boys laughed and then put the peelings and the greens where I had ordered.

Just a couple of days later my mother came home and was very angry with me. She called me a thief and threatened to give me a beating that would prevent my ever going into a person's field to steal turnips again.

Of course I felt bad about this but said to her, "Let me try to explain. Let me tell you why I stole the turnips and you'll see that things are not as bad as they now appear." She agreed to listen and I told her the complete tale—Matt's reading the Book of Moses, the body-measuring stick, and his playing watchdog in the turnip patch. "This was why I did it."

Mother laughed so hard she had tears in her eyes, but she managed to say, "It's still wrong to steal."

I agreed, but said that Matt himself did wrong in accusing us of being thieves, measuring off the turnip patch and then sitting there reading the Book of Moses. "If Matt ever talks to you about this, tell him what I said."

Mother didn't say much more on the subject except to counsel me not to steal again. "I'll forgive you this time," she added.

Soon the entire village knew the story, and I learned that a secret is not a secret if seven boys already know it.

My father continued to send what money he could afford to send from his meager earnings. Mother went to work wherever and whenever her help was needed. She sewed well into the night for others and was busy all day long with five children and a great deal of work around the house. People began to believe that she was hoarding money and had who knows how much piled up. "She goes to work every day." "Her man sends her money and she earns by sewing for others." "She has enough of everything." Such was the gossip in the village.

I recall one day when Mother was away at work. We heard a strange sound above the ceiling. A ladder stood on the porch giving access to the loft. Whatever was making the noises seemed to be working on the fireplace chimney with a continuous pounding. My sisters said it was a devil, so I said, "I want to see." I had climbed half-way up the ladder when a young man stuck his head out of the entryway to the loft. He looked at me. His face was blackened with soot so I couldn't recognize him. He drew himself back inside and began working away at the bricks once more.

"Such a young man to have decided to become a devil," I said. "What do you hope to gain? I not only don't fear you; if you are up to no good I will shoot you."

I went back into the house and after hooking the doors told my sisters, "That is no devil. It is a man trying to scare us. Let him be, but if he comes down the ladder and tries to come inside, we'll hit him with this stove poker. It is no spook. It is someone who has set about being a spook in order to scare us away." I couldn't understand the reason for the incident then, but later on I did. What's more, I suspected a certain young man in the village, but I didn't mention a word of it to anyone.

I remember another incident when the minister and the bailiff came to the house. The bailiff asked Mother if she had a cow.

"No, I don't," she replied.

"You have not paid a personal tax on your husband," said the minister.

"He is in America and has forbidden my paying his tax," she answered. "He does not breathe here and we'll pay his tax where he breathes."

The two of them then came into the house and saw Mother's sewing machine. They listed it to be sold to pay off the debt for the personal tax. The minister announced this forced sale a few times at the church so many strangers gathered at the auction.

The bailiff asked, "What is offered for this sewing machine?"

Our good neighbor, an old man named Juko Tausta, stepped forward and asked, "How much is the debt in question?"

The minister told him and Juko counted out the money on the table. "I don't want to see this sewing machine taken away from the one who needs it," he said. "Here is the money."

Then the bailiff spoke up. "I want my fee also," he said.

A master of one of the estates was present and he said, "The bailiff here has a yearly salary. He cannot demand payment for any service, since he does nothing."

It was then that I had a realization about the nature of those government officials, ministers and the gentry. I was young—barely ten years old—but the opinions I formed of them are the same ones I hold today. Not only have my opinions not changed, but I have become even more convinced that I formed the right opinions of them as a youth.

One day all the children weren't feeling at all well. Some of us even stayed in bed, complaining that we were sick. Mother had to cut grain for someone. A hand-held sickle had to be used and it had to be done in a hurry because the grain was so ripe. After she left I found a piece of dry *kanfaart* in her drawer. "I'll make some medicine that will cure us," I told the others.

I put water in the coffee pot and used a knife to whittle the *kanfaart* into thin shavings. I put the shavings into the water and set the pot on the fire to boil. When the stuff was all melted I gave each child a half-cup to drink, taking a half-cup myself. Later, Mother used the same medicine, saying it was also good for the chills when you drank it very hot.

In Finland in the fall the days are already short and the nights long and dark. Mother was away working again somewhere one night and all of us grew tired of waiting for her and went off to bed. Some time later my brother woke me up. "Get up," he cried, "there is a fire loose somewhere. The house is full of smoke!"

The fire was burning where the floor met the wall. On seeing this we began pouring water on it to put it out. We nearly had it out when Mother came home and suggested that we investigate its cause. She traced the source of the fire and found that a firebrand had been taken from the fireplace and then placed between the wall and the floor. The cupboards had all been ransacked, of course, because whoever did it was looking for money. But why would they try to set fire to the house and burn us up?

Thus we didn't stay there much longer, moving instead to the empty Virtainen house. Here I didn't have any companions to my liking, so I often ventured into the forest on my own. To scare me into staying home, I was told about a certain forest dweller. I laughed and said, "There is no other forest dweller there but me."

The forests I explored were large virgin forests of pine, spruce and birch. I set snares and trapped birds. There were ant hills that reached heights of from six to seven feet. Some of the nests contained no ants but I couldn't determine why they had been abandoned. But in every case a fox would dig three holes under the abandoned hill to make himself a shelter and a hiding place. People said that in freezing weather during the winter the fox would say, "*Ho hoi*, if only I will see summer again, then surely I will build a home for myself." But when summer came he would say, "Ah, I don't really care for a home. After all, I got by last winter, didn't I?" A fox was just that lazy. But every time I saw one of those ant hills I thought, there is at least one fox who kept his promise to himself.

Our nearest neighbors lived at the Iloharju farm, and a little beyond the farm lived a widow named Anna Valli, who had three sons—Jacob, John and Isaac. They were already young men. It was said that Jacob, who had been born blind, could, when traveling alone, sense when he came into the presence of another person. I had seen Jacob and knew him, and I planned for some time to test this sense of his. One day I stood about fifteen feet off to the side of a path and didn't move or make a sound as Jacob came along the path carrying a stick in his hand. When he came alongside me he stopped and asked, "Who's there? Don't harm me."

I didn't answer or move as he began walking toward me, feeling the ground in front of him with his stick. He continued coming toward me saying, "Don't do anything bad now. Say something . . ." I started to flee but he shouted, "Don't go! Don't leave a blind man in the dark. Tell me who you are."

"Don't leave a blind man in the dark." This was something for me to think about. I said to him, "I'll never leave you in the dark, and I promise to always let you know who I am." Whenever I happened to come upon Jacob after that I immediately told him that it was me. It was not necessary to say one's name; he had only to hear the voice to know the person.

Our nearest neighbors, as I said, were the Iloharjus. They had a son named Antti who was three years younger than me, but we often played together at his home. Mother had acquired a cow that she kept in the Iloharju's barn where she would walk to milk it. We had no barn but did have a small shed in which we kept four or five chickens. One of the chickens was brooding and Mother said, "I'd let her sit on the eggs if I could get some from someone with a rooster."

I knew that the high waters in the river had receded and that meant that I could catch fish. This was because during high water the fish swam into small flood-pools where they were easy to catch by hand when the waters receded. I caught three large pike on this occasion and started for home. I hadn't taken more than a few steps when a wild duck moved ahead of me. I saw the nest where she had been sitting on her eggs. I put the fish on the ground, took off my cap and carefully placed the eggs in it. I got home with the fish and eggs and explained to Mother that I wanted our chicken to hatch the ducklings.

"Are they still warm?" she asked with a laugh.

Mother and I got the hen to sit on the eggs. Over a week went by, and then the hen was being followed by nine wild ducklings. The brood followed the hen in her wanderings for some days when they happened to pass by a pit that had been dug to get clay for the bog fields. The pit was now full of water. Naturally when the ducklings saw it, they didn't hesitate but made directly for the water for a swim and a dive. The mother hen began clucking in desperation, as if her life hung in the balance. I ran to see what was causing her distress and saw the ducklings swimming and diving with the poor mother hen clucking madly and flying about. She tried to get them away from the clay pit, but to no avail.

I went to tell Mother. She and the others came to watch. Mother said, "Let them be. Here you see two laws of nature at odds. Mother-love pitted against the wild ducks' natural attraction to and love for the water."

I went again to check on them later that evening and the distress calls had ceased, for the hen had her ducklings back with her. The following day we went back to the pit and the hen wasn't worried about them at all. I often watched the hen as she waited at the edge of the pit. When the ducklings got out of the water she would take over and escort them away. They grew and were quite large when the ducklings finally rejected their adopted mother. Some of them disappeared, and I didn't know what might have taken them. When I last saw them only three remained. Later I blamed their disappearance on an eagle I saw flying in the vicinity of the clay pit.

I remember one day I was playing with Antii Iloharju on the floor at their house. His mother, who was a rather stout woman, was spinning wool yarn at her spinning wheel when she stopped her work and went outdoors. A few minutes later she came back into the house carrying something cradled in the hem of her skirt. A broad smile lit up her face as she approached us. "Boys, see what I have here." And from within the folds of her skirt she showed us the face of a baby. She told Antti, "Go over to the ditch and tell your father that his wife has a newborn baby and that he must prepare warm water immediately. And you, Isaac," she said, addressing me, "go tell your mother to come and wash the baby. Hurry!"

When I got home Mother had her sewing machine going. I opened the door. "Mother . . ."

She interrupted me. "Quiet! Don't bother me. I'm in a hurry to get these clothes done."

"There won't be any such hurry if you'll listen to me," I said to her. "You must go to the Iloharju's and wash Fiia's baby."

She paused and looked up. "What are you saying?" I told her everything and she exclaimed, "Oh, good God! I hadn't been aware of anything like this." Then she left. When she returned all she said was that Fiia had planned to go to an out-building, but as soon as she went outdoors the baby had been born.

I said to Mother, "My sister Anna was born in the Herman Polvi sauna; my sister Hilma was born in our sauna when we were still on the Polvi place; Selma was born in the Saraanpaa sauna, and my brother Viktori was born in the sauna on Kreivi Hill—but where was I born?" I had put this question to my mother before but always received the answer, "Don't annoy me" or "Don't ask these things." I was, therefore, left to ponder a matter she didn't want to tell me about.

One day I caught a young rabbit and brought it home. We fed it and kept it in the house. There wasn't anything too good to give that rabbit, but its favorite food was milk. It drank milk with the cat from the same dish. Once when the milk ran out, the cat and the rabbit began to fight. The cat hurt the rabbit with its sharp claws, but the rabbit jumped three or four feet in the air and came down on the cat's back. The cat didn't like this kind of sport and ran first behind the cookstove and then hid under the bed. It stayed out of sight, as it didn't want any more to do with this kind of leaper. After this we let the rabbit out of the house to come and go as it pleased. Whenever it saw Mother return from milking it ran to meet her, jumping up and nagging her in its peculiar way and coming with her into the house. Once again there was milk for both the rabbit and the cat, which was fine so long as the milk lasted. But as soon as the milk was gone the rabbit would immediately attack the cat. The cat learned to leave when the milk ran low in the dish. You can't blame the cat. The rabbits there weighed between sixteen and twenty-one pounds.

The forest birds were the grouse, the wood grouse and the black grouse. Of the three the wood grouse was the largest. The male wood grouse was called *metso* and the female *koppelo*. A black grouse, or *teeri*, weighed three and one-half pounds, and a grouse, or *metsa kana* weighed two and one-half pounds. The grouse changed color with the seasons quite like the rabbits. In winter the grouse were snow white and in the summer the color of the ground. In the late winter when their mating time commenced, they made such a racket that you would have thought people were present. The noise they made sounded very much like, "*Parta pois, parta pois, viimeen koko, paa pak, kak kaa, aa ha haa.*" It was some racket when there were forty or fifty of them in a group. A bird would start with "*peukka peukka paa,*" and another would threaten to remove its beard if not its entire head.

We trapped these birds with snares attached to forked sticks that were placed near a bush. We placed branches as obstacles on both sides of the snare so the birds wouldn't go around it. In cold weather and during storms these forest birds dropped into soft snow and dug themselves in deep, sometimes clear to the ground, where they were better protected from the elements.

During the winter I traveled in the forest on skis. I always went alone and had many happy and pleasurable times there. Before the snows came in the fall I made shelters for the birds under the spruce trees. I leaned four or five round poles about six or seven feet long against a spruce and then placed boughs and twigs over them. This created a shelter agaist the snow, and the birds were attracted to it by the visible bare ground. In each of the shelters I placed one or two snares.

To catch rabbits I put snares on the trails. I recall an incident when I had a snare set for a rabbit but it wouldn't go in. It always jumped to one side and then returned to the path after it had made it around the snare. This type of trap was a spring snare. Near the path was a tall slender birch sapling. I cut off the top and then bent the trunk over the path. I placed the bent sapling under the branch of another tree in such a manner that, when a rabbit went into the snare and gave it a slight jerk, the sapling was released, and the rabbit was raised off the ground. Each time I saw that the rabbit had jumped to the side and avoided the snare, I thought to myself, one of these days you'll make a mistake.

One morning I went to check the snare and again there was nothing. I continued on and heard what sounded like a barking dog. I stopped to look and saw a fox chasing a rabbit along the path. Surely now it will go into the snare, I thought. But as it approached the snare the rabbit jumped aside as usual, while the fox ran straight along the path and got caught in the snare. The sapling was released and the fox was lifted off the ground. I cannot find the words to convey the joy I felt! I immediately checked to see whether the snare was around the fox's neck or around its body. It was held fast by the neck. I waited until the fox no longer moved, but I couldn't wait calmly in one spot. I got off the skis and made a path just by running around the fox in my excitement. I had heard about how sly a fox is so I decided to let it hang there while I checked my other snares. I had also trapped a rabbit and a black grouse. An hour at least had elapsed before I returned.

The fox was already stiff. I took the fox down and left the rabbit and the black grouse in the woods. The fox was such a prize that I felt I had to take it home and fast. I was in such a hurry that I was soaked with sweat even before I got there.

Mother took the fox to a man named Sapari who trapped fur-bearing animals and received ten marks for it.

With the arrival of spring the fishing began. I made fish traps from willow branches and placed them in that small river. The pike went upstream to spawn when the ice began to flow. After the ice had gone and the flood waters had receded, the pike started downstream once again with the current. They were easy to catch with the fish trap. Once summer arrived the pike moved about very little, although they could often be seen basking in the sunshine. Then I would put a snare on the end of a stick and very nicely arrange the snare into an open position. I moved the snare very slowly in front of the fish and gently slid it back around the fish's body. With one little jerk the fish was landed. I caught many large pike this way, although at the beginning I sometimes jerked too hard and cut the fish in two. If the pike was in deep water it had to be retrieved very slowly.

One day I saw a large pike lying in the sun in shallow water. Its back was just above the surface, and at first I didn't take it to be a fish. It looked like a snag with a branch sticking out on either side at the middle. The fish's back was black and the branches were white. It was that very detail that had first caught my interest, but I was not careful enough and the fish left. I knew then that it was indeed a fish, but the question of what those white branches on its back might be remained on my mind. I thought about it, deciding that I must first catch the fish; then I could examine it and have an answer to my question. I sat and waited but the fish didn't return, so I went home.

I returned to the site the following day and stood waiting for a long time, wanting to be ready because I was certain that the fish would return. Finally I saw it coming, but I realized that my snare opening was too small to slip over that large head. It had come to lie in water so shallow that its belly was on the bottom and its back about half an inch above the surface. It was the same fish though; there were the two white branches, one on either side. I decided to hit it with a stick and found one that was suitable. I put a lot of force into the blow and was successful in stunning the pike. I then jumped into the water, grabbed it by the gills and dragged the fish far enough onto the shore so that there was no danger of its getting back into the deep hole from whence it had come.

Now I began an examination of the two branches in its back. They turned out to be a hawk's feet. Evidently a hawk had sunk its claws into the fish, but the fish was too much for it and pulled it into deep water, where it drowned before it could withdraw its talons. I have no idea how long it took the hawk's body to wear away from the fish's back. I left the talons and legs in place on the fish's back so I could show them to somebody and they couldn't say that it had been an evil spirit. The pike measured four feet, five and one-half inches long, which was the longest I had ever seen.

Once when I was in the forest I heard a sound that sounded a lot like a baby crying. I went toward the sound and came upon a place where two or three spruce trees had fallen atop one another. I began to investigate and found that a large hawk or an eagle had a rabbit in one foot and was trying to drag it out from under the branches. The rabbit wasn't cooperating and screamed as it struggled. I began beating at the bird but the branches were in the way. I wound up not getting the bird or the rabbit either. When I told others about this incident they stated in all seriousness that I had encountered an evil spirit. I thought then that one perhaps shouldn't relate all that he sees, because I went ahead and told Samuli Perala, a man of forty-five or fifty years, about the strange sight I had seen. Of course he claimed it had been an evil spirit.

"Mother," I said, "I want to show the fish to Samuli as proof that one of his evil spirits has drowned."

Mother laughed and said, "Don't tell him about it. Just ask him to come see a large fish you caught."

I caught up with Samuli where he was splitting wood nearby. "Mother has coffee on, and I want to show you a fish I caught. It's larger than any I have ever seen before."

"I don't have time," he said, "I have to leave for home."

"It's not only that I want to show you a fish, but there is something about this fish that is very interesting, and I would like you to see it. If I tell you about it you won't believe me, so please, come and see it."

He came and marvelled at the size. Then he noticed the hawk's legs protruding from the fish's back. "But what are these hawk's feet doing here?" he asked. "Were they there when you caught it?"

"Yes," I said, "just as you see them."

He looked closer and said, "I wouldn't have believed it. This fish was too heavy for the hawk to lift out of the water, so the fish drowned the hawk. How did you catch the fish?"

I told Samuli everything—how I'd watched like a cat watching for a mouse, and how I must have broken it's back since it didn't flop around much after I hit it. I also reminded him that when I told him the previous fall how a hawk or an eagle had sunk its talons into a rabbit and was trying to drag it out from under some branches, the rabbit's cries of distress had sounded like a baby crying. "You said it was an evil spirit. Yet this fish here was the same sort of thing, and it drowned."

Samuli looked at me for a moment and then said, "It may have been so. I concede now that you were right." He turned to Mother and said, "He doesn't fear anything. If I had heard a baby crying far out in the forest, would I have gone to investigate?" Then he himself measured the fish and said, "Yes, it is the biggest pike I have ever seen, too."

I had a squirrel that liked sugar. It was amusing to watch it gnaw on a lump of sugar held in its two paws. It also would come to the table when we were eating, but it began to tear clothing and Mother put it out. It came back in, and when Mother went back to her weaving, she found that the squirrel had cut the warp in many places. The squirrel disappeared. I asked where it had gone, but, because Mother never wanted to lie to us, the only thing she said was, "Don't bother me with questions." I know that it did a lot of mischief and didn't blame her that it disappeared, and I told her so.

Samuli Perala had a dog I liked. It often came over to our house and I was friendly to it. One evening Samuli came to our house and asked me to give him a hand with something. He said he had a small job that wouldn't take long, so I went. He had thrown a long rope over the wall of a shed with one end inside and one outside. He explained that he wanted me to go into the shed with his dog and place a noose over the dog's head. "Then, when you've done that, just say 'good' and I will haul it up. That way I won't have to see the dog die."

The dog came to me without hesitation, and I took it into the shed. There I saw a sturdy old wooden bench used for chopping kindling. I placed it into the noose. I told the dog to lie down and keep quiet and then called out, "Good!" Samuli pulled the rope, and I said, "Raise it a little higher." He pulled again and I yelled, "That's fine," and then went back outside.

"I wouldn't have believed that dog was so heavy," he said. "I was barely able to raise it high enough. How long will it need to hang before I can skin it?"

I told him, "Let it hang there for the night and skin it tomorrow." Then I left for home.

Mother asked me when I returned, "What small job was it that you have come back so soon?" She wanted to know all about it so I told her. She laughed and then said, "It is wrong to leave Samuli thinking that his dog is hanging by a rope."

"Samuli didn't want to see his dog die, and it is not dead," I told Mother. "He will find Shep in the shed. I didn't want to see it die either. Since it was his wish as well as mine, no harm has been done."

Mother laughed again and went to the Perala's and explained to Samuli what I had related to her. His wife Maija said, "It is also my wish that the dog not die. Tell Iisakka that I'll make a cheese for him." Then she went into the shed and brought Shep into the house. They were all thankful that Shep was still alive.

One Sunday morning Mother said, "Today we are having visitors. Put on clean clothing." She proceeded to clean and dress us, and I even got to put on a new shirt. While waiting for the visitors I went for a walk to the edge of the forest nearby. I heard a peculiar sound and saw a bird the size of a blackbird calling and flying about. I also saw that it had a nest in a tree there. I went closer, and the bird flew by and dropped one in my ear. And then came dozens of birds, all of them shitting on me. I realized what was happening to my shirt, so I decided to get rid of the nest. I began to climb the tree but didn't get to the nest before my eyes were so full of that soft shit that I couldn't see. So down I came. They continued to bombard me. I tried rubbing my eyes to allow me to see enough in order to get away, but I was getting hit with fresh hot shit down my collar, on my head and in my ears. Finally I got enough out of my eyes to find my way home.

Mother's visitors had arrived, and I went to her to ask that she put my old clothes back on me. She was thunderstruck by my appearance. The visitors were highly amused and one said, "The trip wouldn't have been anything if not for this."

Mother had a big job cleaning the slime from my head. My clothes were put to soak, too. Among the visitors was an old man who was so amused at what happened to me that he wanted some of the other visitors to go to the nest of the "shit-thrush."

Berry-picking time was at hand and we were harvesting lingonberries. On several occasions I went with the others but I preferred to be alone. Once when I was picking berries a thunderstorm came up. Nearby was a very large fallen tree that was hollow. It was so large that I was able to stand upright in the opening of the hollow. I ventured inside and found it was completely dry. The butt was three or four feet off the ground. There was no seat so I lay down and fell asleep listening to the rain.

When I awoke it was as dark as the inside of a bag. I thought, all is well except for the fact that Mother will worry because I didn't come home. It will be impossible for me or anyone else to pass through the primeval forest in the dark without immediately becoming lost, I thought. Well, I can't do anything but sleep until daybreak.

I didn't fall asleep again right away. Another thunderstorm came up, so I got up and went to stand at the opening of the hollow for a long time, admiring the flashes of lightning, the thunder and the rain. Oh, how I loved my shelter, and I decided that when dry weather came I'd gather leaves and moss for a bed and a seat. Finally I lay down and slept again.

When I awoke the second time I was cold, but it wasn't quite as dark as before. The wind had blown the clouds away, but the air had been cooled by the thunderstorms. I felt like having a drink of water, and it appeared to me that there was water around me. I lowered myself down and took water in my cap and drank, gazing up at the starry sky. I tried to remember the direction my fallen tree had pointed, as it seemed to have turned as I slept. I thought, when I climbed inside the hollow yesterday, the top was pointing west. Now it seems to be pointing east. But this is merely a muddle that occurs when one gets lost in one's sleep. I went back into the tree to think it through. Then I happened to remember that thunderstorms always came up in the west, and that I wasn't lost when I went into the tree. Ah, what do I care? While I'm asleep, perhaps it will turn back again.

I didn't fall asleep, and when it seemed to me that day was beginning to break, I got up and saw that I was right. Where east should be, dawn was breaking and the sun would rise as before. I went out, found the source of water I had drunk from before and washed my face. Soon there was enough daylight to start for home. At full daylight I happened upon a good berry patch. I had one full dish, but the other was nearly empty so I filled it as well.

When I arrived at the edge of the woods an opening allowed me to see the house. I saw Mother coming from Perala toward home. I called to her, and she stopped on hearing my voice.

She had gone to Perala about me, but Samuli had told her not to worry. "Wait until noon, and if he isn't home by then we can begin to think that something may have happened to him. If it were someone else, I would fear the worst. But I'm sure that he will be home very soon and that he has been in no distress. The weather was bad all afternoon, and he has found a shelter and will not attempt to go through the forest at night and get lost."

Mother watched me approaching with my berry dishes in hand. "What a good night's shelter I had!" I exclaimed. "Get me something to eat. I found a good berry patch on my way in and I'm going back to fill my berry dishes today also."

A river flowed through the forest, but the land was quite flat so the current was quite slow. Moss had grown on top of the water. In many places trees had fallen across the river and one could use them to get to the other side. There were deep spots in the river, too, but they were all covered with moss.

It was warm and the sun shown. I was again picking berries along the mossy river. I wanted a drink of water and so with a stick peeled some of the moss off the surface of the river. The water was bright and clear. I took some in my cap and drank. I then went back to picking, filling my dishes and finally deciding to go home. But I decided I needed another drink of that good water before I left.

At the same place where I had taken a drink earlier I found that a large pike had come to lie in the sun. I had a snare nearby so I fetched it and attached it to the end of a stick. Proceeding cautiously, I slipped the snare over the fish and with a slight jerk flipped the fish on the riverbank. I cleared several of these spots of moss and got three more fish. Now I tied the fish on my back with a twisted switch, took the berry dishes up in my left hand, and, holding the switch in my right hand, headed home.

I hadn't gone far when a female eagle began to harass me by making screeching sounds and diving for my head. I tried to hit it with my stick, but it moved out of reach for a moment until it returned and went for my face. Then another eagle joined in the attack, and I thought it best to leave. I noticed then that there were several eagles on the ground, plus there was a nest containing eggs and eaglets of various sizes. The larger ones tried to flee. In the nest were feathers of all kinds, some pieces of sheepskin and a rabbit's paw. I didn't have time to inspect the nest carefully, as the two mothers were trying to get to my face. I fled, and once I was away, one eagle fell back. The other continued to follow me all the way home. It flew high above me and evidently wanted to know where my nest was.

Nearby was a tenant farm known as Iso-oja where the people had a son named Isaac. He was a young man, and he owned a gun. I sought him out and related my experiences with the eagles to him. I asked him if he would shoot them. He agreed, and we went out into the woods. We learned from the older men that the female eagle lays her eggs and hatches them all summer long. And so it seemed, since we had to shoot one eaglet, being unable to catch it otherwise. We killed four eaglets with a stick. One of the eggs was ready to hatch, one had an eaglet inside that was just beginning to form and a third was newly laid. We destroyed everything. There surely had been many different kinds of birds devoured in that nest. There were also fish bones, a lamb's head and a cat's paw. One eagle measured seven-feet-nine inches from wing tip to wing tip.

On these berry-picking outings I began to set out snares for rabbits and birds once again. I also placed dry leaves and a seat in my hollow tree. I never stayed there another night, but my route would always take me past it, and I generally sat there to eat my bread. I say "eat my bread" because I had only a hard, dry piece of rye bread. In Finland we usually didn't bake bread more than twice a year. The bread was then dried. Each loaf had a hole through the middle and was placed on a smooth pole about an inch-and-a-half in diameter and raised up to the ceiling or roof. There were many loaves on one pole. When they were as dry as powder they were taken down and placed in a barrel kept in a dry outbuilding, usually the granary. If the bread was not powder dry it became moldy and then was considered spoiled and unfit to eat. These loaves were about fourteen inches in diameter and an inch thick.

A piece of this bread was usually my lunch. We had a cow, and Mother churned butter and put butter on our bread. But this was not successfully carried in one's pocket. We had no paper to wrap it in, for what little paper we had was needed for something else. My mother usually cut the bread into small pieces, and if she had fat, tallow or pork meat, she would put it into a pot and melt it by pouring boiling water over it. She then put in the pieces of bread with some salt and left it on the fire until the bread was soft. Finally she poured milk on it, and we had what we called *leipa ressua.*

She also cooked porridge. The rye porridge was black, and at meal-time it was generally placed on the table in a single large crockery bowl. She put butter in the middle and we called it "the eye of the porridge." She would then give us each a cup of milk and a wooden spoon. The bowl of porridge was placed in the middle of the table and everyone ate from one bowl but drank their milk from their own cup.

One evening Mother called us to come for porridge. When I got to the table I noticed that she had forgotten to put in the "eye." In addition to the crockery bowl containing the porridge, herring and potatoes cooked in the skins were also on the table. I took a small potato, slipped off the skin and placed it in the porridge for an eye. But I was giggling so that it didn't quite go in the middle. The others came to the table then and my sisters immediately wondered aloud if Mother planned to give two eyes to the porridge today, since she had placed it to one side.

"It's on my side," declared Anna.

"Viktori poked at it with his spoon and remarked, "It hasn't melted a bit as yet." I couldn't keep from laughing and Viktori dug out the potato and called to Mother, "What kind of an eye is this?"

"I forgot to put in the eye," said Mother. She came to the table and saw the potato Viktori had fished from the bowl. She laughed and said, "Isaac must have put it there, but the porridge is not spoiled. It was a clean potato."

She also made porridge from barley flour, but she made it stiff and we called it *akkinainen,* which means unformed. We ate it with milk. We'd put *akkinainen* into a bowl and pour milk over it.

But aside from porridge, herring, bread and potatoes constituted our main diet. Mother also prepared *viilia,* a yogurt-like culture, for us, but it was a very special treat. For Christmas she bought dried cod and soaked it in lye for weeks before it was ready to eat. She also made what we called hot water bread and biscuit. Most of the time she cooked the fish I brought home from the river with milk and potatoes, and some-times with birds or rabbits and potatoes. This was our usual fare.

So, that fall and winter I trapped. In the spring Mother began prep-arations for her trip to America. We sold whatever was worth selling at an auction. There wasn't much besides the cow and the sewing machine.

3

The Beggar's School

MOTHER LEFT FOR America and I went to stay with my grandfather and grandmother on my father's side. Viktori hired out as a farm hand as he had reached the age of fifteen. It was as if I had been awakened from a dream. I came to realize that my mother's family was proud. In their opinion I was no better than a dog. Nobody really cared about me. Nor did the two elderly people with whom I was left please me. My grandfather was old, and I had to work every weekday. When Sunday rolled around, there was nowhere to go. One Sunday a boy named Manu Torkkoola came to me and said that his father had told him to stop by to see how things were going. Torkkoola, I knew, was a large estate, and the fact that the master had told someone to see me meant something. Manu and I went out to get acquainted. After we had talked for a while, I realized that Manu was the black sheep of the family because of his opinions, and because he and his father had opposing views regarding poor people. Before we went into the forest together I asked my grandfather for permission to leave with Manu.

"It depends on what Grandmother says to that," he said. So I went to ask her.

The old lady was good-hearted and said, "It's good that there's someone with whom you can spend time. Go ahead, but try not to be too
late."

Now I had a pal. The more we got to know each other, the more we
wanted to be together. The master of Torkkoola seemed quite polite to
me. He often went to the workers' house and said, "Come to the house
to eat, boys." I noticed it was always the master who asked me over. He
seemed happy that Manu had a companion whom he liked.

At Torkkoola's there was a large flat-bottomed row boat. The flat
bottom made it perfect for fishing. Using the boat we would find the
deepest parts of the river, drop anchor and begin fishing. Large schools
of small fish swam near the surface of the water. We made small hooks
from straight pins and used a #40 sewing thread to make a very fine line.
We used flies for bait and a piece of cork to keep the bait close to the surface. These fish, known as bleak, were three to four inches long, and we
would each try to bring four or five into the boat. In turn we used them
for bait to catch perch which were always in the deepest holes in the
river. When we had our limit, we would go to the Torkkoola workers'
house and there clean and divide the fish. The heads, tails and other remains were given to the cat.

One Sunday morning as we were about to leave on our weekly fishing rounds, the mistress came to ask us to take the old cat to the river with
us and drown it. "It isn't good for anything anymore," she said.

It seems that she had seen the cat at its bowl of milk drinking con-
tentedly. A mouse came to share the milk, and, instead of killing the
mouse, the cat chased it away and went back to drinking.

Manu got a sack and put the cat into it, and on the river's edge we
gathered rocks, put them into the sack and then placed the sack into the
boat. When we reached a deep spot, we dropped anchor and threw the
sack with the cat and rocks into the water. We went to the stern of the
boat and started fishing. That day we had luck, catching two large pike,
a sea trout and several large perch.

As was our custom, we cleaned and divided the fish. Each got half
the fish, but this time I got the trout. "Neither piece will amount to much
if we cut it in two," said Manu. "Take it to Grandma Kartano. It will make
good salt fish." He also handed me the heads and entrails and told me to
bury them in the dung hill. "We no longer have a cat to eat them, since
we took it to the river."

I left, and as I was passing by the barn I happened to glance toward
the window where I was accustomed to seeing the cat sitting. And there
it sat, licking its fur. I found Manu and said, "It is true after all that the

dead come back to haunt us. The cat we sank to the bottom of the river this morning is sitting in his customary favorite place in the barn window. Are you absolutely certain that the cat was in the bag when we dropped it in the river?" I asked him.

"Indeed it was," said Manu, "and, furthermore, it is not to be seen in the barn window any more."

I told him to come with me. "I'll call the cat to come eat the fish guts, and you'll see that the cat is back. It must have torn the sack open, swum to shore and come home. That cat has suffered the punishment of death and that is enough for anyone."

I called the cat, and it appeared. Manu laughed and said, "That cat can live until he dies a natural death."

Manu and I always split the day's catch without any disagreements. When the water was low we sometimes went into the woods to the banks of the salmon stream. We would take switches and poke around under the rocks in the river to see if there were any salmon hiding there. We would watch carefully to see which rocks they hid under. Then we'd take off our clothes and slip into the water. We'd wade to the rock and carefully feel with our hands for a fish. It could be touched anywhere but on the head or tail. We would guess its position by feel, and then suddenly press its head and tail against the rock so it couldn't go forwards or backwards. We'd give the fish a hard squeeze, and then it could be brought to shore. This kind of fishing lasted only for the period of time when the water was very low. The salmon wouldn't take a hook, but sometimes we'd get them with a lure. There were quite a few deep holes in the river from which we couldn't take them due to the many trees and branches clogging them.

There was simply no end to this type of activity. Manu and I also would go to the river when it was muddy, which was whenever we had a big rain, or during the spring floods. We made a scoop net by bending a nine-foot mountain ash sapling into a bow and inserting each end into a hole at either end of a five-foot piece of wood. We wove a loose, sack-like net onto this frame and lay a long pole across the five-foot piece of wood to the bow, tying it in both places. We placed the net in the river and pushed it down to the bottom with the aid of the long handle. Because the water was muddy, the fish were unaware of the net and did not swim away as we pulled them to shore. We usually went scoop-netting in the evening.

One midsummer's eve Manu and I planned to go scoop-netting, so I went over to Torkkoola. Manu's four grown brothers and other older people who were there asked us if we were not afraid to go fishing on the eve of such an important holiday, when "even the grass doesn't dare grow." I argued with them, but someone said, "You'll surely meet that whisk-pants out there."

I told them that I would definitely enjoy meeting him. Of course, they reasoned that we would surely come running home from the woods since the coming night was one in which all the devils were about. I said to Manu, "Don't believe them. I promise you that even if we should meet one with fire and smoke shooting from its mouth, I will welcome it and not run away. Come on!"

So off we went. It was not particularly dark and we were able to catch fish with the scoop net. Our path took us past the Laulaja bridge where the Laulaja estate had burned down. All of the buildings were in ruins with the exception of the sauna, which was located on the river-bank. From within the sauna, across the river from us, we heard a loud clatter.

"Let's get out of here," said Manu.

"Fine," I said, "but first I'll clear up the matter of this noise. I won't leave without looking into it. I've always known that emptiness does not make a sound. There is something in there."

I left Manu there and walked across the bridge to the other side of the river. The nearer I got to the sauna the louder the clatter became. I knew the sound came from inside the sauna, because, when I arrived, it stopped completely. I opened the door. Bundles of rye straw had been stored there. They reached from the floor to the roof and left only a space the width of the door at the entrance. First I felt toward the back of the door with my arms outstretched and didn't find anybody. Then I felt to the left and nobody was there either. But I happened to think that since the door opened inward and did not open all the way to the wall, some-body could be behind it. I reached behind the door and caught hold of someone's hair.

"Not so hard!" he yelled. It was one of the Torkkoola boys return-ing from his night's rounds. He had seen us coming and remembered that I had promised to take care of all the whisk-pants.

I knew him by his voice and told him to pretend to resist. I called my pal Manu to come and help me. "I have hold of a devil and we'll put him in the river."

Manu was still across the river on the other end of the bridge when he saw that I was pulling someone or something along behind me. I called again for help, but his brother began to laugh. Manu recognized his voice, so the joke ended there.

I was at work helping my grandfather in the bog behind a hill where he had undertaken to make a new field. I was going along ahead of him cutting the bog into pieces with a large ditching axe. He came along behind me with a shovel lifting pieces of soil and continuously prodding me on. I wasn't able to stay ahead, so he swore and said, "Move the axe faster."

"I can't," I told him, "I have a headache."

"You're lazy," he said.

I can't recall what I told him then, but he took the axe by the blade and began beating me with its handle. I retreated, and he came after me, threatening me and swearing. On the other side of a nearby fence was a dense stand of small pine trees that stood about five or six feet high. They grew so close together that it was difficult for a person to get through them. I jumped the fence with Grandfather after me. He was swearing, and I kept just ahead of him. His head was above most of those pine trees, but he couldn't see me all the same. I hid myself in a cluster of pines. Grandfather came right by me, and I went back across the fence and crossed the bog. I could hear him threatening me and swearing, but he didn't know that I was already on the other side of the bog. I left the old man there searching for me, and I never saw him again.

I sat in the forest thinking about everything that had happened. I came to the conclusion that I would beg for my bread. If I go back to the village of Mieta, I thought, there are only large estates, and they don't want beggars around. So I set off through the forest.

I had been traveling in one direction for a long time when I heard a cow bell and turned toward the sound. I came to a tenant farm. A couple of children were playing with a puppy. I walked up to them, and their mother came out. "Who are you?" she asked.

"Only a beggar," I replied, "and I would like something to eat."

"Where are you from?"

"From the village of Mieta," I said. "I came through the forest."

"Can't a beggar live in Mieta?" she asked.

"There are only large estates there," I told her, "and they won't even give a beggar a piece of bread. In their eyes I am not even a dog's equal."

"Are your mother and father living?" she asked.

"I believe so," I answered.

"What is their name?" she wanted to know.

"Don't ask," I replied. "I don't want to lie, and I don't want to say who I am. I don't want to steal either, but if somebody needs my help, I am ready to do any kind of work."

"I don't want to call you 'beggar,' " she said. "Couldn't you give yourself a better name?"

"My name is Iisakka, so call me Iisakka," I said.

She said, "Come in, Iisakka. I'll find you something to eat. And you can do a small job for me . . . or will you?"

"If I can do it I will," I said.

She brought out herring bread and made a sandwich. Then she put a small *viilia* on the table and asked me to come and eat. After I had eaten she took me into the barn and told me to clean it. I carried out the manure, and, when the barn was clean, I said to her, "Give me an axe, and I will make a better stanchion for your cow. I could also fix the cow's stall if you have a plank or board of some kind."

"Since it looks like rain, I think I'll put the cow into the barn," she said. "You go ahead and repair the stall, and tomorrow I'll have a good bed for you to sleep on. You don't have to go anywhere." The children were inside, and I sat outdoors on a bench next to the well.

It started to rain. She brought the cow to the barn and asked me in. Once we were inside she said, "You haven't asked our name."

"It wouldn't be right to ask you who you are when I didn't tell you my name," I said.

She paused. After a long time she asked me, "Have you ever heard anything of a man named Kalle Perakorpi?"

"Yes," I answered, "and I know that he is dead."

"I am his widow," she said, "and now I can guess who you are. You are Iisakka and Soffia's son."

"This is true," I replied, "this is who I am. Now ask me whatever you like, and I will answer truthfully. But don't tell anyone about me. I will not go back to my grandfather."

"I have a cow now, and I get milk and butter from it," she said, and I have enough fish to last a long time. There is bread, and when that is gone we can get more. If you wish, you may stay here."

I stayed for several weeks. Nobody came over in that time. I wanted to see Manu Torkkoola, so Mari, which was Mrs. Perakorpi's name, showed me the shortest route to his place. She also admonished me not to travel around begging.

"Come here whenever you feel like it," she told me.

"I will stop in to see you," I said.

So I left, following Mari's directions, as I had never traveled that route before. I went to a tenant farm. When they found out I was begging, the master told me they needed no beggars there.

My next stop along the road as I continued my journey was a small cottage where children were playing outdoors. The children's mother wanted to know my business, so I said, "I would like something to eat."

She immediately began to prepare some food. "How far is it from here to the village of Mieta?" I asked her.

"My dear child," she said, "you are many *virstas* off." (A *virsta* equals 1.067 kilometers.) You won't be able to make it today."

Nevertheless, later I found myself on the Kauhajoki side of the river, so I turned around, reversing my direction. It was getting late, and I came to an apparently well-to-do place. I made my way to the house but received a most unwelcome reception.

Before I had a chance to say anything, the lady of the house snapped at me: "We don't need beggars here!"

I turned on my heels and left the woman behind me. She kept asking me if I was a beggar. Then I heard her calling a dog and telling him, "Chase that beggar away!" The dog barked, and I stopped to look. "Bite him, Shep," she cried, "he's a bad boy."

The big dog came toward me, and I said to him, "Come here, Shep. Shep, you won't bite another 'Shep,' will you?" I stroked its head, and it wagged its tail for me.

Seeing this the woman called out, "*Hus!*," which means "sic 'em."

But instead of attacking me, the dog simply left. I said again, "It is a wise Shep who won't bite another 'Shep.' I, too, am somebody's beloved 'Shep.'"

The woman said something, but I didn't listen to what it was and instead walked away. It was quite late when I finally came to a road that turned to my left. It didn't make much difference which way I went, so I continued on ahead. I could make out a building in the darkness which turned out to be a threshing shed. I wondered whether I could find a place to sleep inside. In the rear section of the shed, I found some oat straw, and there I made my bed.

When I awoke the sun was already high. I immediately left on the same road. At the same time, I saw a house near where I had spent the night, but I knew that I needn't go there as it was a home of the wealthy. Then I found a creek and lowered myself down to the water, dipped my cap and took a drink. As I was washing my face, I heard somebody walking on the bridge. When I saw it was a young girl about my age, I went back up on the road.

The girl looked at me and exclaimed, "You're covered with straw! Where have you spent the night?" She began brushing straw from my coat with her hand. "Were you in the Ahtos' threshing shed all night?"

"I don't know whose shed it is, but that's the one," I said, pointing to the building.

"It is the Ahtos' shed. Where are you going?"

"It doesn't make any difference where," I answered, "but I should get something to eat."

"Keep going along this road, but not too fast," she said. "I have to get our cow, and then I'll catch up to you. Surely Mother will give you something to eat."

I waited where I was, and the girl eventually came back. We walked along together for a while and shared some dried meat and a *viilia*.

I continued my journey. It was summer, and one could spend one's nights in sheds or wherever one happened to be. I wasn't concerned about where I went and simply passed my time wandering here and there. Once, when it was well past mid-day, and I hadn't eaten anything yet, I found myself alone on a road that had been made through large forests. Nor were there settlements along the way. I was hungry when I came upon a small house and a stable near the road. I approached the door. It was open, and I saw four men inside, one of whom was bringing a bowl of porridge to the table.

He looked at me and asked, "What do you want?"

"I would like to share that bowl of porridge with you," I answered.

He turned to someone and said, "What does the master say to this?"

The master was the eldest of the group. His face was covered with a beard. His eyes were mild and happy. He had the look of a man who welcomed fun and moved gracefully. "Let the boy take my place at the table," he answered after looking me over.

He took a spoon and marked the bowl of porridge into four equal parts. Leaving the spoon on one of the portions he pushed the bowl to the center of the table, saying, "This is your share. I will begin checking out the *penkki velli* ["bench-soup"] to see how it is."

Everybody laughed, and we sat down at the table. The man who had carried the porridge to the table now brought a butter dish over. He took a large spoon of butter and stuck it in the middle of the bowl of porridge.

"There it is," I said, "an eye for the porridge."

They all glanced up at me, and one of them said, "The boy is from Kurikka. There they give the porridge an 'eye.' Here we call it a 'driver.'"

"I heard the master mention a moment ago that he intended to see how the bench-soup was doing," I said. "I wonder what bench-soup is."

They laughed, and the master said, "It is a soup that is cooked on and under the bench." He searched under a bench there in the room. "Where has that flagon of bench-soup been taken? Renki Matti, where is the flagon?"

They all laughed again, and the one named Matti said, "Wait, let's eat first. I don't want you to start anything with it now. You'll certainly get the flagon later."

"You didn't place it on top of the chimney, did you? It will begin to do crazy things up there."

"No," replied Matti, "It isn't up there."

Then the master changed his tone. "The boy is hungry. Matti, bring out some dried meat and spread butter thickly on his bread. When was the last time you had something to eat?" he asked me.

"I had a little food yesterday," I answered. "It wasn't much, but I'll manage with this porridge."

The master regarded me kindly and said, "My child, food will not end by eating it. Go ahead and eat all you want."

Matti brought meat and buttered bread to the table and I dug in. "Are you truly from Kurikka as Heikki said earlier?" the master asked me.

"Yes, I am."

Now the bench-soup was brought to the master. When he touched it, the cork began to sizzle. Instantaneously the cork flew into the air and bench-soup squirted up to the rafters. He placed his mouth over the bottle's neck and got his beard, face and eyes full of soup. It was literally everywhere. When he pointed the neck of the bottle down, not a drop came out, but when he turned it upright toward himself, it sprayed out, causing everyone to laugh.

Matti said to me, "Now you see what bench-soup is like."

"It seems rather like *syoma juurta*," I said, "which is made in Kurikka from an edible root."

"Matti," said the master, "bring this boy a dish so that he might enjoy the flagon's bench-soup with me. The others don't know what is good."

Renki Matti brought me a dish and said to the master, "The next time you can go into the woods with your flagon. Do I always have to clean up the mess left by you and your flagon? And this isn't the first time. Every time we come here that soup squirts up into the *lehteri*."

I asked what a *lehteri* was, and they showed me an open sleeping loft built up high at the roof line. The steps leading up to it had been made by drilling holes into the log wall and by driving a ten- to twelve-inch peg into each hole. These pegs made a nice ladder. "In Kurikka," I said, "this is known as a *komppeli*."

I was given a two-quart wooden bowl of bench-soup. It was still bubbling when I took a drink. "Why, this is *pontikkaa* [moonshine]!" I exclaimed breathlessly.

They all laughed.

I collected myself and said to them, "What I mean is that the stronger it is, the more effective it is against hunger. Mmmmm. Good. This will surely keep a man on the road. It is exactly what my soul craves."

Now they went into convulsions of laughter. Eventually, the master wiped his eyes and said, "If I ask you a few questions, will you answer me honestly and not lie to me?"

"If I cannot tell you the truth, I also will not lie. A lie leaves a short trail, so it is better to say nothing."

"I would like to know who you are," he continued.

I gave him a brief account. "I am a beggar. During the entire time that I have spent begging, I haven't told anyone my name, except a widow who is the mother of two children. You have been obliging to me and have given me what you yourselves have, so if you have time to listen, I will tell you the events of my life."

The master said, "We're here cutting grain, but it is now wet. Because of the rain we have the time, so do tell us."

I told them where I was born, how my father went to America, how Mikko Perapolvi freed me of all fear and how I showed the other boys that I didn't fear evil spirits or sorcerers. I told them how I was left with my grandfather when my mother went to America, and how I had been treated while begging; about how I had spent nights in threshing and hay barns, and about many nights spent alone in dense forests.

"But tell us," one of the men said, "where in the world did you get those clothes? They are so patched that it is impossible to tell the patch from the original material they were made from."

I laughed and said, "I had rather good clothes when I ran away from Kartano, but as I traveled around begging people said, 'The beggar is certainly wearing good clothing.' One day I went into a cottage where a widow was patching these trousers. There were six children there. A boy my age and size sat on a bench waiting while his mother sewed this patch here." I pointed to the patch and they all nodded. "She said, 'Here they are. I don't know where I'll get clothing for you. These are already so patched that I don't want to see them on my son anymore.' So she tossed them on the floor.

"I picked them up and said, 'They should be on me.'

"The widow had a coffee pot on the fire, so I said to her, 'Give me bread and a cup of coffee, and he can have my clothes. They'll fit him.'

"'That can't be,' she said. 'Then what will you do for clothing? Have you stolen them?'

"'I am a beggar,' I answered, 'but I don't steal, nor do I lie. These clothes are too good for me. People always complain that the beggar has such good clothing.'

"I took my trousers off, saying to the boy, 'Try these to see how they fit.'

"The widow said that it wasn't right, but I insisted that her son put them on. He did as he was told. I put his trousers on in turn and said, 'Your coat and cap.'

"The boy said he didn't have a coat, but he did have a smock. 'Bring them to me, boy,' I said.

"And the boy brought them, and we made the exchange. I then asked the widow, 'Do you have a piece of bread to give me to seal the bargain?'

"'If you are hungry,' she replied, 'then you can have whatever we have.' She put bread, herring and a long draught of home-brew on the table. I ate and was nourished.

"I thanked them and started walking, but a few days later I noticed that I had lice. I recalled my mother telling us that a louse says, 'Cook me in ashes and lye, but don't take me to the sauna.'

"Thus I had to get to a sauna so that I could hang my clothes over the sauna stove, throw water on it to make a lot of steam and get into the steam myself. I was sure that I hadn't raised such long-tailed lice myself. I sat in the bushes talking to myself while picking lice and dropping them in the grass. 'It is enough that I have to beg for my sustenance. I shouldn't have to support you, too. You can learn to eat grass like a cow. I refuse to feed you anymore.' I put my smock back on and then continued my travels.

"A few days later I noticed a sauna that was being warmed at a tenant farm. I walked in and said, 'I see you have your sauna warmed. May I share some hot steam and have your permission to wash my shirt here tonight?'

"The head of the household added sarcastically, '. . . and give you food this evening and again in the morning, and why not a warm bed for the night while we're at it, eh?'

"'I'm not begging anything from you except a sauna bath,' I said. 'I will leave immediately after my bath and after washing my shirt.'

"'You don't need to go anywhere,' said the man's wife. 'We have food to give you if you are hungry. Feel free to spend the night, too, as we have a spare bed that is nice and warm.'

"I said, 'I haven't slept in a bed for a long time. Nor do I crave one. But a hot sauna will do me more good right now than even food and lodging.'

"Why is that?' asked the housewife.

"I told them the whole story and ended it saying, 'I don't want to leave my lice with anybody, but I want to be rid of them.'

"This was a young couple with one child. The wife said to her husband, 'Matti, is there a place over the sauna stove where this boy can hang his clothing? He seems to be honest, and he was so forthright about his situation. Where do you come from? What's your name?'

"I answered, 'I am merely a beggar. Iisakka is my name, but I don't want to say any more about myself, and I don't want to lie. Please be so kind as to not ask.'

"But the woman continued with her questions. 'Is your mother living?'

"I didn't answer her and Matti said, 'He begged you not to ask. I'll go into the sauna with you to see that you get everything you need there. But first let us eat.'

"The housewife prepared food for the table, and we sat down to eat. The child, I noticed, was sleeping in a cradle to which the wife had added two boards to each side. Now should the baby awaken when we were in the sauna, it wouldn't fall out. And then the three of us went to the sauna. I took off my clothes, and Matti picked them up and hung them on hooks over the sauna stove. His wife said, 'You need entirely new clothing.'

"'These will do if only I get rid of the lice. They should fall on the stove due to the steam.'

"'But that shirt is so dirty and sweaty. I'll give you another shirt I have. I'm sure it will fit you.'

"And we three threw water on the rocks and climbed up on the benches. Matti even gave me a whisk. I said to them, 'I haven't been in a sauna for almost a year, but I've been swimming often. I've tried to wash away the dirt and sweat, but swimming is not the equal of this sauna.'

"We washed up and the wife said, 'Take those clothes in the house and put them on there. Leave the shirt here. I have another, and I think I'll find a warm, clean smock, too.'

"When we got indoors Matti had another shirt which I put on. His wife showed me a bed which was an upper bunk. I slept well and awakened near mid-day the next day. They fed me again. Yes, I got this smock you see on me here. I thanked them and left, but the woman stopped me and asked if my mother was living, and, if so, why I had left her.

"'My mother is living,' I replied, 'but far away. I didn't leave her. She was forced to leave me. I am going to see her soon.' So I started walking and now I am here before you."

The master stroked his beard thoughtfully and said, "You really don't fear anything by day or by night?"

"This is true," I said. "I'm not afraid. Even a dog won't bite me, so I don't even have to fear that. All dogs are my friends."

To this the master replied, "Listen, boy, I have a good place for you if you wish to stop this traveling about. My sister lives alone and apart from people with only her dog. She has three cows, a few heifers and a calf. She needs a boy of your type there. She says that she's afraid living alone like that. You see, her husband is dead, and her fifteen-year-old son died seven months ago. She'll even have clothing and shoes to fit you. I know she'd be happy to have you come and stay with her."

"I don't know how to get there," I said.

"Well, then," he replied. "I will take you there immediately, if you'll go."

"How far is it?" I asked.

"We'll go there by horse. I'll stay there the night and come back tomorrow." He then said to the others, "You boys can cut oats if the weather permits. I will be back tomorrow." And to me he said, "What do you say? Will you go?"

"I will go," I answered.

"Renki Matti," he said, "harness the black and we'll be there before dark."

The black was hitched to a very light two-wheeler and we left straightaway. We went over the Kauhajoki River, and I told him, "I have traveled through here before—as far as the village of Kirves."

"We'll go through there."

The black wanted to run, so it didn't seem to have any problem getting us there quickly, even though the last stretch of road was very bad.

I could see a small threshing building, a sauna, a barn and a hayshed. There was even a granary. He drove under the shed roof and grabbed an armful of hay for the black.

A woman of about forty-five came out of the house and greeted her brother. "John! I didn't expect you at all this time. Who is this boy?"

John said, "I brought him here to you so you won't always be alone. He is good and honest. His name is Iisakka. You'll like him. You still have Eric's clothes and shoes. Iisakka doesn't have shoes, and from now on he should have them."

A dog was barking and making a big racket inside the house. "Why don't you let the dog out?" I asked her.

"No, no," said the woman, "it is vicious and will bite you."

"Bite me?" I said. "It won't bite me. No dog has bitten me yet."

John urged his sister to let the dog out. "We'll see how the dog and Iisakka relate to one another."

I went toward the sauna away from John, and his sister reluctantly opened the door to the house. The dog started to go to the horse and John, but I clapped my hands to attract his attention saying, "Come here and I'll stroke your head. We're friends."

The dog came and sniffed me. Then its tail gave a friendly wag. John and the widow laughed. The dog ran toward John, but the woman quieted it down.

There were two heifers, three milk cows and three calves in a small fenced-in area. John put the black in there with them. Then he went into the house, and the dog followed after me, always on my heels. The dog's name was Hupi. The woman, John's sister, was named Sanna.

"Where did you get the boy?" Sanna asked John.

"I am a beggar," I said to her, "but I have promised John that I won't beg any more, and I promised him that I will be your good boy for a time. I am not afraid of anything—not even evil spirits. You can use me as bait to catch a hobgoblin if you like. Not even a hobgoblin's tooth can touch me. What I mean," I added, "is that there aren't any hobgoblins."

Sanna asked me if I knew how to read and write. "I sure do," I answered. "My mother taught me."

"Where is your mother?"

"My mother is in America," I told her, "and I am going to be with her when my mother and father send me a ticket."

John then came in with some sheers and said, "I want to shorten your hair. Tomorrow Sanna will dress you like a young lord. You won't need your official uniform, as you no longer hold the office of beggar. You are now Sanna's good boy."

And, as he began cutting my hair, he said to Sanna, "This boy has slept in threshing sheds, straw sheds, hay barns, forests, saunas—wherever he happened to be. Wash his head and neck. It would even be better if you took him into the sauna."

"Do you have lice?" Sanna asked.

"No," I replied, "and I don't believe I'm very dirty. I've done a lot of swimming."

Sanna inspected me carefully. She wiped my head and neck with a clean towel. "I'll give you another shirt and fresh clothing that you can put on in the morning. Now I'm going to bed. You can sleep with John."

When I finally awoke nobody was in the house. I put my clothes on and went outside and was immediately greeted by the dog. John and

Sanna came from the cow barn. John already had the black in the shed and was about to harness up.

"Let's eat first. You can't leave without eating," Sanna said to him. John asked me, "How did you sleep?"

"I slept very well," I replied. "I like it here much better than in the forests or barns."

After we had eaten, John said to me, "I'll be seeing you again, Iisakka. Try to be a good boy, and Sanna will see that you have a good home." And then he was gone, and I was left alone with Sanna.

She turned the cows and heifers loose in the woods saying, "Those calves should also be let loose in the woods, but I'm afraid they won't follow the cows."

"I'll go with them and see that they do," I said.

"No, not so fast," she said, "but maybe later. I hardly know you yet. And you'll get lost out there in the woods."

I said to her, "Those cows will come home without our getting them. But in any case, I will stay with the cows to see that the calves don't wander away."

We went into the house. "If you care to listen I will tell you about myself," I said, "so that you can't say that you don't know me. I really want to tell you everything from as far back as I can remember."

"I was just about to suggest that you do just that," she replied.

So I told Sanna about my family, saying all I could possibly remember about how my mother taught me how to read, about my being left with my grandfather, how I ran away, and how I traveled about begging. At last I said, "If there is something more that you wish to know . . . I want to tell all there is to tell."

We talked together all that day, and she told me about herself. I found out that the place was called Takamaa.

The dog Hupi stayed close to me. Sanna was surprised that Hupi had accepted me so readily. "A dog always knows another dog," I said. "Once somebody tried to sic a dog on me, but it went away. They couldn't get the dog to bite me, as all dogs are my friends." Then I asked her, "Where are my trousers? I want to wear them tomorrow when I go into the woods with the cattle. The clothes you gave me are too good to wear in the woods."

"Oh, I have lots of clothes for you," she replied. She got up and began collecting them. She brought clothes, plus shoes and stockings for my feet.

The next morning I was ready to go. Sanna gave me a knife and sheath and offered me some food to take along. "A piece of hard bread is all I need. I don't want anything else." But she did put butter on the bread. Then she brought out some cheese wrapped up in white cloth, which she put into my pocket. Together we turned the calves out with the cows.

An entire new world opened up before me. I was very curious to learn what forest animals there were, so I went to a spruce tree to look for signs of birds or rabbits. Under the very first tree I found signs of black grouse. I also found ptarmigan feathers and saw a rabbit. But I didn't dare leave the calves alone, so, therefore it was impossible to be very far from the cattle. Indeed, I kept a sharp eye on the calves, and they seemed to follow the cows and heifers.

I sat under a spruce tree eating my lunch. The cows had changed direction, I noticed, and the calves followed them. I got up and ran after them because they quickly disappeared onto the lower ground. They stopped to drink at a small creek, where I found many hazel grouse. Then, after they had drunk their fill, the cows turned in the direction of home but didn't go far before they lay down. From my position I saw a small opening on the other side of the creek where there was low ground. When I got to it, I was astonished at the abundance of the whortleberries there. I set out to look for a birch tree, and when I found one, I made a berry basket from the bark. Soon I was picking whortleberries.

Eventually the cows stood up, one after another, and since my basket was full, I decided to follow them. When I found that our destination was not far, I took a shortcut to Takamaa and presented the basket to Sanna. "Do you like these berries?"

"Yes," she said, "but where did you find such large blueberries?"

"They're whortleberries," I told her. "Blueberries grow on short bushes. These grow on tall ones."

"Did the cows come home?" she asked.

"They are near," I answered. "The calves followed the cows, and I haven't once had to hurry."

Hupi stayed at home to protect Sanna. Sanna had told me that she was afraid to be alone, but with Hupi there she felt safe. When the cattle came home, I opened the gate to the night pasture from which we let them into the barn. Sanna milked them and left with the milk. I turned them out and then cleaned the barn. Finally, when we were eating supper, she wanted to know if there were a lot more of the whortleberries and whether the berry patch was far off.

"Do you think you could find it again?" she asked. "I would like you to take me there."

"We'll turn the cattle out in the morning and go there by the shortest route," I said. "I don't doubt that the calves will follow and come to drink at the creek at midday. We'll have our baskets full by then, too, and I'll bring you home. Hupi can come with us as well."

The next morning Sanna prepared a lunch for us. She had dried meat and cheese for us and even considered taking a coffee pot and such. But I thought this would be too much. "We'll have enough to carry with the berry baskets. Plus we have good water there, so we'll manage." Then we turned out the cattle, locked the doors and left on our trip. Hupi was happy that he could come along.

"When I go out," said Sanna, "I always leave the dog home to watch. But he also likes to get away sometimes."

I took her along the shortest route, and soon we were picking berries. There certainly were a lot of them. It was not long before our bark baskets were full.

"Now we must eat," Sanna announced. So we went to sit beside the creek and had our lunch.

Time passed, and we still didn't hear the cows, so I said, "I'll go to a higher place to check whether I can still hear them."

I hadn't gone far when I heard the soft tinkle of a bell. I returned to Sanna's side and told her, "They're coming. We'll wait here awhile to see if the calves are still with them."

In the meantime I told Sanna how I used to snare birds in the woods when I was with my mother. "If I could get some long horsehair and flax, I will make some snares."

"I have plenty of flax," said Sanna, "and I think that we can get horsehair at the neighbor's."

Right after we got home, Sanna took berries to the neighbor's and said, "I have a herd boy my brother John brought to me. He says he needs some horsehair to make snares to catch the birds he has seen in the forest. He is just a youth, but I hope to keep him with me. I've brought you some of the berries we picked. He found a berry patch yesterday and got me so excited about it that I went along with him today. There certainly were a lot of berries there."

When she got back home, I learned from her that some people would be coming over to pick berries. "You must take them to the berry patch," she ordered.

"You must accompany us," I said, "so that they'll have less of an opportunity to question me."

Sanna laughed and promised to come.

In the morning a man and his wife came over. They were master and mistress of the estate. I already had learned that they did all the horsework at Takamaa. The man's name was Mikko. He brought some horsehair and left it at the corner of the cow barn. As we were leaving for the woods, I showed them the manure pile and discussed how important it was that one put twigs in with the manure. "I'll cut them a little at a time as time allows." Then the four of us were off for a morning of berry picking. And once at the patch we again filled our baskets. Thinking I would stay with the cattle, I asked if they could find their way back.

"No, you can go home with us now," Sanna said. "The calves will come home later this evening. We needn't be concerned about the cattle."

When we got home Sanna gave me some flax, and I set about making snares. It was Saturday, and it was my job to warm the sauna. In my spare time, I twisted snares. I made fourteen in all from the horsehair and flax. The cattle came home as usual. I carried water to the sauna and got everything ready. Sanna milked the cows, and, after we had eaten, Sanna and I went into the sauna. She brought me another clean shirt, and, after we had taken steam, she washed and cleaned my head, feet and body.

"I'm so happy to have such a nice healthy boy," she remarked. "You won't run away, will you?"

"If I can stay here with you, I promise that I won't run away," I said. "But next spring I will visit Mieta. No, I won't run away, and you know I don't lie. But sometime next summer they will send me a ticket, and I will go to America to be with my mother. Just when the ticket will arrive I don't know."

"Because tomorrow is Sunday," Sanna said, "I want you to dress yourself up and stay home. There is talk in the village that I have a boy here, and people will surely come out for a look at you."

"As you wish," I replied.

In the morning Sanna brought me some clothes. They were of good quality, and they were clean. She began preparing food. I helped her get the cows into the barn and later helped her turn them out again. When this was done I decided to see what literature Sanna had in the house. It was all church literature. I found an old hymnal and showed it to Sanna.

"Do you read this?" I asked her.

"I don't know how to read it," she replied. "It came to me as my mother's legacy."

"My mother taught me to read from this very book. It was my first ABC primer."

"You know how to read this book?" she asked.

"Yes," I replied. "I read the Bible history four times in all before I ever saw another book. The entire Bible history is in the last part of this hymnal. In the present-day version some chapters are interpreted in an entirely different way. For example, in this old version we read that Christ died on the cross and descended into the kingdom of death. However, in the present-day version we read that He descended into hell. To me this is contradictory. Why was it changed to read, 'Christ descended into hell'? He died with a clear conscience. He couldn't go to hell. I'll never accept this passage."

Sanna didn't respond, and I didn't know what she thought of my saying this about the Bible history. But later, when the visitors from the village were there, I was still looking at books.

"Can this boy of yours read?" asked a woman visitor. "I see he has books open before him."

"Ask them the question you put to me earlier about Christ's death," Sanna suggested.

I said, "Well, I have here a Bible history that is a text of an 'original' translation into the Finnish language. It reads as follows: 'Christ died on the cross and descended into the kingdom of death.'" I set that hymnal aside and opened another hymnal. "And here in our present-day version of the Bible history it states, 'He descended into hell.' This is a contradiction. Why should He, Christ, who had no sin, who died for our sins of His own free will, and with a clear conscience—why should He have gone to hell? Isn't that dictated by a person's conscience? Everything good within us is of God."

A man in the group said, "I think you're too young to judge the Bible."

"But I wasn't judging the Bible," I answered, "I was criticizing the fabrication in this Bible history. The thought comes to mind, how many times has this history already been falsified? And how was the 'original' history written? In your minds this is something that must be overlooked in silence. I don't agree with that."

The moment I closed the book, they began to ask where I was born, where I went to school, how old I was. Above all they wanted to know how I had learned to read that old hymnal, since they didn't know how.

My answers to their questions were very brief. Sanna noticed that I was reluctant to say anything, so she intervened. "Iisakka, how would it be if you were to see if the cattle have stayed together? I'm a little concerned about the calves."

"They should be at the drinking place by now," I said. "I'll go and meet them there."

I excused myself from the company, changed clothes, picked up my snares and went directly to their watering place. The cattle lay down, so I crossed the creek and set some snares. Then I went a little beyond as well, since I wanted to set a few more snares and get the lay of the land. I again crossed the creek and placed two more snares under a spruce. I decided to return with an axe to make a winter shelter for the birds there.

When I got home, Mikko and his wife were there from the farm. I again said to Mikko, "If I could get evergreen branches, I could chop them up a little at a time. I saw a good spot there, only we lack branches and a chopping bench."

Mikko said, "I'll be coming over with a horse soon to drag in winter wood. At that time we can collect branches and set up a chopping bench."

The other visitors left, but Mikko and his wife stayed. Sanna served us all a *viilia*. After Mikko and his wife had gone, I asked Sanna, "What did our visitors think of me?"

"They don't think badly of you," she said. "In fact they paid you a compliment by saying, 'That boy should get some schooling.' They liked you. And they said your mother was a learned and wise mother."

"When I was with my mother, I didn't know it," I commented, "but when I left her care, I then realized what a good mother I had."

The following day I went into the woods with an axe and began preparing shelters for my snares while looking for the best place to make a trail. When I got home that evening I said to Sanna, "In a few days we'll be eating fowl."

"Not so fast," she replied. "Don't expect too much. I haven't eaten fowl in years."

"We'll be eating it this very week," I promised, "and I expect that we'll also have some fish. I saw a fish in the creek where the cows go to drink, so I made a fish trap from branches. I didn't find any willow, but I should get a few fish with it anyway. I believe it was a pike I saw, and it isn't alone. There are others."

Sanna told me where to find willow, so I went there the following day and made another fish trap. After a few days passed I took it to the creek, setting it in the water much further downstream. When I checked the first trap I had made I found that I had indeed caught a pike. In the snares were two grouse and two partridges. I gave the bag of game to Sanna. She fried fish, while I cleaned two of the birds for our meal.

"Should we give the other two birds to Mikko?" I asked her.

She promised to take them to him, and after she did so Mikko urged her to bring him all the birds I caught, which he said he could sell for a good price. I got more horsehair from him to use in making snares, plus I made another willow fish trap. I went downstream and found better places for the traps and the snares.

I spent most of my time in the woods. Every other day I checked my fish trap. We had fish every day. There was even enough for Sanna to take some to Mikko. He took all of the birds I caught to town.

Mikko came to cut firewood for Sanna. He also brought branches for me to chop up for the manure pile. I set myself a certain amount of branches I was supposed to chop. I also cut firewood into stove-length chunks. Mikko brought me a saw that was in good condition, measured off the length the firewood should be and gave me a couple of splitting wedges for the larger blocks.

As I said, I got so many fish from those traps that Sanna could take some to Mikko. And, Sanna took all the birds for Mikko to sell in town. One day Mikko came over and said to me, "I have the money my selling the birds brought in."

"Don't give it to me," I said, "give it to Sanna. She's my mother now. She gives me what I need. Take it to her. It belongs to her. Nothing belongs to me. From her I get shoes, socks and clothing. She provides my food . . . everything I need. I don't need money, but she does, so give it to her. It's hers, not mine."

He went in, and I was left there chopping branches at the bench. He hadn't been in the house long when he returned and said, "I left the money with Sanna."

"That was the right thing to do. She needs it, and I don't," I told him. But when I went in, Sanna immediately began to talk about the money.

"It belongs to you," she said.

I went to her like a little boy, hugging her and crying. "Please don't say any more about it, not another word. If you knew everything I've experienced since I was separated from my mother; if you knew the treatment that has been my lot while begging. . . . There's no money— not all the gold in the world—that could equal the sympathy and love you've given me while I've been here. I love you, Sanna, like my own mother."

Sanna encircled me with her arms, and I was as a child, even though I had already reached the age of fourteen. "I will write to you after I go to my mother in America," I said.

We both cried and Sanna said, "I've had such a lonely time these seven months since my son has been dead, until you came into my life as if by fate. You are my happiness. At first I was afraid that you'd leave me and go away, but I'm not afraid any more. I feel so fortunate that you are with me this winter."

The following morning I again went into the forest for the day. From the snares I collected eight grouse, two ptarmigan and two partridge. The fish traps yielded four pike. This was my biggest single catch yet.

"I didn't even check all the snares," I told Sanna that evening. "I'll go out in the morning to check the rest. These birds should be taken to Mikko, but it's too late now. When are we going to dig potatoes?"

"Mikko is coming over tomorrow morning to open up the rows with the horse and cultivator," Sanna answered, "so they'll soon be picked and bagged."

"In that case, it would be best if I didn't go into the woods tomorrow," I said. "I'll stay at home so that we can get all the potatoes picked."

In the morning I showed Mikko the fish and birds I had caught. When he learned that I hadn't yet checked all the snares and that I intended to do so later, he asked me why.

"I want to help you pick potatoes today," I answered.

"My wife is coming with her sister and her sister's son, plus the boy who helped them pick potatoes yesterday. We'll get them all picked today. You'll do much more good in the woods than in the potato field. Just go into the woods," Mikko said.

"First I'll check with Sanna to see what she says," I replied.

She and Mikko both urged me to go into the woods, so I left, taking an axe with me. Once in the woods, I made snare shelters and set more snares. I caught two large pike and four grouse. Later, when I came home they were eating fish *keitto*, which is fish, potatoes and milk boiled together. All the potatoes were stored in the root cellar. Mikko received the birds and said he would take them to town. Sanna prepared a fish dish and gave Mikko what was left over.

One evening when we had finished our chores, Sanna's brother John drove into the yard. I ran to greet him, telling the dog Hupi to stop barking, which he did immediately. "You arranged a good home and a good mother for me," I said. "I thank you."

Sanna also came out to greet her brother. I took the horse to the stable and gave it fresh hay and water. I heard Sanna explaining my enterprise to John. When I finally went inside they seemed very satisfied with me.

John began the conversation by saying, "I saw you when you first showed up at our cottage door, but I didn't pay any attention to you. But on hearing those bold and at the same time friendly words, 'Could I share in your porridge bowl?,' I was ready to give you what we had. The more we talked, the more I was impressed by you. Now I'm most thankful that I brought you here. Are you content? Is there anything you need?"

"I like it here," I said, "but when we get a lot of snow I will need a pair of light skis. I won't take them with me when I have to leave. I'll leave them here. When summer comes I am going to Mieta, but that won't be until early June."

"Don't worry about the skis," John said. "I'll bring you two pairs I made. You can use both pairs. I have half a dozen made."

The evening passed pleasantly, and it was quite late when he left for home. Early the next morning, I hurried to cut winter wood, and to split and pile it. I didn't go into the woods for several days.

In the meantime, Mikko brought the grain to the shed in front of the threshing building so that it wouldn't get wet. He said, "Soon the fall rains will begin. Put this grain into the shed when it's convenient. It will be dry here."

The next morning I went into the woods again to check the fish traps. I caught only two pike, even though I hadn't been there for four nights. I went downstream and found a small lake where I decided to sit and eat my lunch. To my surprise I saw a fish going upstream into the creek. I watched the water for a long time and saw both large and small fish going upstream. I thought to myself, my fish traps are set for fish going downstream. I must construct a throat trap, which is a fish trap with a small, funnel-like opening. I can't catch fish that are traveling upstream with the traps I have.

After that I went to look at my snares and had caught eight birds. It began to rain, and I was soaked by the time I got home. Sanna felt bad. I laughed and said, "This is only the beginning."

She brought me some dry clothes, and I told her my plan. "I must make throat traps, but there's more work in making them than in the traps I've been making."

The next morning it rained lightly, but I still managed to get willow and start work on the traps. Sanna came to watch me tie willow into hoops with willow bindings.

"Why don't you tie them with some sort of cord?" she asked.

"It would have to be cord made of flax," I said.

"My husband used to make nets, and the cord he used is in the granary. It's flax. I think it'll work well." She then brought me a large ball of net lacing.

"This will do fine," I said. "I'll have a throat trap in a couple of days."

I worked hard on the project and then saw that I didn't have enough willow to make as many hoops as I needed. I went to get some more willow, and, on returning, asked Sanna if I could work indoors that evening so I could complete my work. Sanna gave me permission, so at ten that night my throat trap was finished.

In the morning I started off for the creek with the new throat trap. It was heavy, and I soon got tired, but I eventually made it to the site of my lowest trap. I removed it from the water and there was one pike in it. I put the new trap there in place of the old one and placed the old one under a spruce tree to wait for the spring run. I did leave an old trap in the water to catch everything that attempted to go downstream, and I told the new trap to catch everything that attempted to go upstream. Again, when I checked my snares, I had three grouse. It rained lightly all day, so I was wet once again when I got home. Sanna again brought me dry clothing. "I expect a big catch tomorrow from the new fish trap," I told her.

"If it rains I don't want you to get wet again," she said.

"So long as it isn't cold, the rain does no harm," I replied.

It wasn't raining in the morning, so I went directly to check the new trap. In it were eight turbot, which I took home. I asked Sanna to take four to Mikko and to have Mikko get the birds from me himself, since there were too many for her to carry. Mikko came over even before Sanna got away. He was pleased to have more fish, and he even presented me with a larger leather pouch to use to carry my catch.

"My neighbor is going to town tomorrow," said Mikko. "He came to see if I had more birds."

"I won't be going into the woods tomorrow," I said, "since I have to chop up and pile the branches you brought, plus saw more firewood."

"Forget the branches for now, but go ahead and try to cut up the stumps. In a few days I'll bring over some dry firewood to mix in with the green for burning. When we get snow I'll bring more logs and another load of branches. I should also put firewood near the threshing shed. The sauna has enough."

After Mikko left, I started sawing the wood into blocks. The saw was in good condition, and it seemed to me that there was no difficulty here. The wood seemed light. I even moved heavy logs easily with my pry bar.

I had cut up half of the tree trunks when Sanna came around and said, "There is fish *keitto*. Come and eat." She had cooked a turbot, along with the milk and potatoes. It was almost better than pike.

After supper when Sanna went into the barn to complete her chores, I asked her if she needed me. "If not, I'll saw up some more of that firewood. It's coming along fine."

"Go ahead," she answered, and so I stayed at the pile of firewood until well after dark. Eventually she came out to get me saying, "You're tiring yourself out."

It was the same thing the next day. Right after we were through in the barn, I went back to the woodpile. Before dark, I was through making firewood. It was all cut up and piled. And Sanna had once again made *keitto* from turbot.

That having been accomplished, the next morning I went to check on my fish traps and my snares. Oh, what wonders there were to behold when I pulled up my fish trap! It was full of turbot. But what was even more amazing was that there were four wild ducks in it as well. I couldn't understand how they fit in the throat of that fish trap, but I later decided that they probably bent the willow hoops back and forced their way in. When I got the whole thing on shore, I quickly put all the small turbot back into the creek, but the four ducks and twenty-two turbot I put into my pouch. The pouch was so heavy that I decided then to make for home with my catch. I didn't put the fish trap back in the creek. Why take more than is needed?

It was noon by the time I made it home. I said to Sanna, "My fish trap was completely full. I even put ten smaller turbot back into the creek. What should we do with all these fish? The ducks are plump and they'll be good to eat, but there are so many fish. Plus they're too heavy to be carried around."

We were discussing it still when Mikko drove up, his horse pulling a wagon-load of firewood. When Mikko heard about my catch he said, "Take all the fish you can. I will use them to pay the men in the village when I need help with the threshing."

I agreed to do it. "I'll go check my snares tomorrow, plus re-set the fish trap." I said to Sanna, "There are enough fish for us. Mikko should take all the fish I brought home today, plus two of the ducks. I'll probably get a few pike from my other fish trap. I didn't check it today."

After Mikko had gone, Sanna said, "I should have given Mikko money for the firewood and his labor, but the money from the birds belongs to you."

"It's your money," I told her. "Use it for all of your needs. I wish that I could make so much we wouldn't ever have too little money. When I came here I had neither clothes nor shoes. All I had was hunger and a good appetite. You gave me a home, put clothes on my back and shoes on my feet and gave me everything I needed. But the most precious gift has been your gift of motherly love, your sympathy." I hugged Sanna.

I knew how fortunate I was. We wept for joy.

But there was firewood to pile. I went out and put up the wood Mikko had brought, working quite awhile before I went back into the house.

The next morning I went into the woods and set my fish traps. A large flock of ducks flew upstream, just above the water. Shortly, while I was checking my snares, I noticed more and more ducks going in the same direction. I wondered if a lake might not be their destination, although I couldn't be sure, as I hadn't previously gone upstream very far.

My second trap yielded a couple of large pike. Altogether there were eight birds in my snares. It was still early when I got home. Sanna took the pike to Mikko. When she returned, she told me Mikko had the money the birds brought. She paid Mikko twenty-two marks for the firewood and his labor; then she gave me forty-two marks.

"You earned the money."

I said to her, "You don't need to give an account of this money. Today is Sunday. Tomorrow I would like to walk up that creek to see what is up there that the turbot swim upstream and the ducks fly in that direction. I believe there's a lake up there."

In the morning Sanna prepared a lunch for me to take along. I went up the creek about three miles and discovered that I was right. There was indeed a lake in the forest. It was six miles from the lower lake I knew about. The turbot were trying to get from the smaller to the larger lake for winter, because the latter was the deeper of the two. There were lots of ducks there, too. I hurried home and arrived by two o'clock.

We had visitors, Mikko and his wife. Mikko urged me to catch a lot of fish. He was about to start heating the threshing shed. "Wednesday will be threshing day. There'll be five or six men here."

"Are you coming tomorrow morning?" I asked.

"I'll be here early. Why?"

"Because my fish traps will be full. You can accompany me and help carry the load. I should check my snares, too," I added.

Mikko came over with the two men. They were there to load the threshing shed and place grain on the racks to dry. Mikko and I went to the fish traps and found we had around thirty turbot. Again there were ducks; two large ones this time.

"The ducks will be good for the threshing crew," I said to him. "Give them to Sanna. I'll get a lot of fish tomorrow. Take these and give them to whomever you wish." I went to a place upstream and placed more snares, so that now half my snares were downstream and half upstream. I placed my fish traps about half-way in between my two groups of snares. I caught another pike and five birds this way.

And so my time passed.

Mikko, it turned out, was a brother to Sanna's late husband, which explains their close relationship. He regarded her as a sister, and she treated him as a brother. He brought me a pair of shoes in payment for the fish I had given him. He had had them made at the cobbler's. "The shoes you have on need half-soles," he said. He took them to the cobbler as well. We had a feast of fish and duck on threshing day. I had enough left over so that I could give a couple of fish to each helper.

Before the snows came, John Salo brought over two pairs of skis. I gave him two ducks, two turbot and a pike. When the snows did come, I filled a large box with snow and took it into the granary to use to store fish and birds in. We stored the fresh catch, and ate the earlier catch. Turbot went into my fish trap until just before Christmas, but in fewer numbers. When the creek froze over, I found it difficult to work with the fish traps because of the cold and the icy water. So I put them away until spring. There were lots of rabbits as well, but I didn't catch many, since I didn't have the kind of snare wire I needed. The turbot stayed good in the snow box. We were still eating fish when February came around.

Sanna decreased her herd. For winter she sold a cow, a heifer and one calf. She was quite fond of the remaining cows, as they were home-bred. Mikko was the one who bought her cattle from her.

Now, with snow on the ground, Mikko brought dry firewood, tree trunks and more evergreen boughs. I made it out to check my snares only twice a week. Nor did I catch as many birds as before. They probably had better feed in some other area. In early February I removed some snares. By early March I had only six out. Moreover, I didn't take the birds I did manage to catch to town any more; Sanna and I ate what we caught.

Sanna and I spent all the long winter's nights in deep discussion. Sanna was one of those persons who had been frightened as a child, so she wouldn't go out in the dark on a dare. This was a never-ending source of discussion between us. I often repeated Mikko Perapolvi's encouraging talks, and I made light of her fears. I also read her the Bible history in the old hymnal. I showed her how the wording had been changed. I should say "falsified," for falsification it is! "Now the question is, how many times has the wording changed before this edition was printed. What did the original say?"

When we held discussions like this, she would toss a cloth over her head when the Bible came up. I didn't believe in that. Once I said, "The person who wrote that statement into the Bible declaring that the wife who prophesies must cover her head, demeans the wife. I hold that a wife and husband are equals, but the wife does greater things than the husband—and is therefore more worthy than a man—because she raises the children and teaches them."

In March I ran without skis far out on the crust of the snow and found a small bog where there were numerous exposed hummocks. So, too, were the cranberries exposed. I tried making a birch bark container, but since the bark didn't come off the trees easily, I only made a small one. Thinking I would go home and bring a basket back with me, I picked the small container full and started off. Suddenly I found myself in the midst of a heavy snowstorm. I walked a long way and found some tracks, realizing that they were my own. This signaled me that I was lost. So I began to examine the trees. Lichen grows on the northern exposure of the tree, I thought, so I should head north to find the creek. I started walking, eventually coming to a large lake, which I began circling. Eventually I found the creek I was looking for, but I couldn't seem to get oriented. The wet snow was falling by the skyful, and I was soaked. Gradually the snow got even thicker, and the weather turned cold.

Finally, I saw a spruce tree I thought I recognized, because a small shelter was leaning against it. Sure enough my snare was there, and there was a grouse inside. In my mind, however, was the strange sensation that the shelter should be on the other side of the tree. Since I knew how disoriented one can become when lost, I sat there in the shelter with my eyes closed for a long time. When I opened them my sense of direction had returned. I knew the way home, but, when I got there, I was in wretched condition. My clothes were frozen, so I could hardly get them off. Sanna built a large fire in the fireplace and once again brought me dry clothing.

When I finally warmed up, I said to her, "Don't worry. I'm well. I don't even have a headache. I didn't know there were wood grouse here. This is the first I've seen. I couldn't get to my other snares because I got lost in the snowstorm. That means there are five I left unchecked. Cook the grouse in a large, covered iron pot," I suggested, "just like you cooked the ducks on threshing day. What do you say we invite Mikko and his wife over for a midday meal?"

"I should think Sunday would be fine," Sanna said. "We'll do just that. So you clean the bird, and I'll go over to their house to let them know."

When she got back home she was carrying a lot of pork fat with her. "Do you want me to cut it up?" I asked.

"That would be best," she said, "since it's too big to fit in the pot whole."

On Sunday Sanna was preparing the grouse when her brother, John Salo, and his wife came over on horseback. Soon Mikko and his wife were there, too. I hadn't seen John's wife before this.

She was very friendly. "John has told me so much about you that I suggested to him that we come here together, so that I could meet you, too," she said.

"I don't look at all what I looked like when John first met me. Sanna burned those clothes of mine in the sauna stove. Now I look entirely different," I added.

John interjected, "What we want, Iisakka, is for you to tell us about yourself, just as you told us there at the cottage. It was most interesting."

"Fine," I said, "perhaps the story will go well with this grouse dish." Then I added, "This time I'll tell you a little more—like how I feel toward Finnish ministers."

And so I began. I told them of my family's life, explaining my father's departure for America. I very carefully related to them how Mikko Perapolvi freed me of all fear. I told them what experiences I had when I heard or saw something—how I would always investigate to determine what caused what. I told them about the body-measuring stick, and how I went into the field and stole the turnips, despite Matt's watching and reading the Book of Moses. I told them how the minister demanded that my mother pay Father's breathing tax and how, when she refused to pay it, he advertised her sewing machine for sale at a forced auction. I told them that at that time I became aware that ministers don't give a damn about saving our souls; their minds are on money. "I have always tried to follow my mother's advice," I said, "to listen to the voice of my conscience. It tells me when I am doing right, and when I am doing wrong. Keep your conscience clear, and you will have no fear of death, for you'll be living a life that pleases God. I didn't dare say this to you back at the cottage for fear that you'd declare me a heretic."

I went on to tell them all the small happenings, including how I was treated when begging, up to the time I arrived at the door of John's cottage, at which door my occupation of beggar was terminated. "I am thankful for having been a beggar," I said, "for I learned a lot. When I looked people in the eye, it was as though I could read their thoughts and their opinions. Yes, I could tell who would give me charity and help. I noted well that I didn't get so much as a polite word from well-to-do people. The poorer and more wretched the household, the friendlier the reception. Such people are ready to share their last morsel with you.

I am also thankful to John for bringing me here," I added. "I promised you then that I would be Sanna's good boy. I feel the love between us has grown continuously and not faded a bit. Sanna feared that I would run away. You know when I'll be leaving, but it won't be before June. Then I'll go to Mieta."

"Whether you want to go there at the beginning or at the end of the month, I'll take you," John declared.

"If it's possible, make it between the first and the tenth," I said.

Now John's wife said, "Wasn't that just like a novel? And you tell the story so well."

Mikko then began to tell the Salos how visitors came to find out if I knew how to read. "And he knew how to read something we didn't—the Bible history—in the back of that old hymnal!" he exclaimed.

"The midday meal is an hour late," Sanna said, but I just couldn't bring myself to interrupt the story. Now, everyone, to the table with you!"

When we were at the table I asked everyone, "Well, how does the story taste with the grouse dish?"

"If the story doesn't exactly have a taste," said one of the women, "it certainly is to be long remembered."

I had a suggestion to make to Mikko. "If you want fish after I leave, you can catch them with those fish traps of mine. I took the traps out of the creek for the winter. When the spring floods subside so that it's possible to set the traps again, you'll get as many fish as you need or want from them."

Mikko had once again brought a lot of tree trunks and evergreen branches for me. Thus, there was no shortage of work. As spring approached, I piled all the wood. One morning, though it was quite cold, the frozen snow made walking easy. I told Sanna that I was going to pick some of the berries from the small bog I had found in the wilderness during the period when I brought home the grouse. "I'll take a basket and go pick cranberries."

I went to where it should have been, but no matter how I ran around looking for it, no such bog was to be found. I was still deep in the forest when the sun, which had risen high in the sky, began to thaw the crust of the snow. I began to fall through. I tried to quicken my pace, but the crust had thawed to the extent that it wouldn't support my weight at all. I was falling through up to my armpits in the wet snow. Soon I was all in and soaking wet, but I tried to make progress. The sun began to fall, and I knew that soon it would be cold and a good crust would appear on the snow once again. But I was wet. I would freeze to death out there.

I sat in the snow where I had fallen the last time.

Voices carry a long distance in Finland's air. I heard a voice! It was Sanna. I called in answer and waited. The voice drew nearer. At last I could see Sanna skiing at a rapid clip with another pair of skis over her shoulder.

"And now you have saved me from a certain death," I told her.

By the time we got home, the sun had set. I quickly removed my wet clothes and received dry ones from Sanna. She told me, "I still have cattle to take care of. While waiting for you to return, I walked out onto the snow. When the crust didn't support me, I knew it wouldn't support you either. I got another pair of skis and went to take them where I thought you'd be. I went into the deep forest calling your name. Oh, how good it felt when I finally heard your voice!"

"I was wet and tired from struggling onward," I said to her. "I knew I'd freeze to death because I had gotten wet, and then I dropped into the snow up to my armpits once again. I sat there and then heard your voice. It was as if I had heard the voice of an angel. That it was; my angel, my rescuer!" I ran to hug Sanna, and we both cried for joy. Neither of us said any more, but our hearts spoke of the love of a mother and her child. This united us.

Later Sanna served me coffee. "I'm going to the barn," she said.

"Wait a little, and I'll go with you. It's quite dark."

Sanna answered, "I'm not afraid any more. You have talked all fear out of me this winter. I'm thankful to you for that. I'm just going out to give the cows some hay. Then I'll come back. After we've eaten we'll go back to the barn together." She didn't stay in the barn long when she came back in the house laughing.

"What's going on?" I asked her.

"As I was leaving for the barn," she said, "I assured you that I wasn't afraid any more. When I opened the barn door, there before me was some sort of creature. I was frightened, of course, but then I remembered that you told me that whatever frightens must be examined. And that's what I did. I stepped into the barn, took hold of it and discovered that it was a new-born calf. It was already quite dry. Very likely it had been born by the time I left for the woods to take the skis to you."

We went into the barn together so that we could get the calf into a pen. I reminded her that it was a good thing that she had examined the creature. She had made her fear disappear. As she examined the cow she said, "Yes, she has already cleaned herself."

She tossed hay for the cattle, and we went back into the house to eat. Afterwards, we went into the barn again, and I cleaned it and brought evergreen twigs for bedding. Sanna milked, watered and fed the cows. I had an *amme*, or barrel, in the barn and another in the house. I saw to it that there was always plenty of water in these barrels.

Spring was coming. The snows had melted, and there was so much water everywhere that I couldn't get around much. Toward the end of April I made an attempt to get to the creek to set my fish traps, but I didn't succeed. We turned the cattle out every day for a short while, but they didn't go into the woods. "They won't go back there until the waters recede and the ground dries," said Sanna. "You needn't try to go back into the woods until you see the cattle do it."

I counted off nine days before the cattle went into the woods. I followed shortly thereafter, except the creek where I wanted to set my fish traps was so flooded that I couldn't get near it. I went back home and waited another fifteen days before I could place my fish traps in the creek. I still found large snowdrifts in shaded places in the woods where the sunshine didn't penetrate.

The morning after I had set my traps I went to check them early, for the days were at their longest. A cuckoo called and the birds sang. I got eight large pike and two turbot. A couple of the pike were real whoppers. I was home early. Sanna was just getting back from milking. I asked permission to take half of the fish to the manor. She told me that Mikko was on his way to our house. "We'll cook these two turbot right away," she said, "as we had our last fish *keitto* in February." The turbot were also good-sized, and we ate our *keitto*.

Mikko arrived and inquired after my catch. I told him to help himself to the fish *keitto*. "We have eight fine pike. Tomorrow I'll get more." One morning Mikko accompanied me to the fish traps. I didn't know when John Salo would be coming to take me to Mieta, and I wanted to show Mikko where the traps were.

On the first of June I went again to check my traps. This time they were full of pike and turbot. Mikko started going regularly to get the fish from the traps. What he didn't need himself he gave to the people who helped him with his work. He asked me when I thought John Salo would come for me.

"I believe he'll come on the tenth, a Sunday, or perhaps on Saturday evening, in which case he'll stay the night," I answered. "In fact, I'm quite certain."

"What if he doesn't come?" Mikko argued.

I told him in that case I'd wait a few more days and leave on my own. "But I know he'll come if there are no obstacles. There could be a reason why he can't leave home, but I don't expect him before the evening of the ninth. Come over on the tenth," I told Mikko, "and bring your wife. We'll have a fish *keitto*. I can't get any birds because they're preparing their nests."

He turned to Sanna and said, "If you like, I'll bring a smoked pork roast."

"And I'll prepare it, if you wish," Sanna said.

Time passed, and the ninth came. I had just brought in a large load of fish. I asked Sanna if I should warm the sauna.

"If you wish," she said.

"I believe John Salo will come tonight," I said, "and he likes the sauna. He's been planting in the fields, and a sauna would be of great importance to him. If he doesn't come, then you and I will have a good sauna—we two together—but I believe he'll come."

So I carried in water and got everything ready. In the evening I started warming it up. The sauna was no sooner ready than the dog began to bark. Salo and his wife drove up with a horse and buggy and parked under the shed roof. Sanna and I approached them. I announced that the sauna was ready and that we had already taken care of the cattle.

"Should the horse be taken to pasture, or what?" I asked.

He said, "I have some oats to give it now. Let it remain in the stable until we get around to it. We're all going to take a sauna."

When we had finished with the sauna, Sanna prepared a fish *keitto*. We ate and then chatted awhile afterwards.

Then we went to bed. I woke up early—at three a.m.—and went to check my traps. Nobody else awakened. I left them all sleeping there in the house. This was to be my last trip to the memory-filled forest where I spent many happy times.

I love this forest, I thought to myself, and I love the creek and everything here. A cuckoo flew into the top of a tall tree and began to cuckoo as though it wanted to speak with me. I told it, "I love you, too, and your beautiful calling." When the small birds chirped, I said, "You have arranged a farewell for me. Thank you for all of this."

When finally I arrived at my fish traps, as I stepped on a log to get to a trap, a nightingale sang, "Don't fall, don't fall; careful, don't fall."

I took the trap out of the water and there were fish in it. After putting the small ones back in the creek, I had nine large pike and four turbot left. This was enough for me to carry, so I placed the fish trap back in the creek, saying, "Mikko will check you from now on."

I started back, and when I got home I saw that the cows were in the barn. I dropped my fish pouch near the well and went into the barn to find John Salo and his wife there. Sanna gave me a large bucket and said, "Here, put the fish in this. I know it's what you need."

Mikko accompanied me when I went to take care of the fish. He marvelled at their size and beauty. Sanna had raised his expectations by telling him of my early departure for the woods at three in the morning. While Mikko exclaimed, I drew cold water from the well and poured it over the fish. Yesterday's fish were in a separate bucket, so I poured cold water over them, too. I also had some sacks, which I placed over the fish to shade them from the sun.

I said to John, "You can have a share of these fish, but how can we keep them?"

"It's best to clean them right away and put them in cold water. As soon as you can, you should salt them, wet the sacks with cold water and wrap the fish in the sacks. They'll still be good tomorrow."

We were asked to come into the house for breakfast. The women had baked two large pike from which they had removed only the heads. I asked Sanna how they had been prepared, and she told me that they had been baked on a spit over an open flame, and basted with butter and salt. They were very tasty.

After breakfast John went out of the house and then returned presently with a pair of sheers. "Come outdoors," he said to me, "and I will shorten your hair."

The midday meal was ready by eleven o'clock. Mikko and his wife were there along with two girls, who were the only young people I had seen the entire time I was there. One was fifteen and the other was sixteen. They said they had heard I was about to leave so they came over to see me. One of them said, "No one in the entire village knows where you came from or who you are, but they are singing your praises as a good and able boy."

This moved me, so I took each by the hand and thanked them, saying, "I'm not much of anything, really. First I was merely a runaway, then I became a beggar, and now, at last, I have been Sanna Takamaa's dear boy. I don't know what will become of me now, but my begging days are over. I've had my fill of that. Will you girls come to see me if I return to Sanna's?" They both promised they would, and Sanna sat them at the table for something to eat.

I continued, "It has been almost a year since I ran away from my grandfather's. Nobody in the entire village of Mieta knows where I am. I probably have letters waiting there for me from my mother and father in America. I have to go to Mieta now to get some word of my mother and to answer her letters. But I won't go to my grandfather's. In Mieta there are many well-to-do families, but I learned not to expect humane treatment from them. They treated me and they treat all poor children worse than a mongrel dog. Perhaps I'll be there in Mieta for some time, but if I don't find it to my liking as a place to live, I'll come back to Sanna. She and I love each other. I'll never forget her."

"Well," John Salo finally said, "I think it's time we began our journey."

"Take the fish you need," I told Sanna. "Do these girls also want to take some fish home with them?"

Mikko answered that he would take some. John said he already had his share, and he encouraged me again to get going. "You should start dressing," he said.

Sanna helped me dress and put my everyday clothes in a bag. John had driven the horse to the end of the steps, and I said a quick goodby to the girls, thanking them for coming to my farewell party. Then I turned to Sanna, who stood at my side. "I want to thank you for all the good that I've shared in," I said.

She was carrying a small cloth bag which she held out to me. "This is your money. There're eighty-eight marks. I've used a lot of it."

I said to her, "Sanna, I wouldn't have been able to earn one penny without your help. Plus you have given me a good home and good food, not to mention clothes. And you've always watched out for my well-being. The money belongs to you, not to me."

"Take at least half," she said.

"Give me sixteen marks then," I replied, "in case I can't find a desireable place to live; and so I won't need to beg right away. Or I may come back to you," I quickly added.

"You are welcome here day or night," she said simply.

I took the bag from her hand and counted out sixteen silver marks. I put them in my pocket saying, "No matter what happens, I will come to see you again one more time—if we live."

Taking hold of one another, we both cried. Then the two girls began to cry. Soon Mikko and his wife cried, and John Salo and his wife as well. As I became aware of how it must look with all of us weeping, I began to laugh. "Why are you all crying?" I asked them. "Neither Sanna nor I are crying out of sadness. It is our love that cries, but even that doesn't cry any more. We must be strong. Crying doesn't make matters better."

I clasped Mikko's hand. Then I wished his wife well one more time. I took Sanna's hand again and promised her that I would see her again if it meant having to walk. They were left standing there as John, his wife and I rode away.

We had driven a good distance when I asked John, "What time will you get back home? Seems like it's getting late."

"I don't know," he replied. "But I should water and feed the horse before I start back."

"Do you know the boundary between Kurikka and Kauhajoki?" I asked him.

"Yes," he said, "we aren't far from there now."

I urged him to feed his horse on the Kauhajoki side at Lahiluoma. At the first group of buildings on the Kurikka side there was an old hostelry whose doors were always open. "Anybody can go into the living quarters," I said. "I will go there and find a bench to lie upon. They don't know me there. In the morning I'll leave for Paloluoma where the post comes."

While en route John drove into the Harju yard and gave water and oats to the black. The hired boy came up to me and asked me if we wanted something to eat. I told him we had eaten so much already that we wouldn't need anything more.

"Let's get some coffee anyway, if there is any," John suggested. So we went in and drank coffee. "Do you want to leave soon?" he asked.

"I'm in no hurry," I replied, despite knowing that we still had a long way to go.

John told the hired boy to give a bunch of hay to the horse. "We'll sit and drink another cup of coffee before we leave," he said.

And so we stayed.

The hour approached eleven at night. I directed John to the building I had mentioned. He drove into the yard in front of the stables. We got down out of the wagon, and I retrieved my bag of clothing. I set it down to thank them.

John's wife approached me, saying, "I have a small gift for you. I'll give it to you now that we're about to part." She put a belt around me. On it was a sheathed knife. They were beautifully made.

I thanked them for all the love they had shown me. "You've been so good to me. I'll remember you as long as I live."

The woman took me by the hand and said, "I wish you luck . . . and success."

John had my other hand. He said, "I didn't know then what a treasure I brought to my sister when I took you to her. She tells me that you talked her out of being afraid. There is nothing she fears anymore. Love of that kind can't be rewarded with material things."

"I promised I would do as much for her when I went there to her place," I said, "so I was merely fulfilling a promise."

We embraced one another and said good-night and wished each other well. John and his wife got into the wagon. He turned the horse sharply, and as he did he said, "Take good care of yourself."

"I will," I answered, "I have nothing else to do." We all laughed happily.

When the black was turned toward home, it began to trot at a fast pace.

4

A Good and Able Boy

I TOOK UP my bag of clothing and went inside. No one was about that I could see, so I took off my coat and hung it on a nail. Then I lay down on a bench, placing my clothing bag under my head for a pillow. I hadn't been there long when I heard someone come in. It was someone I recognized—Matti, the hired hand. He walked up to me and looked me over closely. Finally he said, "Iisakka, it's you, isn't it? I overheard your conversation outside awhile ago. Who were those people? The man is so hairy he reminds me of Esau in the Bible."

I told Matti that they were friends. He had gathered as much from our conversation.

"Get up and come with me," he said. "I have a clean bed. You'll be able to rest more comfortably." He picked up my bag, and we went into another room. "Here in our village there has been much speculation about your having vanished. I don't believe there's a person here who hasn't offered an opinion as to what happened to you. You have been a constant subject of conversation. Where have you been all this time?"

"Please don't ask," I replied. "I haven't been up to anything bad. I've been with good people. I feel well, and I'm healthy."

". . . and such fine clothes!" he exclaimed. "You're quite the gentle-man, judging from your wardrobe."

"I have no desire to be gentry," I said.

The next morning I woke up as Matti was getting dressed. "I'm on my way to the stable," he said.

I also got up, dressed and went out into the yard. Seeing there was some activity back inside the house, I decided to find out what was going on. The mistress of the house was there with a servant girl. The mistress looked me over. "Who is this young stranger?" she asked.

The servant girl laughed. "Here, now, is the much-talked-about Kartano boy."

I told them I had spent the night with Matti at his request. "I have a bag of clothing here. If someone asks for it, give it to them. I'm going to Paloluoma to inquire about my mail." With that I hurried out.

The woman hurried after me. "Wait until the food is ready at least," she said.

But it wasn't food I wanted. "I want to get my mail," I explained. "It's been over a year since I heard from my mother. Don't try to detain me."

I made quickly for the road and had to travel the entire length of the village of Mieta to get to Paloluoma's trading post. I met some of the men from my mother's family along the way, but they had always been so haughty toward me that I didn't allow them to engage me in conver-sation. Though they spoke to me, I just kept going. Then I saw a young boy whom I knew well. He was walking ahead of me. He turned in at Kakkari, where my mother's sister lived. He recognized me immedi-ately when I called out his name. I asked him to take a message to my aunt right away. "Give her my greetings, and tell her that I'm healthy and doing well. Tell her also that I arrived last night and slept at the inn. Now I'm on my way to the post office." He took off on a run.

When I arrived at Paloluoma, Ista Paloluoma said, "Aha, the lost sheep. There are some letters for you. Nobody knew where you were, so I couldn't do anything but wait for your return." He handed the let-ters over. Some strangers were in the shop and were listening to our con-versation. They were curious to know who I was.

"Let me read my letters," I said to them. "They're from my mother. It's been over a year since I've heard from her."

"Come here," Ista said, and he took me to his wife, telling her that I was Isaac Polvi's son. "Let him read his letters. He will probably have to answer them as well, so if he needs help, give it to him."

From the letters I learned that I had a new baby sister. My parents asked me to write them and tell them where I was so that they could send me a boat ticket. And, of course, they asked what I had been doing since they hadn't heard anything from me.

I thought to myself, now I must write to them, but what to say? Mother wants to know where I am, and she has always said, "If you can't tell the truth, don't say anything. You must not lie." I thought deeply about this. "I don't want to say that I've been begging," I thought. "That is absolutely out of the question. Plus, I don't want to tell Mother anything about my travels and my stay at Kauhajoki." Then—at last—it came to me. "I now know what to say." I thought, "and I won't have to lie." So I requested pencil and paper, which were given to me by Mrs. Paloluoma.

I first off greeted my mother and told her how happy I was to have a baby sister. "Be good to her," I wrote. "I am now sitting in the Paloluoma house writing to you. I'm happy that you're sending me a ticket. I'm healthy and doing well. For the present I don't lack for anything. This is written by your son Iisakka. I remain waiting for the ticket." Then I asked the housewife for an envelope.

"Have you already written your letter?" she asked.

"Yes," I replied, "but I'd appreciate it if you'd address it. My handwriting isn't that good."

"Sure," she said. She wrote the address on the envelope and then added, "I know you haven't had any schooling. Will your mother be able to understand your letter? Why don't you show it to me?"

I unfolded it and laid it in front of her. She glanced at it and remarked that it didn't look too bad. "Try reading it to see whether there are any corrections that should be made," I suggested.

She read it over. Then she said, "You didn't mention anything about where you've been for almost a whole year."

"Mother doesn't know that I've been away from here," I told her, "and I don't want to tell anyone anything about my journey." I then thanked her and tossed a mark on the table, asking that she put a stamp on the envelope. "Take something out for the paper and pencil as well," I added.

"Put your money back in your pocket," she said. "I'll pay for the stamp." I was about to leave, but she said that the coffee was hot and poured me a cup. "Where are you staying that you didn't tell your mother?" she asked.

"I was brought to the inn yesterday evening," I replied. "I stayed there the night. I've been at Kauhajoki where I had a good home with a widow. I may go back there."

"I can see that you've had a good home. You're dressed in good clothing. If you go back there, be sure to write to Ista Paloluoma and give him your address, so that we can forward your letters to you."

I thanked her and left, but I didn't exit by way of the shop, slipping out instead through a side door. I got to the road and started back to the inn, thinking to myself that I should have eaten first. But I wasn't about to approach a landowner for a bite to eat, because they are so high and mighty. So I turned onto a side road I knew. There were tenant farmers living on it. I walked quite a distance until I finally came to a small, dilapidated house where an old couple lived. They had a single cow in a tiny fenced-off area. I went into the yard and could see the old man repairing shoes. "Good day," I said.

His wife who was standing nearby looked at me. "Good day," she said. "Does the young gentleman have some business with us?"

"I'm not gentry," I answered, "and I don't intend to become gentry. We belong to the same class. I walked all the way here from the main road to find people like myself. I am the child of poor people, and I want to be with poor people."

"Where do you live?" she asked. "Who are your parents?"

"My parents are Isaac and Soffia Polvi. They are in America," I told her.

"Oh, so that makes you the boy who has been the general topic of conversation around here. When did you return to the area?"

"I was brought to the inn yesterday and spent the night with the hired hand. I went directly to the post office and there were letters from my mother. Could you give me some food? Herring, bread, soup—whatever. It doesn't make any difference. I'll pay for my food, but I haven't eaten since noon yesterday, and then all I had was a cup of coffee at Paloluoma's."

The old man, who had been taking all this in, turned to his wife and said, "You have eggs. Cook them."

"A little herring bread is enough," I said.

"I'll fry you some eggs," said the old woman. "They'll be ready in a minute." It wasn't long before the food was ready. She even brought a *viilia*. I sat at the table and ate well while they both quizzed me. "I've been at Kauhajoki with a widow. It was a good home. If I don't find a desirable place here, I'll go back there."

'Aren't you going to your grandfather's?"

"Not even for a visit," I replied.

By the time I finished the meal, it was noon. I stood up and laid a mark on the table. The old woman said, "Not money, my son. I don't want your money."

"At Paloluoma's I laid that mark on the table for the mistress, and she said she'd pay for some postage stamps. Now you refuse to take it as well."

The old man picked up the coin from the table and then handed it to me, saying, "Put the money in your pocket and come here again. We are happy that you are so healthy and well-dressed. And I am happy that you are aware of class distinctions and know yourself to belong to the proletariat."

"Thank you," I said.

"Where are you headed now?" he asked.

"I have a running mate at Torkkoola. Since I haven't seen him in a while, I'll go there first."

I said my goodbyes, thanked them all again and started walking. Amazingly, I didn't meet a single person I knew. Near Hakuni, I took the hill road to Torkkoola. I was sure I wouldn't meet anybody along the way. Nor did I. When I turned toward the house, there was still no one in sight. Once inside the house, I realized even that was empty. So I sat on a bench to wait.

Soon I heard the master coming. "Kartano boy!" he exclaimed on seeing me.

"I'm not the Kartano's boy," I said. "I'd rather beg for my bread than go there again." For some reason this struck him as extremely funny, and he started laughing. "Why are you laughing?" I asked him, but he couldn't contain himself. Then some of the boys came in and he pointed at me, laughing all the harder.

"Look at the Kartano boy—ha, ha, haaa. . . ."

"Does it please you that I have no place to go?"

At last he was able to speak. "No . . . I'm glad you're here. You see, these boys ordered me to go to Kartano and ask you to come here. I just bought a horse, and I need a driver for it. But I sure didn't want to ask Herman Kartano if you could come here to work."

"Good," I said simply. "My work clothes are at the inn. The bag is heavy, and I didn't feel like carrying it."

The master looked me up and down and said, "You have on the clothes of a gentleman—just as we have already been told. Yet you have work clothes." He smiled. "Don't worry about a thing. I'll fetch your bag for you."

Then Manu came in. I walked up to him and took his hand saying, "I've often thought of you. Now we can be together again. I have already arranged it with your father."

"How far away did you go?" Manu asked me.

"Not far really," I answered. "I've been over at Kauhajoki with a widow. I had a good home and a good mother there. I'll never forget the friends I made on my sojourn. I was treated like a human-being—not a bad word from anybody. The man and woman who brought me to the inn even gave me a gift of a belt with a knife and sheath."

The master said, "Look, Jaska, get the horse ready for me. I'm going to the inn to get Isaac's clothes."

Shortly after they went out we saw the master leaving in a light rig behind the horse. I chatted with my old pal Manu until the master returned, and Manu went to him to get my bag of clothes. We went upstairs and began taking the clothes out of the bag.

Manu marvelled at the quality of the clothing. "Three outfits, and none has holes! Three pairs of shoes, and the fourth pair on your feet! Where in the world did you get all these clothes?"

"I didn't ask for them," I answered, "but the woman I lived with kept bringing me new ones. I'm leaving for America soon, and I'm taking only the clothes I have on now. You can keep what's left. And here, take this." I handed him the sheath and knife I had used while at Kauhajoki. "Here's the belt, too." I put on the clothes that were the most worn. The shoes didn't look bad. I asked Manu where I could hang my clothes, and he arranged a place. Together we hung them up on a row of nails. "These clothes will fit you well," I said, "and I can't wear out the ones I have on. I'm going to America before winter. Care for these as if they're your own, and they'll be left to you."

We went downstairs and the mistress said, "His clothes still don't look like work clothes."

"He has three more outfits," said Manu, "and they're all like new."

"They aren't brand new," I replied, "but the mother I had always cleaned them. When I came in wet, she always brought dry, clean clothes for me to put on."

The mistress commenced to question me. "Where did you come from?"

"I came from my work."

"And what work was that?"

"Anything that had to be done and that I could do."

"Ah, you probably just ran around the village with the other boys," she said.

"I was with that widow for nine months," I said, "and during the entire period I didn't see any young people—except for the two girls who came to see me. They were at my farewell party."

"And you really had a farewell party?"

"Yes, I did," I answered her, "and when we had eaten dinner, a couple came to give me a ride to the inn. When we got there, they presented me with this belt, sheath and knife. They urged me to return to Kauhakoki if I don't find a place I like."

"So, a real farewell party was held," said the mistress. She sounded a little sarcastic.

The master glanced my way and then said, "And why wouldn't they like you, boy? I don't see any reason why it wouldn't have been proper to have a farewell party."

With this I ceased explaining myself to them, and although they continued asking me questions, I wouldn't answer them. Manu later asked me why I wouldn't tell them anything.

"I've said too much already," I told him, "and I won't say any more."

The master now explained the situation with respect to the horse. "That new horse I bought—the one you're to drive—is sound in every way. It's a good horse; pulls well, tender mouth, a splendid trotter. And young. But it has one fault, a bad one. It won't let you catch it. It takes a gang of men using ropes—every time!"

"You've got to be good to it," I told him. "If I can drive that horse and be allowed to feed it by myself for the rest of the week, I am sure that the horse will come to me. But only if you don't hurry my fieldwork."

"If you can remedy that fault," the master said, "then you will have done a good deed. You can feed it whatever we have. Bread . . . oats . . . and if by next Sunday it comes to you and lets you take hold of it, you're a better man than anyone here."

"Who drove it today?" I asked him.

"I had to," he replied.

I asked him if he had been angry with it, and he replied that he was.

"You must be good to it," I told him. "I would like to be on a separate field with that horse, because I want to stop now and then and give it a piece of bread and talk to it. Only then will we be able to understand one another. A tenant farmer said something to me one time, and I think it is true. Whether it's a cow, a horse, or any creature—it will reward its benefactor."

"Right you are, and you can depend on it," said the master.

The next morning all the men went out with ropes to try to catch the horse. Finally, they brought it to the stables. Manu had orders from his father to harness the horse and tie it to the hitching ring. I waited until the master and the others went out to the fields.

I had been talking to the horse for just a short time when the master returned, saying, "It will work out well. You will be in another field where there are a couple of long plots already harrowed. But there are still lots of clods. Hitch the horse to the raft, and you can stand atop it. I believe you can grind those clods into fine soil and at the same time level the field. I can then start planting and then use a horse to cover the seed."

So I hitched the horse to the raft. "Give me a loaf of bread," I said. "I want to keep the horse in a good mood."

He got the bread for me and said, "I'll go with you. I have to give you a few more instructions, and at the same time I want to see what the raft will do to the field." Then when we got to field, he added, "Drive up close to the ditch, but take care that no soil goes into it."

I gave a little bread to the horse and then drove to the opposite end of the field. Then I stopped and talked to the horse, again giving it some bread. The master waited there watching as I came back. I gave the horse some bread and started another round. "Yes," the master said, "the field will turn out fine, and I believe the horse won't get any thinner. I'll bring another loaf."

I made another round with the master watching as I turned the horse along the strip we had dragged. The horse stopped and turned its head toward me, waiting for me to give it a piece of bread. The master laughed and shouted to me. "I'll put the bread on a fence post here." He laughed again. "The field will be fine, and the horse will be even better. Take your time. I'm going to see about the seed." And so he left for home, laughing the entire way.

By noon the horse was already on the second loaf of bread, but we were on the second field and had already made one round. The other workers had gone in for lunch, but I started the next round. I didn't hurry the horse, but I noticed it was working faster, so at the end of the round I gave it another piece of bread. Then I took hold of the snaffle and walked alongside the horse back to the stable. Manu called to say he had set out oats and hay but first for me to take the horse to the well where the water was ready. Afterwards I put the horse in the stable and went inside. My horse and I were the objects of much laughter.

I told them, "Tomorrow I'll get the horse into the stable and won't need ropes or anyone's help to catch it. Say what you will." Some of them were curious as to whether I liked my work. "I like it fine," I answered. "And why shouldn't I? I have it better than you. You have to walk while I stand on top of the raft. I'd like it better still if I had a seat so I wouldn't always have to stand up."

Everyone laughed, and one said, "There's so much dust I wouldn't want that job."

"This is a good job for my horse and me," I said simply. "I can't complain at all."

After we had eaten, I noticed that the boys were laughing among themselves. Manu said that he'd feed the horse, and I told him I'd get it after he had gone back to work.

As I lingered there at the table the master began to chat with me. "So, you've finished that field?"

"Yes," I said, "and I'll do another. Perhaps even a third."

"No need to hurry," he replied. "It'll be sufficient to plant one field today."

I went out to see if people hadn't already started to go back to work. Two of the boys were just coming back from my field, hammer in hand. I sat down on the steps and waited for them to leave. Manu watered his own horse, and, as he was leaving said, "I've drawn enough water from the well for your horse, too."

I got my horse and left behind the others. When I got to the field, I found that a seat had been attached atop the raft. There was nothing to say, so I simply sat on the seat. The tenant farmers were going by carrying sacks of seed to the first field. They laughed.

Then the master showed up with some more bread. "Here's a loaf for your horse. And you have a seat now?"

"Yes," I replied, "but it seems they forgot the backrest so I can't lean back. And there should be a small box where I can keep the bread so I don't have to carry it in my shirt. Plus it should have a cover so the bread doesn't get dusty. Otherwise, the box will be full of dust in no time."

The master laughed and went to plant the seed. I finished the second field and drove the horse to the third. I was over half done when I saw the master with two horses he got to cover the seed. "Take your horse to the stable," he said. "I'll come and give it some hay. Manu can remove the harness. The other workers will be in soon. Offer the horse some water."

When I got to the house, the master told me to clean the dust off myself over by the sauna. "I want to clean the horse up first," I said.

"The other boys will gladly do that," he replied, "so long as they don't have to be in that cloud of dust."

Later, at the sauna, I removed my clothes and beat them against the wall. The dust came off easily but I was covered with dust that wouldn't brush off. The master brought me a bucket of warm water and helped me wash my back. It was as though I had taken a sauna—it felt that good. From then on the sauna was warmed daily during the entire planting season. The horses were given hay and oats before they were taken to the pasture for the night. As the others started for the pasture with their horses, I gave mine a piece of bread and followed the others. Before I turned it loose, I gave it another piece of bread. It went some distance away, and I said, "Look, boys, I'll catch it again." I walked up to it and gave it a piece of bread. Then I put the bit in its mouth, along with some more bread. I led the horse to them, took off the bridle and gave it another piece as I patted it. The boys marveled and Manu asked me why I placed my hand on the horse's withers before putting the bit in its mouth.

"It's a gesture of friendship to an animal," I said, "a promise to be a friend. Be friendly to your horse, boys. Don't jerk it around or swear at it. Speak pleasantly and the horse will surely serve you willingly and well."

One boy said, "You've already shown it to be true. I believe every word that you have said."

The next morning I brought the horse to the stable. I went into the house and said, "I've already caught the horse. How much oats do we give it?"

The master laughed and said, "You've done the work of nine men. We always needed eight or nine men to catch that horse."

One of the boys explained how I had caught it the previous night and told everyone how to treat a horse, repeating all that I had said.

"We'll abide by this rule," the master said, "which is simply to be good to a horse. We can do that. Oh, but I feel good about this. I'm thankful to you. We'll follow this rule from now on: Be good to the horse."

"I'll feed your horse for you," said Manu.

When I got to the field that morning I found that they had attached the back of an old chair to the seat on the raft so that I could lean back. And they had made a box to keep the horse's bread in. They had provided the box with a lid on leather hinges.

"All is good," I said. "If things were any better, it would be extravagant." They all laughed, and we began to plow the fields.

Immediately after the planting, ditches were opened and deepened. The plowed fields were planted in rye. This usually took place around the end of August or the beginning of September. The rye reached a height of two or three inches before the ground froze, and the snows came. The frost wouldn't destroy the sprouts after they were covered with snow, and in the spring when the snows melted, the rye began to grow from the same shoots. If the larger snowdrifts didn't melt, people tossed wood ashes on the snow to speed the melting, for if the snow stayed too long, it killed the rye and nothing grew there. The rye crop was very important to the Finnish people. It was their bread, porridge and soup. Rye was also used in many other ways, as it was an especially healthful food.

Manu and I were always together, and the master gave us work to do together. Once I recall he had us hoeing the soil that had been dug up from the ditches. He paced it off saying, "Boys, when you hoe up to here you can go wherever you please."

The tenant farmers were making a ditch nearby. We were on good terms with them and asked for a helping hand so that we could get our work done and go about our business. They came over, and this trick worked for a while. But one day when the farmers were helping us, the master appeared. He said, "I'm not demanding too much work from any of you, and I haven't belittled anyone's efforts. But I want these boys to do by themselves the work allocated to them. It's not too much for them. I've not demanded anything of them that isn't reasonable. They have to do it themselves."

The farmers went back to their ditch, and we didn't get their help any more. "You must do it yourselves," they said.

My aunt had come to Torkkoola to visit me, but I was out fishing with Manu, so Manu and I went fishing at the Kakkari flour mill where my aunt's husband Ojaniemi was the miller. She wanted to know where I had been during the year after I ran away from my grandfather's. I told my aunt that I hadn't told anyone everything about my journey. "But I'll tell you," I said, "with the stipulation that you don't tell others. I'll tell you the good and the bad of that time."

She promised not to tell.

I related how I left Maiju Perakorpi's place to go to the Kauhajoki area. I told her how I began by begging, and how I spent nights in threshing sheds, fields, ditches, under bridges, in the woods, in haybarns—wherever I happened to be. "Sometimes I had to leave my sleeping place because of the rain or the cold. And I was barefoot the whole time."

I described the wretchedness of my existence, telling her everything, including how they had sicked a dog on me as though I were some sort of evil-doer. "But a dog has never bitten me when I've been able to say a few friendly words to it." I told her how people were friendlier in poorer homes, ready to share their last morsel with me. I told of my hunger, and of the cold reception I received at the homes of the well-to-do. I said to my aunt, "I don't regret begging, however. On my journey I came to know the differences in people. It was a school for me, and I learned a great deal."

I told her how I came to a cottage, chilled and hungry, where people were friendly to me, and how I had explained for the first time who I was. "I told them my life's story, and a certain John Salo took me to his sister's secluded place. Then I had it good."

I told my aunt all about this woman, Sanna, how I tried to be of help to her, how I snared birds and made money. I told her about our mutual love. "She loved me as her own son, and I loved her as a mother." Tears came to my aunt's eyes when I told her about the moment of our parting, and how I promised to see her once more. My aunt asked if I was going to see her or not, and I replied, "As surely as I am here now, I will go to see Sanna—even if I have to walk the entire distance . . . and if I live." My aunt asked me if I wrote about all this to my mother, and I said, "No, I don't want to tell her. Mother doesn't even know that I've been away from the village of Mieta, so she doesn't need to know that I've been a beggar. You're the only person I've told about my sojourn, and no one else needs to know about it."

"Have you fulfilled your mother's wish? Do you remember what it was?" she asked.

Indeed I did remember. "My mother told me to listen to the voice of my conscience," I replied. "It will tell me when I'm doing right and when I'm doing wrong. 'Always keep a clear conscience, and you will be acceptable to God. If you can't tell the truth, don't say anything. You must not lie.' These were my mother's wishes and urgings. I've always tried to follow her advice."

My pal was waiting for me, so I said goodby to my aunt and we left. I said to Manu, "I want to go the village of Krukula where there is a woman with whom I had a home when I ran away from Kartano. I promised I'd go to see her before leaving for America."

The following week I was still working with Manu, hoeing the dirt dug from the ditches and spreading it around. The master came and asked me who I planned to see in Krukula. I answered that it wasn't exactly in Krukula, but rather nearby at Maiju Perakorpi's farm.

"You can go with me tomorrow morning," he said. "I can leave you there and pick you up in the evening."

"Good," I said.

That evening the master saw me cleaning my clothes, and he said to me, "You have three outfits upstairs. Why don't you put one of them on?"

"I'm not going there to display my clothes," I said, "I'm going as a sign of friendship. Besides, she'll know me better if I'm in work clothes."

In the morning our journey began. Along the way, the master told me he didn't want me to go there on a Sunday, as Manu needed my company. When we arrived, he brought me into the yard, and Maiju came to me immediately. "I've brought you a visitor for a while," he said.

He left after a short greeting, but Maiju and I didn't have time to exchange many words before a cow got into the potato patch. We went there together, and after getting the cow out, we began repairing the fence. Maiju only wanted to work until noon, but I said, "The fence needs rebuilding, and if a job is worth doing, it's worth doing right or not at all."

I made new stakes and twisted new ties. Maiju went to the house, made coffee and brought back herring bread for lunch. We talked while she helped me with the fence. She didn't know that I had been away from Kurikka. I was glad of that, as there wasn't much time for chatting. We weren't half done with the rebuilding of the fence when the master returned. Maiju told him that I had said that a job worth doing is worth doing right or not at all. The master said nothing, going to look at the old fence and then at the new.

He said, "I don't know how I would have fixed that fence any other way but to tear it down and build it anew. You've done a good job. Now, let's close up the fence. You and Manu can have the horse tomorrow to come here and repair the entire fence for her, just as you've done with this section. I'll give you a lunch to take along."

Maiju asked us into the house for coffee, saying she could have it ready in no time. Once inside, she said to me, "You've been at Torkkoola, Isaac?"

"I'm at Torkkoola," I replied.

The master laughed so hard that Maiju turned to him and asked, "What's going on? What's there to laugh about?"

"I'm only laughing at Isaac," said the master. "He's rather cleverly evaded your question, since he doesn't want to lie to you, but neither does he want to say where he's been. I know he hasn't been up to anything bad. He was so well-dressed that there isn't a boy in Kurikka as well-off as he is. He has three outfits that are like new, and money jingles in his pockets." He laughed again. When he stopped, he said, "He left you and came to Mieta on the tenth, but that's as far as the explanation goes. Asked to explain further, he replies that he has said too much already. I would have done exactly the same thing. He had been away for a year, and when he was telling about his journey, Mrs. Torkkoo made some disparaging remarks, so he didn't say any more. I don't blame him. I can assure you that this is one honest and capable boy."

"Praise me or criticize me," I said, "and I won't become any different."

"Has he been at your place all this time?" Maiju asked the master.

"He's been there two weeks," answered the master. "He came on the eleventh. Today is the twenty-eighth."

"I urged him to stay with me," said Maiju, "but he had promised to go see Manu Torkkoo." She then turned to me and asked, "Where have you been?" And when I didn't answer, she said, "Why don't you answer?"

I told her that my mother had taught me that if I don't want to tell the truth, I shouldn't say anything—"One must not tell a lie."

"He wasn't into anything bad," said the master. "We won't bother him."

So we drank our coffee and then left. Maiju was grateful when the master promised to send Manu and me there again the next day. When we got home, the other men had already eaten their evening meal. The master told them that we wanted, and needed, our supper.

One of the boys replied, "What? Been on a pleasure trip and you didn't get fed?"

"I've eaten well," said the master, "but as for this pal of mine . . . I'm afraid Maiju didn't have much to give him . . . or did you get lunch?"

"Yes," I answered.

"What did you eat?" he asked.

"Maiju brought me a piece of bread, herring and a cup of coffee."

The master then explained to them what I had done, and that my work was unfinished. "Manu and Isaac are going there tomorrow to complete the fence for poor Maiju. There doesn't seem to be too much there . . . and with two small children. We must help her a little. It's better that you leave early in the morning, so that you have time to finish the fence. We have some potatoes, so, Manu, you fix up a sack tonight, and I'll find something else. These growing children need food, and Maiju's food supply seems very low."

Early in the morning we were on our way. There were bags behind the seat, but we didn't know what all they contained. When we got to Maiju's, we found a kilogram of coffee, the same of sugar and flour (the latter to make porridge and soup), dried meat and a dried side of pork. "Put it all away," I told Maiju. "Torkkoo has sent it from the goodness of his heart."

Tears came to her eyes. "I am very thankful to him. I don't know how I can repay this."

"He didn't send this to you in order to be paid," said Manu. "Don't worry about it."

We put the horse in the yard to graze and then went to look at the fence and started to work. Maiju cooked potatoes for us but we told her that we didn't want anything but whole potatoes and herring bread. "Cook some coffee then, when we leave." She did have a small *viilia* to give us. We finished the fence early, and then even cut some wood. We gave the horse its oats and then went into the house for our coffee. Maiju asked me when I was leaving.

"Mother wrote that they will send me a ticket, but it will be fall before I expect it to come. And I have a new sister who was born there."

We chatted like this for a while. Then I said goodbye to Maiju and we started back.

Even by the 1890s in Finland, hay was still cut with a scythe and grain with a sickle. The women were generally involved in the haying—mostly with a rake in hand—but not much, since they took care of preparing food for the workers, plus milking the cows and caring for the cattle. There was a cream separator in the village of Mieta where the milk was separated and the skimmed milk then brought back to be drunk by the workers. The servants had much poorer food than the landowners, and the former even sang about it in ditties. I only remember a few, but one goes as follows:

> The creamery turns on three wheels
> in Santi's rapids.
> Could this be why the village landowners
> are hard pressed for money?
> Ranta swindles with the food offerings
> on the table,
> and the salted herring is rancid.
> The landladies nag noisily
> that the servant girls are haughty.
>
> *Translated by Bertha Kurki*

Before the women were through with their barn chores, the hay was already dry, and they started raking it together with hand rakes. The hay nearest to the haybarn was carried inside by hand, while the hay in the outlying fields was brought in on a horse-drawn sled with a platform on it. The hay was lifted onto the platforms and then pulled to the haybarn door and pitched into the barn with a fork.

The master sometimes sipped distilled spirits. He would then take the horse that was a good runner—the same horse that had been assigned to me—and he jerked at the reins unmercifully. I felt sorry for the horse. Once I knew he was going to Kyttala's, so I ran along the riverbank and went into the Kyttala yard, where I found the horse tied to the hitching ring. No one saw me as I untied the horse, jumped into the church buggy, turned into the road and drove to Torkkoola. There I unharnessed the horse and took it into the pasture. The mistress asked me what I thought the master would say.

"I don't care what he says," I answered her. "He knows that he didn't do right in tearing at that horse's mouth. He knows that he was wrong to get himself drunk and then to abuse one of God's creatures. I can't stand idly by so long as I can do something."

I did this many times, staying out of his sight until he was sober. One day at the dinner table, he was criticizing all of his boys and giving them hell. He accused them of being dishonest. "You steal from the farm, drink at the farm's expense. . . ." He made all manner of accusations at each of them. Finally, he turned to me and said, "You! You horse thief. Ha, ha, ha. I can't criticize you. Even though you're a horse thief, you still have a clear conscience. I don't blame you. I haven't heard you tell a lie to anyone. I hold you up as an example. You have always fulfilled your obligations, and I can't criticize you in the least."

He was always good to me. I don't recall that he ever said a bad word to me. When the hay was put away, he came to me and said, "We need a herd boy at the Kainasto bog. Have you ever been there?"

"I have," I said to him, "but I haven't been to Latomaki where you and the others have fields."

"Will you go there to help take care of a herd?"

"That depends on what kind of people will be there."

"They are just like yourself," he said, "no class distinctions; everybody is equal."

"When must I go?" I asked. "I want to stop at Laulaja."

"I think you'll go there tomorrow in the evening."

At dinner the master said, "I myself will take you in the morning. I don't have anything so important to do that I can't go there."

Now I began to think about the trip and how I could get him to swing by Sanna's. I decided to try. I thought it best that I present the idea frankly, in all its nakedness, without hiding anything.

Later while I was cleaning my clothes once more, the master asked me what I was doing. "Since you have clean clothes why don't you use them?"

"I don't want to do that," I told him, "as I am getting a ticket to America before winter, and I have one outfit that I will wear. All of my clothes fit Manu well, so he can have them. Why should I use them all when I'll get along very well with what I have on now?"

He gave a slight smile and went into the house. In the morning we started on our trip. The master talked, yet I gave him only curt answers. Finally he asked me what was wrong. "Is it against your wishes to go to Kainsasto? You are so uncommunicative. What's wrong?"

"No, not at all," I said.

"So what's on your mind?"

We arrived at the Kauhajoki bridge. I asked him to stop in front of the store. "I'll tell you what I'm thinking," I said. He stopped the horse. "The road that crosses that bridge goes through the village of Kirves. On the other side of Kirves is a cottage on a farm where the widow lives with whom I stayed after I left the village of Mieta. I promised her that I'd come to see her once more—if I lived—even if I have to walk. That woman is just like my mother to me. But if you don't want to make the trip, don't do it, as I believe that I can arrange a trip from the Kainasto bog. I've always noted that if I have a genuine desire, no power on earth can change it. I believe it is at least six *virstaa* (a *virsta* is .6629 miles), or it may be as many as eight or nine. If we go there now, we'd have to spend the night. This is the matter I've been pondering since yesterday. But if you're in a hurry to return, I don't want you to go."

A man came out of the store, and the master asked him how far it was to Kirves. "Seven or eight long *virstaa*," he replied. "But wait, I'll be more accurate." He thought awhile and then said, "It isn't over seven *virstaa*."

The master turned to me and asked, "Is that woman well off?"

"We didn't lack anything," I said, "but I did trap birds and fish. We sold the birds in town, and then we had money to buy things. She has three cows now."

"Well," said the master, "it probably would be best if we went there. I don't want you to go there on your own from Kainasto."

"I'll buy some coffee and sugar for Sanna," I said.

The master tied the horse and followed me in. I asked for a kilo of sugar and coffee. When I started to pay, the master said, "Put your money in your pocket. I'll pay for it." Some pastry was brought in for sale while we were there, and I took some and started to pay for it. The master took some as well and said, "I'll pay for everything. Does she have butter?"

"Yes," I replied, "and I believe she has fresh fish. We needn't bring anything else."

As we were leaving the store, I started to laugh. The master asked what I was laughing about, and I told him to ask me when we got to Takamaa. "I'll tell you then." We covered the distance quickly, and it wasn't long before I told the master, "We're in Kirves. It isn't but a few rabbit hops from here to the house. Turn there and let the horse walk. The road is in slight disrepair."

We arrived at our destination. Hupi barked and came to greet us. I told the master that the dog was mean to strangers and that he should stay on the wagon until I told the dog to lie down. I stepped down, and the dog was so excited that it wanted to lick my face. Sanna then came out, and we hugged each other. The master told me to command the dog to lie down. He wanted to get down off the wagon.

"Is there anything in the stable," I asked Sanna, "or can we put the horse in there?" She said to put the horse in the stable, so I told the master to drive under the shed roof. Sanna and I followed. I commanded Hupi to lie down and introduced the master to Sanna. I told her that I was waiting for a ticket to America, but for now the master was taking me to Kainasto to be a herd boy. "I told him I wanted to come to see you, so he brought me. We'll stay overnight and leave in the morning for Kainasto."

I drew water from the well for the horse. Sanna brought some hay. I asked her, "Has Mikko brought you any fish?"

"No," she replied, "he hasn't always had time to go for fish himself, but he has arranged for some other men to get them. Right now Matti Ylinen is out and should be coming back soon. I've had plenty of fish. They're brought to me for first pick, but I don't need many since I'm alone. Now that we're making hay it's good that there are plenty of fish."

We went into the house, and I asked the master, "What has become of the things we brought?"

"They're under the cover in the rig," he said. He went to get them. I told him to stay where he was and went to get them myself. When I returned, the master and Sanna were engaged in a spirited conversation. "What was it you laughed about earlier?" the master asked me. "You promised to tell me when we arrived at our destination."

I gave the coffee, sugar and pastry to Sanna saying, "Here's something for you on my homecoming." Then I added, "I laughed when I thought about the blessing that is on the sixteen marks I have in my pocket. Listen, I'll tell you." I took the silver coins from my pocket and put them on the table. "Sanna, here's the money I took from your bag."

"Why, it's all your money," she said. "There were eighty-eight marks. You took only sixteen."

"True, but hear what a blessing is on this money. I wrote a letter to Mother, and the mistress of Paloluoma said, 'Put your money in your pocket.' She bought the stamp.

"I went to a cottage where an old man was repairing shoes, and his wife asked if I had any business there. I asked her to give me something to eat: 'Herring bread or soup—I'll pay. I don't want it for nothing.'

"'Who are you?'

"'I'm Isaac and Soffia Polvi's son.'

"'Are you the one who ran away from Kartano?'

"I answered that I was.

"The old man said, 'Try to find some food for him,' and the old woman fried chicken eggs for me and brought me a *viilia*, and so I ate. I tried to pay for it, but they said, 'Put that money back in your pocket.' I thanked them and started walking.

"Then, several weeks ago I was fishing with Manu and we were thirsty. The river water was warm, and we didn't want to drink it. We went to Kreivi Hill trading post and bought a bottle of lemonade. When we went to pay for it, the shopkeeper said, 'Isaac, put the money in your pocket. I'll pay for it.'

"Now, when I got the master to come here, I wanted to buy coffee and sugar for you. He said to me, 'Put your money in your pocket. I'll pay for them.'

"I thought I'd buy some pastry, so I took one. But he also took one and said he'd pay for them both. What else can I do but laugh and be glad that the money has been blessed in this fashion? Sanna, I want you to have the money. It belongs to you. I wouldn't have been able to earn one penny without your help. I'm giving these coins to you, as I don't need them. I'll keep only three marks. I believe this amount has as great a blessing as the whole. I'm very much indebted to you for providing me with such a good home."

Sanna said, "And I've been so thankful to you. I've thought about you with great love. Awhile ago when Hupi was barking, you were on my mind. I looked out the window and saw you petting him. I couldn't seem to get out of the house fast enough. I didn't care about the stranger. I came to embrace you, so great is my love for you—for all that you have expressed to me."

Sanna made coffee, and Matt Ylinen came in with twelve pike. Sanna took two, and I cleaned them. She told Matt that we would be staying overnight and asked him to tell Mikko that I was there. I didn't know Matt. He had been away during the entire time that I was with Sanna.

We went into the barn. Sanna had sold a cow, leaving only two. When she finished milking, she brought some dried meat and a fish *keitto* to the table. After we had eaten, Mikko and his wife came over. The evening passed pleasantly. They said that the two girls I knew were staying with relatives somewhere and were not at home. We had a good time, the master taking part in the conversation.

The master talked about conditions in Kurikka and explained the class distinctions that existed between the landowners and the poor people. He said, "I have a different view on the matter than most. We landowners wouldn't be able to manage without the workers, and it is better to give credit to those who do the work. They deserve the thanks.

I have never looked down on the poor, and they have always treated me well. When I want workers, they are always ready to come. I don't need to coax them."

It was midnight by the time Mikko and his wife left for home. Mikko said, "Isaac is just a boy, but we have learned much from him."

Sanna said, "He has given me a greater gift. Since I was a small girl I have been very afraid, but he talked the fear out of me. Every evening last winter we held discussions. Sometimes we had the Bible or Bible history before us. He always found, and showed me, the proof for his arguments. It's just too bad that he hasn't had the opportunity to go to school."

"I don't feel that I'm better than anyone else," I said, "so don't brag about me."

The master laughed, saying, "I do know that he's not afraid. He's always been willing to be bait for a hobgoblin."

We said goodnight and went directly to bed. In the morning we were on our way early. Sanna urged me to take the money I had left, but I refused, saying that I had a job and knew that I'd have enough food. The master went to get the horse ready, and Sanna and I followed him to the stable.

The master took Sanna by the hand and thanked her. "I'm glad I came here," he said, "and as I said last night, we couldn't get him to tell much. But what little he told was true. If you should ever come to Mieta, don't forget to come to see me."

He took up the reins, and I embraced Sanna. I said, "I believe that this is our last farewell. I'm glad I could be with you once more. I thank you for everything." Sanna cried, but I reassured her, saying, "We don't need to cry. We shall be friends as long as we live." Sanna wished me everything good as I jumped up next to the master. He had tears in his eyes as he started to drive off. I continued waving my cap. Sanna waved her hand.

When we had traveled a short distance, the master wiped his eyes and said, "That was very moving, seeing your parting with Sanna. May I tell about this at home?"

"Go ahead," I replied, "until someone makes fun of it . . . then not another word."

He laughed and said, "People are insensitive. The mistress has regretted her comments. I know. I've heard it from her own lips. She only started thinking when you told us that you'd already said too much."

We had driven a good distance and had hardly spoken at all. My thoughts were still back on where we had been. I saw that Torkkoo was eyeing me. I said to him, "I'm content after getting to see her. I think a great deal of that woman. I suffered through so much cat-yowling before I got to her place. She was good to me and treated me so well. I respect her and the treatment I received. I searched my mind for a way to repay her. I really wanted to do something. I don't believe anybody could have done any better by her than I did. There is another example of a desire and a will so strong that no power on earth could stop it or alter it. I'm glad that she got so much monetary help, but what she was to me cannot be rewarded with money."

"Where had you been before you wound up with her?" asked Torkkoo.

"I'll tell you, if you don't talk about it," I said. "Everybody doesn't need to know." I told him briefly. "I begged my bread, slept nights wherever I happened to be—in threshing sheds, under bridges, in the woods—wherever. I suffered cold, hunger and the unkind treatment that people had for me in great quantities. I learned a lot. It was a great school for me, and in spite of all this, I don't regret it. I came to know the world and its people, came to know the differences among individuals. It is a school where you come to know your god, come to know that money, goods and wealth are not measures of a man's true worth and add nothing to his fame. Rather, his deeds and works establish his worth. My mother advised me to listen to the voice of my conscience, that it would tell me what is right and wrong. 'Live honestly. Live so that none can criticize you for having done wrong. Don't do anything that will not stand the light of day. Live always in dignity, and remember to respect others.'"

Torkkoo asked me to tell him how I came to Sanna's home. I told him how I met her brother, as I related earlier, and we talked quite animatedly for the entire trip until our arrival at Latomaki, our destination.

5

Equals

T HERE WERE two houses so close together that they shared a common yard. A woman of about forty came out and greeted the master. "I brought you another boy, Maiju," he said. "He will herd the cattle. He is good material. Take care of him."

Maiju didn't know me. "Who are you?" she asked.

"He's Isaac and Soffia Polvi's son."

"Is he the one who ran away from Kartano?"

"He's the one."

"Oh," said Maiju, "then he's my old friend Soffia's son. Your mother was a servant at Laulaja, and I am Laulaja's daughter, Maiju—an old maid. That's what they call me. I was always good friends with your mother, and you still need a mother. Can I be a mother to you? But where in the world have you been all this time that you've been away from Kurikka?"

I told her I hadn't been up to anything bad.

"So you say."

"Maiju," the master interrupted, "don't doubt him. He always speaks the truth. I wish my own boys were like him. He has been with us since

July eleventh when he returned, and I have yet to see anything bad in him. Yesterday morning we left to come here, and I have only now come to know him. We drove to where he stayed for that year, and the people there greeted him with love and friendship. We stayed there a night, and I came to know him."

"Where was it?" Maiju asked.

"It was at Kauhajoki, on the way here. We made a fifteen *virsta* round trip. I lost a whole day of my time, but I don't feel bad about it. I'm glad I went there. I can assure you that you can depend on what he says and what he promises. You can rely completely on this boy. Just take good care of him."

Maiju said she was glad I came with such a good recommendation. "We have excellent rules here, and there is no class distinction. We are all equal, and we must all try to help one another. We can't sing lewd songs, swear, lie or steal. Not one person is better than another. We are all created by God. Now what do you say about this?"

"That rule should apply everywhere," I answered.

The master laughed, and Maiju asked him why. "I am laughing because Isaac's hope is beginning to be fulfilled."

I asked the master, "Will you try to get my mail to me here when I receive some? I don't really expect any until the latter part of September."

"As soon as any comes, I will personally put it in your hand," he said. "I won't leave it to anyone else to bring, you can be sure of that."

When his horse had eaten, he prepared to depart. I went to him and thanked him again for the trip he had made. He said that he needed the trip himself, and had enjoyed it as much as I. Then he left, and Maiju remarked that I seemed to be in his good graces.

"What have you heard of your mother?" she asked. I told her that I had a baby sister born over there. Then she asked me one thing after another, and I answered her. I asked her if she didn't have something that I could do, but she told me to relax. "You don't need to do anything but wait for those boys to come in from the bog. They'll be here in about an hour."

The cows began arriving, and I went outside to wait. The gate to the paddock was open. Two cows had gone in, and another was about to. Maiju walked past me, and I asked her how many cows there were. "Around fifty," she said, "and five horses. There are four boys at the bog, and you'll be the fifth." The cows were coming now in groups of five or six. The boys rode horses and drove the rest of the cows, trying to hurry the stragglers along. When they had them all in the paddock, the gate was closed and the horses stabled.

Maiju went to milk the cows. First they sent in those cows that weren't giving much milk, followed by those that would freshen in the fall. Later, we had a good meal of dried meat and *viilia*. Maiju churned butter and always set out good meals. No herring at all!

I introduced myself to the boys. I told them my name, and said Ylitorkkoo had brought me to be a herd boy. "Will I fit in with your crowd, or must I start walking back?"

The boys laughed and yelled, "Welcome!"

After Maiju had asked us to come and eat, the question of horses came up. The boys all had their mounts, but the fifth horse was only a colt around three years old and had never had a bit in its mouth. "It is tame, and we have named it *Kakara* (which means 'brat'). It is fun to play with. You can have it for a mount," said one of the boys.

I asked them to help me train it for riding. "But we must be careful with it. We can't hurt or hit it."

The boys laughed and said, "Here we don't even spank a cat. The Old Maid of Laulaja is law and order here, and we must heed her commands. If you drive the cows, you must be sure that the cows don't run, or you'll be called to account for it by Maiju." The boys all laughed again, but Maiju was silent, as though she hadn't heard what the boys were saying.

When we had eaten, we decided to go and put the bit in Kakara's mouth. A boy went in front of the horse and bridled it. It didn't take long. It was led first by one and then by another. Then the reins were attached, and we tried driving it from behind, but it wouldn't start walking, so somebody took hold of the side of the bridle and led it. We trained with the horse for quite a while that evening.

The next morning when the cattle were let out on the bog, the boys left on horseback. I drove Kakara from behind and followed them. When we arrived at our destination, the horses were turned loose to eat for a short while. We then called Kakara and placed the bit in its mouth. Each boy took his turn on its back while the horse was led around. It wasn't difficult to do. It seemed to understand that it shouldn't hurt us and was as gentle as a lamb. We raised its hooves and simulated nailing on shoes with a wooden club, and then we again jumped on its back. We had a good time, and on the evening of the first day, I rode to Latomaki on Kakara's back. Later we harnessed it and asked the master of Latomaki for a grain cart from which we removed the wheels. We first led the horse, but it wasn't long before the five of us were on the cart platform riding all over the yard. We then removed the harness and again rode on its back by turns. It progressed rapidly.

I went to Maiju and asked her for a piece of bread. "I want to give it to Kakara."

Maiju laughed and said, "We have more bread than anything else, so go ahead and take some."

The next day I, too, had a mount. We trained with it all day, until one of the boys reminded us that we hadn't given it time to eat at all that day. Another said, "Oh, the poor creature. It's so hungry." He went to our knapsack and fed all the bread from our lunch to it. We ate our lunch without bread on that day.

In the evening we again hitched the horse to the grain cart without wheels. We drove in the yard until one of the boys suggested that we go to Metsala's store to buy chewing tobacco. This tobacco was in the form of leaf twisted into a rope about one-half inch in diameter. It was coiled up and soaking in licorice water and served as chewing tobacco.

One of the boys asked if Maiju would give us the money. Another said, "She hasn't refused yet when I've asked." He went to Maiju and came back with fifty pennies, so five boys left on a grain cart in a terrible cloud of dust. I drove along the sandy road. The distance was only about a mile.

I recall another time when we were again going after tobacco, and I was driving. I saw three girls on the road and said to Anttii, one of the boys, "If only the girls would pass on the right side so they won't get caught up in this cloud of dust." And indeed they did, whereupon I recognized two of the girls I had known in the village of Kirves. I stopped the horse, gave the reins to Anttii and told him to take care of everything. "I'm staying here until you get back." I gave him some money and told him to bring back some sweets. Then I jumped down.

"Didn't you go to Kurikka?" asked the one named Alma.

"I did go there," I replied, "but they brought me here to Kainasto to be a herd boy. These are my friends—Anttii, Matti, Jussi and Akseli. These girls are my friends—Alma and Etla. What is your name?"

The third girl said, "My name is Mari, and I live nearby. Alma and Etla live in Kirves."

"No, no, Mari," I said, "don't tell these boys too much."

Everyone laughed, and Anttii asked, "How many sweets should I bring? And what kind? Who are you going to give them to?"

I said, "Twenty-five pennies worth of confetti, candy and 'belly buttons' of mixed or equal parts for each of these girls. And you know what I want, Anttii."

"Chewing tobacco," Anttii said, "which is sweet enough for you."

We laughed, and the boys drove off.

The girls and I sat down on the side of the road to talk. I told them, "I visited Sanna, and we stayed a night. I also saw Mikko and his wife. They got word that I was at Sanna's place, so they came there. They said that you girls were somewhere with relatives, and now I find you here. I was very surprised when I glanced up and saw you. I could hardly believe my eyes."

"Do you know when you'll be leaving for America?" asked Alma.

"The end of September or the beginning of October," I replied.

Now the boys returned, carrying the sweets wrapped in paper. They gave them to me, along with seventy-five pennies. "Did you bring the tobacco for me?" I asked.

The boys laughed and said, "You'll get your tobacco tomorrow."

I gave the sweets to Alma and told the girls to divide them among themselves. "I don't want anything that sweet. Chewing tobacco is my candy."

The boys said, "Well, Isaac, aren't you coming with us?"

"No," I replied, "I want to be with these *kakaras* for a while yet.

Anttii laughed. "What about this other *kakara* of yours?"

"You take care of that one," I said. "I have three here."

Alma opened the paper wrapper and said, "There's so much candy here, it would be wrong not to give some to the boys, too." So she walked over to the boys. They laughed, thanked her and left.

"Which way is your home?" I asked the girls.

They laughed and said that they wanted to know where I lived. "We'll come to see you, and then we'll show you where we live. We'll take you home today, so we'll know where to find you."

So we walked to the Latomaki road intersection. The girls didn't want to go to the house but promised to come to see me in a few days. We again sat for a short time, and then bade one another good night.

The boys asked if I had brought the "brats" home. I told them that they had brought me as far as the intersection, promising to come again some evening. Maiju wanted to know who they were that I might know them from here.

"Two are from Kirves," I said, "the village where I stayed last winter. They are visiting here. They are the only young people that I came to know there, and I was very happy to see them again. They promised to come and see me again before they return to Kirves. They are good, decent brats."

Now, after a few days, my mount was as good as the others. In fact, it was better, because when I called Kakara it came to me immediately, running so fast that the other horses had to get out of the way. I would put the bit in its mouth, jump on its back and take off at a gallop. It was a pleasure to be on its back; just like a rocking chair. In the evening we taught it to pull, but we noticed that the grain car was getting shorter at the end where it dragged along the ground. That end was badly worn, so I went to the master of Latimaki and told him about it.

The master came to look. He laughed, saying, "There is no great harm done. I'll nail a new bottom on this and extend the platform. You can put wheels under it. Use it with wheels, and I'll repair it tomorrow morning. You have made a horse out of this colt. There is no harm done."

In the early evening of the next day, having finished our work, we started off for Latomaki. But we found that we had left our knapsack and lunch bag far out on the bog. I went back to get them while the boys went on towards home, slowly driving the cows that hadn't already gone. I picked up the bags, and when Kakara saw how far behind the others we were, it started after them at breakneck speed. I didn't even try to stop it. I felt as though I was flying, and thoroughly enjoyed the ride. The other boys were leading their horses to the stable through the cowshed. Only then did I see the danger that awaited me if I couldn't stop Kakara. I pulled back on the reins and said, "*Tpruu, tpruu,*" but the horse lowered its head to its chest and didn't slow down.

The roof of the cow shed was so low that only the horse would clear it, so I grabbed Kakara's mane and tried to plaster my body against its side with my left leg still stretched over the horse's back. My leg hit the eaves and I flew around in front of the horse. Kakara jumped over me but immediately turned around to sniff, as though asking, "How badly are you hurt, pal?"

In a moment my four pals and Maiju were gathered around me. Maiju wanted to take me into the house, but I asked them to check for broken bones before the leg had a chance to swell up.

"Where are you hurt?" asked Maiju.

"My left leg hit the eave," I said. "I couldn't stop Kakara. See if there are any broken bones in the knee."

Kakara continued to sniff me, and Maiju slapped the horse, saying, "This is all your fault. Go away!"

"You can't be angry with Kakara," I said. "If the boys hadn't taken their horses into the stable, this wouldn't have happened. But they didn't think. This is only an accident. It just happened, that's all."

Maiju was examining my knee and said, "You have hit the knee-cap and bruised the tendons. I don't find any damage to the bones. Well, it won't take long to heal, but I can feel that it is beginning to swell fast."

Maiju now took me in her arms and said, "Put your arms around my neck." She took me into her bedroom and checked me over again. "Your right arm is hurt also, and there is a black and blue mark on your back."

"They don't mean a thing to me," I said. "I'm not concerned about small black and blue marks, just so my leg gets well. It doesn't seem to have any feeling, but if there are no broken bones, I believe it will wake up. It's as though it has gone to sleep. There's no feeling in it."

Maiju again began to check my knee and said, "It's swelling fast. The tendon was hit. I believe it'll get well, but we must apply a cold compress, because it is so hot."

"Leave me here," I told Maiju, "as the cows are still unmilked."

"True," she said. "I'll put them in the barn and arrange for the neighbor lady to milk them."

But the neighbor lady had already come, thinking that Maiju might need help. "Akseli has already put the cows in the barn. I'll tend to the milking. I've done it before."

Maiju bathed my leg with cold water, then rubbed it with liniment. I told her to toss a sheet over me and go about her own work.

"I'll get you a long shirt to put on. And now while you're in bed, I can clean your clothes." She left the room briefly and then came back in laughing. "There are so many helpers in the barn that I'm not needed." This time she had warm water. She cleaned me up and put the shirt on me. As I once again examined my knee, she asked me, "Is feeling returning to your leg?"

"It feels better."

"A cold bath is good for the swelling, I think," she said, "but hot water is probably better for the tendons." She got some hot water and bathed my leg with it. Then she asked me what I'd like to eat.

I didn't feel like eating. "Nothing now," I said.

"Surely you must eat something." She left and then returned with bread, butter, dried meat and milk. "Should I bring *viilia*?" she asked.

"No, nothing," I said. "I'll eat just a little. Not being mobile, I'm better off hungry than with a full stomach."

"Here's a pail for you to use when you must attend to your bodily functions," she said. "I'll help you. You needn't feel ashamed. Are you?"

"No, there's no part of my body I'm ashamed of. Since I know I'm like other people, why should I feel ashamed?"

"That's right," Maiju agreed. "If you must go, let me know. I'm always ready to do whatever I can for your good."

I thanked her.

There was a good deal of activity in Maiju's room the entire evening.

The boys came to see me, as did the neighbors. Maiju bathed my leg again with hot water and rubbed the knee with liniment.

When we went to bed, Maiju asked me if I was in any pain. I told her it was still numb. "It's no trouble when it's asleep," I said. I lay awake for a long time and was glad that Maiju slept. After I slept, I awoke to find the leg hurting. The feeling was returning. I was glad and said to Maiju, "Now my leg has awakened and will start to heal."

She checked it and found that it had become swollen again. "Shall we rub it?"

"Let's leave it alone and see what it wants to do after that long nap," I told her. Maiju laughed, and I told her that I had been waiting for the pain. "Now it will begin healing." Since the leg wouldn't bear my weight, I asked Maiju to help me to the pail. "I can't put any weight on it at all," I said.

"Of course not," said Maiju. "It won't get well that fast. This morning the feeling has returned. Tomorrow morning it will be a little better, and the next morning better still. That's how it'll get well—a little at a time."

Maiju went about her work, but it wasn't long before Akseli came in with coffee. Soon the other boys came in to inquire about my condition. I asked the boys to use Kakara as much as possible as a mount and to leave the old steady horse in peace. "Don't forget. I'll be well soon, and Kakara is still my mount."

Maiju called the boys to eat. The neighbor lady came into the bedroom, too. She stayed only long enough to say that Maiju had gone to milk and to ask me if I needed anything, which I didn't. The neighbor girls came over, and the master even showed up that evening. I had many visitors.

A couple of days passed this way. And soon I was able to place some weight on the leg.

When Saturday evening rolled around, the boys were there with me. Maiju came in and said, "You boys get out of here. There are three girls who want to see Isaac."

"They're the ones Isaac called the 'good brats,'" they said laughing.

"I presume that's who they are," said Maiju. The boys left, and Maiju called the girls to come up to her room. She found a seat for everyone, explained my accident and added that we had high hopes for a complete recovery.

I introduced the girls to Maiju. "This is Alma. She and Etla come from Kirves. Mari lives around here somewhere, and I got to know her just a few days ago." Maiju asked if they didn't have surnames. "I don't

know anybody's surname except yours," I said. "It's the Old Maid of
Laulaja. And you're now my mother." Everybody laughed.

"How many mothers do you have?" asked Alma. "There's one in
America, and another is Sanna Takamaa."

Maiju laughed and said, "—and the Old Maid of Laulaja is the third."

"I always have had the luck of the waif," I said. "When I need a mother, one is provided. I don't need to look for one. When I injured myself,
Maiju immediately came to me, took me in her arms and carried me to
her bed. She's cared for me like I was her own brat."

Alma told Maiju the girls' surnames, but I don't recall them. It is
enough that I remember their given names.

Maiju then left us alone. The three girls and I talked and joked, and
the evening passed pleasantly. Maiju served us coffee. When we had
finished with it she said, "Let's see that leg. I'll bathe it in hot water now.
It isn't that swollen any more."

She went to get the water, and the girls said good night to me. I
thanked them for coming, adding, "Come tomorrow afternoon . . . or
do you have somewhere else to go?"

Alma was quite bold. "We'll come only on the condition that your
mother doesn't serve coffee. We don't want you to bother with coffee
on account of us. There's no need to serve us. We don't want that."

Ten days and nights later I still lay on Maiju's bed. The girls had
come to see me often. This time they demanded that Maiju bring my
clothes.

"I want to put Isaac's trousers on him," said Alma, making us all
laugh.

Maiju brought my clothes and went out. The clothes were all clean
and in good condition. The girls had a good time bringing me down from
the bedroom and walking me around, although they soon realized that I
should have a crutch.

The neighbor lady who had showed up said she had one, but it was
too long. She disappeared into the house and soon the master appeared
with the crutch and cut it down to just the right size. Using my new crutch
I went back into the house with the girls, this time without their help.

Maiju was glad to see me stumping about with the aid of a crutch.
She told the girls that she'd like them to prepare coffee and call the
neighbors to the table. "We'll drink this coffee in Isaac's name, because
he's finally getting around after ten days in my bed." The girls began
preparing the coffee, but Maiju said, "Use a larger pot. The boys will be
coming in from the bog. We'll put them at the same table. It'll be a surprise."

There was humming as I perfected the use of a crutch.

After supper a man who called himself "Shoemaker" Jaska came over with an accordion in hand. We gave him a chair, and he started to play, quietly at first, just squeezing the accordion softly, but before long a dance was in full swing. The girls danced with the herd boys. The neighor and his wife and Maiju were there. Five or six strangers were there as well. I still don't know how this dance was arranged. When I asked Maiju, she laughed and told me it was something I'd have to figure out myself. She served food and coffee to everyone. It was midnight before Shoemaker Jaska's accordion was quiet.

Afterward Maiju took me up to her bedroom saying, "It's best if you come with me. It's a joy that you have finally begun to get around, even in this manner. I'm grateful to the girls, too. They've been a great pleasure to you. Let's examine your leg again. When she looked at it, she rubbed it with liniment and determined that the best medicine now would be a lot of movement. The master of Toiska had already told me that the more I used it, the sooner it would heal and regain its strength.

Maiju helped me down from her bedroom in the morning and up again in the evening, but I wasn't too happy about sleeping with her any-more. When I mentioned it, she told me that she was afraid to be alone in her bedroom. I immediately told her that I'd come with her. When we were in bed I asked her what it was she feared. "Is it true that you fear the unseen?"

"Yes," she answered, adding, "but in addition I also fear what is seen."

I told her that I was totally fearless. "An angry bull is the only thing I fear. I'll tell you now, Maiju—and what I say is true—I was full of un-founded fears until Mikko Perapolvi freed me from them. Since then I haven't been afraid. He told me to examine the source when I see or hear something strange. So I started doing that. It was difficult, but this was the only way I could stop being afraid. Maiju, I'm telling you truthfully— I have slept nights in threshing sheds, in field ditches, under bridges and in the forest. I've never been afraid. It's been over a year since I ran away from Kartano. Just don't tell anybody that I was a beggar for about three months before John Salo took me to his sister's place.

"My existence was most wretched until I went to Sanna. She was a dear person. I believe that God was inside her, she was that good. Look, in every person there are two separate beings, one good and one bad. The bad is what we should reject, and all the good that's in us is of God. I was very happy staying with Sanna. I made her fearless, too. I assure you that emptiness doesn't do anything. A void will not go 'bang.' Since you don't have to fear emptiness, what else is there to fear?"

"There are those who travel by night and knock on my door when I don't want anyone here," she said. "I should open the door for them. When you're here it is as though I already have a sweetheart whom I love, so they leave me alone. Stay here, and I'll make your stay as comfortable and pleasant as I possibly can."

I finally agreed to continue to sleep with Maiju. She often called me her boyfriend.

I walked with the aid of the crutch for twelve days. I had been away from the bog for three weeks and still couldn't get on or off a horse. When I went back to work, I was given an old steady mount and was helped onto and off of its back.

I had been back on the bog for several days, with the boys helping me to get on the horse whenever I had to turn the cows. While driving them back, I had to cross over a ditch. When I jumped the horse over it, I saw several large pike moving in the water. I rode down to the river and saw that the ditch was dry on that end. The fish apparently had swum into the ditch during high water, perhaps that very spring. I knew that there were other ditches, and that they probably all had fish in them as well, but I wasn't in any condition to get into the ditch to catch them. When I caught up to the boys, they asked me why I had ridden so far before coming back. I said, "I've often thought, aren't there any fish in the river? You've never mentioned it, though you've all fished before."

Akseli replied, "If there were fish we'd have seen them sometimes, but the people who live here have never mentioned that there were any."

"Now we'll go fishing," I said, and everybody laughed. "But we must eat first, and then we'll take that birch bark knapsack to put the fish in. We'll catch them bare-handed. There are large pike that swam into the ditches in the early spring when the water was high, and they can't get back into the river now. There's a fair amount of water, but we'll make a sheaf of sedge-grass and we'll drive the fish into shallow water with it. Two boys will go into the ditch to stand and wait, and when a fish comes by, one will grab it and throw it on the bank. If a few fish get by, there'll be another boy there to grab them."

We ate lunch, and then one of the boys went to collect the sedge-grass, out of which I made the sheaf. We found a couple of sticks at the river and tied a stick to each end of the sheaf. We then called the horses and went fishing.

Jussi, one of the boys, said, "All this fuss seems crazy to me. I haven't even seen a frog on the entire Kainasto bog, and now we have a birch bark knapsack to put fish in."

Everybody laughed, and the knapsack was given to Matti, but he said, "Give it to Isaac. I don't believe we'll be putting any bloodheads in it. It is crazy—fishing with a sheaf of hay."

I remarked that it was at least a grand effort; five boys on five horses going fishing. "But I'm sure we'll have luck and won't come back empty-handed." Once we had arrived at the ditch, I showed them that where they saw water the depth was around two feet. "But it appears to get shallower the closer we go toward the bog. When two boys drag that sheaf on the bottom, as they move forward, the fish will move ahead of it. Then two boys should go on horseback to where there are only three or four inches of water. Get into the ditch and stand there quietly with your hands ready. When a fish swims near you, snatch it up quickly and throw it on land." Everybody laughed, but I urged the boys on. When they had gone a short distance, they saw some large pike ahead of them.

They called for the others to get ready. "There're so many fish in here it's like a boiling pot of porridge." And soon the boys were throwing fish on shore. But when the boys moved, the school of fish turned back and all of the large pike jumped over the sheaf of hay. We tried chasing them once again, after which we counted how many we had. There were thirteen, four of which were three feet long. There was nothing under two feet, but the biggest got away.

"We must devise a better method," I said. "Those fish are slippery. I saw Jussi lose a couple of large pike when they slipped from his hands."

Jussi laughed and said, "But I was trying to take two at a time and ended up with none. What if we try again?"

"No need to try now. We have enough. With thirteen pike the knapsack is almost full."

The boys decided that I should take the fish to Latomaki so that Maiju could fry fish for supper. "Put the horse in the stable," they said, "you don't need to come back."

Once I was astride the horse the boys hoisted the fish pack onto my back. It was quite heavy, and, when I got to Latomaki, I couldn't get down. Nor could I ride through the shed, so I went out through the gate and into the night paddock so I'd see somebody. I saw the neighbor girl and told her to get her father, who came to my aid immediately, taking the pack off my back and helping me down off the horse. They looked in astonishment at our catch. Maiju came over and I told her, "Give the fish to everyone. They should be cooked soon. We'll bring more tomorrow."

I explained to the master how and where we had caught the fish. "I have a scoop net," he said. "We could take off the long handle and put on a short one. We'll put it topside down so that a straight side is on the surface and the curved side will fit well into the bottom of the ditch. Use it tomorrow." The master took the fish. "I'll do my part," he said. "I'll clean them."

His wife excused Maiju from making supper this time. "I'll fry the fish," she said.

Hilda, her daughter, added, "If I can share in the fried fish, I'll go and set the table."

I laughed and told her that the boys had warned me that the fish belonged to all of us.

"And it could happen that this may yet turn into a dance tonight," said Hilda.

I asked her who had arranged the last dance. She whispered in my ear that her father got Shoemaker Jaska and a few visitors to come over. Then she laughed.

The members of the two families were once again at the same table. It seemed to me that some of the food had come from the Toiska house— coffee, bread and meat. But nobody wanted meat. We always had dried meat to offer, so everyone wanted fried fish. They knew how to prepare it well. And when Maiju came in from milking, she was able to go directly to the table without having to prepare the food. The girls cleaned the table afterwards. I told the boys that tomorrow we would have a good scoop net.

After we had eaten, we took the grain platform for a ride. It now had wheels under it, and Kakara behaved like a mature horse. I told the master that I would like to have his church buggy, "The four-wheeled '*Turku.*' It's such a steady horse, we should see if it is anything special. If so, we can then say we've made a horse out of a '*kakara*' (brat)."

The master agreed and soon Kakara was hitched to the church buggy. Once again we were five boys going after tobacco. We drove Kakara at a trot, then let it walk, and once again drove it at a trot. The master waited for us, and I suppose he was a little concerned.

We sometimes took the grain rack and sometimes a lighter, two-wheeled rig. Every evening we drove and trained Kakara. Sometimes we each took our own mounts and rode along the roads.

This was, I believe, my life's happiest time. No want. No oppression. We were all equal. None of us wanted to know the others' past. I came to know that at least one of them was a boy from a big house, but he was our peer. He didn't try to be better than the rest of us. Class distinctions were nonexistent.

We fished every day, but we didn't want to take any more fish than we could use at the time. They were easy to catch in the ditch with the aid of the scoop net.

One evening when we got back to Latomaki, there was a man there waiting for us. My leg was well now, and the master of Latomaki was grinning when he called to us.

"Boys, what have you done with this?" the stranger said, indicating the grain platform.

"That's what has become of it," I answered.

"What of the horse?"

"Kakara? Oh, it has turned out to be a good horse," I said.

He then said that he had come to take Kakara home. "I've arranged for a man who will begin its training, but the master of Latomaki insists that you have it trained. I want to see you drive it."

"We'll eat first," I replied. "Then we'll give you a ride on the grain platform—or that four-wheeler, if Latomaki will give it to us."

We went in and had baked fish, which we also gave to the visitor, who was the master of Antila. He gave us each a mark.

"Now we'll go again to get tobacco," I said. I brought Kakara out, and the other boys helped with the wagon. I offered the reins to Antila, but he told me to drive instead.

"I understand that it is your horse," he said. "I'm only coming along to see for myself."

There were six of us in the "*Turku*." Kakara trotted at a handsome pace, head high, neck slightly arched. I was proud of its style. I bragged about Kakara, much as a gypsy would brag about a horse he was selling.

I stopped the rig and said, "Now I'll show you how good and obedient it is." I jumped down from the buggy, dropping the reins on the road. I went to the side of the road and picked up a rock, which I gave to the master. "When we start to drive, you can drop it. See how this horse waits for me?"

I took the reins, tightening up on them a little as I got up into the buggy. When I loosened the reins, the horse started again. I told him that I had seen how some train horses. "They jerk the reins, and they have long whips they hit the horses with. We haven't hit or jerked this horse. See how good and obedient it has become? A horse can't be trained by a lot of swearing, whipping or jerking it around." We got to Metsala's trading shop, and I continued, saying, "Look! Any of its hooves can be raised." I raised one hoof and tapped it with a rock, much as in horse-shoeing.

"Let's go get the tobacco," said one of the boys.

"Don't we need to tie up the horse?" asked the master.

"When I toss the reins on the ground, it won't move," I said, "but to be safe, I'll tie it so that we don't do any damage. We've already worn out the grain-cart platform, and I don't want any more damage done to Latomaki's equipment."

He laughed and said he'd pay for the tobacco, so we came back with some. I unharnessed the horse and told him how faithful it was. I jumped on its back, rode off a bit and dismounted, dropping the reins on the ground. I walked away, saying, "It will stand there for at least an hour."

I was away from it for a long time before I went back. I said, "If there were no reins, it would run to me when I called. I never go to get it without it running to me immediately." The master inquired as to whether it would pull, and I said, "That grain platform wouldn't be worn like that if it couldn't."

Everybody laughed, and Latomaki said, "If you don't need that horse, I can assure you that it will be in good hands here. It's already well-trained. I have been very pleased when I have seen how these young boys have worked with the colt. I haven't seen that they've even once jerked on the reins, let alone slapped it or given it a bad word."

Antila said, "On second thought, I'll leave the horse another two or three weeks until I must take some cows from here as their time to freshen nears."

Kakara was left there. The master was quite satisfied as we went to the bog. He had taken some money to Maiju so that we could buy tobacco, and a couple of days later, the master of Torkkoo came with a letter from my mother. It read: "Prepare the minister's papers, the bailiff's papers and the official passport. Have everything ready. We are sending you a travel voucher. We can expect that you'll be here in early November."

This was, as I recall, the early part of September. "How do things stand?" asked the master. "Will I need to arrange for another boy to take your place?"

I said, "I don't think so. If you get those papers and a passport for me, it will be three or four weeks before I can get a ticket. By then the cattle will be so few that I won't be needed. Cows are taken away from here every week when their time to freshen nears. I like it here. In my life I haven't had a happier time. I will have my clothes ready. When the ticket comes, come and get me. At that time we'll see whether there are many cattle left. I don't believe you'll need a herd boy to replace me."

As the master of Antila prepared himself to return home, he promised to handle my affairs. He said he'd check on the departure schedule, so we wouldn't make an unnecessary trip.

One evening, several days later, we were eating when the neighbor girl came over. "A bearded man and a beautiful lady want to talk to Isaac. They are asking for Isaac Polvi, the herd boy from Kurikka."

"It must be John Salo," I said, getting up from the table.

"Just sit there," said Maiju, "I'll ask them in."

So they came in, and I left the table to greet them. "I'm so happy to see you here."

"We have some sad news for you," said John Salo. "My sister Sanna died. We buried her yesterday. Saturday I went to the village of Mieta to take you to the funeral, but I was told at Torkkoola's that you were here. It was already late, so I couldn't get you any more. Yesterday at the funeral I met the two girls you know well, Alma and Etla. They talked about you. Only then did I learn that you had been to visit Sanna and had stayed a night there with Torkkoola."

I hadn't seen Torkkoo himself, but rather his son. "How did Sanna die?" I asked. "She was always healthy."

"She died suddenly," said John. "The mistress of the big house had gone there at noon. She was well and happy, but complained of a headache. She lay down on the bed and died instantly."

"I'm sorry," I said. "I loved her as my own mother. She was so good to me."

Maiju prepared food for the visitors. I thought that I couldn't talk. It seemed so sad. Finally, I got up and said, "These two visitors here are my good friends John Salo and his wife. These four boys are my good pals. Maiju Laulaja is our housekeeper. I took a sacred vow when I said goodbye to Sanna that I would come to see her once more if I lived. When Torkkoo left to bring me here I remembered how good Sanna was to me and that I had promised to see her, even if it meant having to walk. I was thinking about the fact that I would soon be traveling to America, but I didn't say anything to Torkkoo. Finally, at the end of the Kauhajoki bridge in front of the trading shop, I told him."

I recounted how I'd kept silent on my whereabouts for the past year, but I told him about the widow in the cottage near Kirves whom I had grown to love as my own mother. I told him about the sixteen marks I had taken from Sanna that couldn't be spent, and how three were still in my pocket because others would pay for whatever I tried to buy. "The money in my pocket is blessed," I said. "And despite the fact that it was seven long *virstaa* to Sanna's place, Torkkoo said that he'd take me. What's more he bought the coffee and sugar I wanted to take to her, plus some pastry.

"When we arrived, I gave Sanna thirteen marks and kept three, and they have increased. That blessing never seems to end. I'm glad Torkkoo so generously agreed to take me there. I realize now after hearing that Sanna has died why I had such a burning desire to go to her. Once I had embraced her, I felt content. Now I know that it wasn't any too soon, but at least I kept my promise to her. I can't say any more but 'Sleep in peace, Sanna. I'll remember you with love. . . .'"

And then I cried.

The visitors got up from the table. John Salo asked where we got the fresh fish. "Who is it that catches them?"

Maiju answered, "The boys bring the same amount every day. The neighbor lady prepares them, and we all eat them."

I asked Maiju if she knew whether the neighbor had any fish, so I could give some to Mrs. Salo for her to prepare at home. Maiju sent me to ask her. She did have two large pike, so I was once again able to give the Salos fish. They inquired as to how soon I would be leaving, and I said I didn't know for certain. "But at least not for another two weeks." We talked for a long time. John promised to visit me again. Maiju fixed coffee, and the neighbor joined us. I went out with John and his wife and told them, "This is a home where everyone is equal. There is no class distinction."

"The girls explained that to me," he said. "I know everything the girls know. Tell me, has your leg healed?"

"Yes," I replied, "Maiju is a good doctor."

I continued to sleep with Maiju, as she wanted it that way. Whenever the boys came and tried to get next to her, she would say she didn't want anyone there, as she already had a boy there whom she loved. They said they'd like to see him, so she opened the door, and they came to look. "He's very young for you," they said. Maiju laughed and said that she could wait until he gets older.

At other times she explained that I had hurt my leg and that she was caring for me. And so she was. Maiju was very good to me, but when I suggested that I sleep with the other boys, she asked me to stay with her, insisting that she was afraid to be alone. So I promised, as I saw nothing bad in it.

6

From Finland to America

TIME PASSED QUICKLY. When Torkkoo came to get me, he had a registered letter with him. Inside was a ticket indicating that the boat would leave in two days.

"We have to hurry," said Torkkoo, so I said goodbye to the boys and all.

"John Salo and his wife didn't get to see me," I told Maiju. "I have to leave sooner than expected, so please take them in as your guests when they come." I also told her that since there were only around forty head of cattle left, another boy wouldn't be needed to replace me. When we drove away, my thoughts remained with Latomaki.

"Say something," said the master. "Don't be so quiet. What are you thinking about?"

"This life of mine is like a dream," I said. "Being here at the Kainasto bog has been my happiest and most pleasurable time. When you brought me here, I didn't know anyone. Now all the people I've come to know are very dear to me. Once again, I'm on a journey into a totally unknown future. I know that my family will be there when I arrive, but on the long journey I won't know anybody, nor will they know me. I will be like a

115

wood chip taken by the river's current. Sometimes the chip happens into an eddy of the current, whirling for a while before moving on. Thus it has been for me since my mother left me at Kartano. Soon I'll be on my way on wider waters. What I will encounter over there across the seas, only the future will tell. I will be among people of a foreign land. I'll know neither their language nor their thinking. No doubt there will be many an obstacle besides the language barrier, but I'm not afraid at all. With the will and desire to conquer all difficulties, time will shape me into someone who can learn to avoid problems, and to get rid of those that do arise. But why do I worry about problems before they arise?"

I told him that John Salo brought word that Sanna Takamaa had died. The master said, "I thought she was the one, although I didn't talk to the man. When I heard that they came to take you to the funeral of a widow in Kirves, it was immediately clear to me."

We talked spiritedly the entire trip. It was quite late when we arrived at Torkkoola. Torkkoo said that he had arranged my minister's papers, as well as the bailiff's papers. "We'll get the passport when we go to the harbor," he added. When we got there he said, "The ship you're leaving on should be here, but it isn't. We'll get your passport anyway, but you'll have to do it. I don't really want to talk to the man."

"Just show me the door," I said, "and I'll do it."

I opened the door to a large room lined with benches. At the rear there was a small room with an open door. I asked if there was anybody there I could speak to. A well-dressed man came out and asked me what I wanted.

I'm from Kurikka," I said. "I'd like to get a passport. I'm on my way to America. Can I get it here?"

He turned around and said, "Come with me and show me your papers."

There was a counter in the room. I went over to it and said, "Here they are. I'm afraid I missed the boat. There was no ship where there should have been."

He looked out the window and said, "I don't see it either." Then he examined a schedule and said, "You won't get to leave for a week. Come here. The boat leaves in the evening, so don't be late." He was very friendly, even asking after my mother and father.

I told him about them without once calling him "sir." When I got my passport and had paid for it, I thanked him, pulled my hat down on my head and went out. Torkkoo asked me how it had gone.

When I told him how friendly the man was, Torkkoo said, "There must be some *good* places on that sheep's head, too."

Time passed once again, and I learned that Mikko Ylihakuna was going to town. I went to Torkkoo and told him that Mikko Hakuni was going to take a load of planks to Vaasa. "I can ride on top of the load. You won't have to make that long trip again, if you'll talk to them about it. They're so haughty they won't listen to me. I don't care how I get there, so long as I get there in time for my evening departure."

He went to see Mikko, and the latter promised that I could ride on top of the load. Antila heard that I was leaving and sent me five marks for training the colt. Mother had sent me ten dollars. Based on the rate of exchange at the time, it amounted to fifty marks, fifty pennies. All told, I had sixty marks, so I went into a store and bought some wide-topped boots. I didn't want to go to America wearing shoe-pacs. The boots cost me seventeen marks, fifty pennies. At Torkkoola they provided me with a lunch in a burlap bag. It was a good lunch consisting of a few hard loaves of bread, a small carton of butter, dried meat and a small cheese.

Torkkoo took me to Haukuni with the horse. I heard him tell Mikko, "Take care that the boy gets away." Mikko promised, but I saw the disdainful look on his face. He was one of the boys from a haughty family and didn't care about me any more than a dog.

The journey was long. We stopped frequently to rest and feed the horse. When I was hungry I ate from my bag atop the load. We had nothing to talk about. I thought: I know who you are. I won't beg for your friendship if you don't want to say anything.

By that time I knew that we weren't far from Vaasa. He stopped, fed and watered the horse, and drank a cup of water. I was thirsty and asked him for a drink. He laughed derisively and poured the water on the ground. He started the horse, and when I realized that I wouldn't get any water, I climbed back on top of the load.

When we arrived in town, we crossed a river on a bridge. He stopped the horse and said, "Get down. We're in town."

As I was getting down I said, "Aren't you going to help me find an agent or the White Star Line offices?"

"I don't know them any better than you," he yelled. Then he turned the horse and went into a place where I saw a lot of planks and boards.

Ahead lay a wide road that led into the town, so I tossed my burlap bag over my shoulder and started walking. I was in a depressed mood. Thirsty. Hungry. Tired from traveling, too. But I knew that people were not all like him, and I knew I would find people I could talk to.

I arrived at an outdoor market square and saw an old lady serving food, coffee, pastry and such. Planks had been set up as a table and seats.

There were many people there, but I found a vacant place and thought that I'd first buy a cup of coffee.

The old woman came over and said, "Farm boy, are you alone?"

I said, "It now seems that I am truly alone in this big world. My mother and father are in America. When my mother went over a couple of years ago, I was left with a haughty family that didn't think I was as good as their dog. Now I'm on my way to be with my mother, and one of the boys from that family brought me across the bridge and then told me to get off his load of planks. My mouth is so dry and dusty, I can barely speak. Get me a cup of coffee. I'll pay for it."

The old woman brought me the coffee and said, "My dear child, I don't want any money. I'll give you all that I have. Eat freely. You don't need to pay. Tell me what you want, and I'll prepare it immediately."

She brought food and set it before me. I asked her where I could find the White Star Line's office.

"Don't worry about that," she said. "Just eat. I'll take care of it. Do you want more coffee?"

I noticed that she kept an eye on passersby. Suddenly she raised her hand and called. A uniformed police officer came over. She spoke fluent Swedish to him and pointed at me.

The policeman told me in Finnish to relax. "Your ship leaves this evening. Enjoy this old woman's hospitality. I'll come to get you and steer you in the right direction. Stay here and don't worry."

The old woman said, "I also have a son in America, but I haven't heard anything from him for many years. I don't even know if he's still alive. I don't understand how he could go so long without writing."

I stayed at the woman's table until the policeman came for me. The old woman offered me everything good, and I thought again about what differences there are among people; how obvious this is in their faces, before they say a word. Right away, at first glance, I can see if the person warrants my esteem.

When the policeman arrived he said, "Let's go to my office."

I took the old woman by the hand and said, "Thank you for the good will you have shown me. I will remember you for a long time for your help in my overcoming my loneliness. I thank you!" The old woman wished me luck in getting to my mother in good health.

We walked a short distance, and the officer turned to me and said, "Here it is." He waited until after I had shown my ticket and passport and then asked the agent, "Does this boy have all the letters and papers required to travel to America?"

"Yes, he does," replied the agent, "and we'll take him to the ship at eight o'clock this evening." When the policeman had gone, the agent called me into another room and said, "Do you see that door across the street, with the two men standing in the doorway?"

"Yes," I said. "There's some writing on the door, or rather, printing. 'Beer Shop,' it says."

He looked at me and said, "Can you see it from here, or do you know that it's there?"

"I can see that it's there," I replied.

"You have good eyesight," he said. He then gave me two empty bottles and some money and told me to go in through that door. "Put the bottles and money on the counter. Wait until they give you two full ones, and then bring them here to me."

I didn't like it, but I did as he said anyway. When I got back to his office I said, "I've traveled all night getting here and I'm tired. Couldn't you take me to the ship earlier so that I can get some rest?"

"That isn't permitted," he said, "but I'll give you a place to lie down here." He opened the door into another room where there was a sofa bed. "Lie on that, and I'll wake you when it's time to go." After he showed me where the toilet was, I fell asleep immediately. I dreamed that I was still with the old woman at the outdoor market.

The agent came to wake me, and we went to the ship. It was dark, but a few lamps illumined the street, and there were a lot of people about. I asked the agent the name of the ship I was to sail on.

"*Veikko (Brother)*," he said, "but it is so small they should have named it *Little Brother*. It arrives in Hanko tomorrow afternoon, where you'll board a larger ship."

When we arrived at the ship, an official was there to meet us. The agent said, "Here is a cleared passenger to America. His passport is in order to go to a foreign country."

I asked for a bed right away and was given one. I slept well, and when I awoke it was full daylight. The ship rose, fell and pitched. I climbed on deck and saw that we were approaching land. When the ship weighed anchor at that port, whose name I have forgotten, among the new passengers was a small, bearded man who was drunk and carrying a canteen of liquor. Some of the sailors were at his heels begging for a drink, but the man said, "No, I need it all. I want to be crazy drunk the entire voyage, so I won't get seasick. I won't part with a drop."

The sailors were having fun, and they urged him to go below. "The ship will be leaving soon, and it pitches so badly you could fall into the sea," said one.

Another sailor said, "If he falls into the sea it will be no great loss, except that he will take the canteen with him."

Still another said, "Let me carry the canteen."

But the old man was adamant saying, "You go below. I'll take care of my canteen, and I alone will drink it so that I won't get seasick."

The ship tossed then, and an officer ordered the boys to remove the man from the deck. "He's drunk. Take him below and see that he doesn't fall down the stairs."

A couple of men grabbed hold of him, and soon he was below. The boat still swayed, but the drunk swayed even more. He lay down on his back using the liquor canteen for a pillow. One seaman was left to guard him, and when he saw that the man was asleep, he notified the others and they gathered around. One placed his hand gently under the man's head and raised it up. Another took the canteen out, while a third placed a block of wood under his head for a pillow. Another came in with two empty bottles and a funnel, and the liquor was transferred from the canteen to the bottles. Still another came with a bucketful of salty North Sea water and refilled the canteen. Then his head was raised again and the canteen exchanged for the block of wood.

The cook brought a couple of liquor glasses and poured liquor for the sailors, always checking to see how much was left in the bottle after each glass. Finally he said, "There are just a couple of drinks left."

"Take it to the 'old man,'" one said, probably referring to the captain. The last of the second bottle was sent to the helmsman. They also rationed some out to the passengers, but nobody got more than one drink. One man was assigned to watch when the man woke up for a drink. He didn't have long to wait before the drunk struggled up into a sitting position and found his canteen. The stopper was screwed on so tight that he couldn't get it open. The seamen there offered to help, but the old man didn't trust them.

A stout passenger said, "It will surely open if you let me do it. I promise before you all that I don't want a single drop of that."

"So open it," said the drunk, handing the canteen to him.

The man twisted it open and gave it back. The drunk raised the canteen to his lips. The canteen sang, "*klu-klu, klu-klu,*" as he took a long drink. Then he set it down and said, "What the hell . . . ?" He tasted the contents of the canteen once more, and everybody laughed. "What's in this, sailor?" he asked.

"It's what you brought aboard. Isn't it liquor?"

The drunk swore, and the sailor said, "Don't swear. Swearing is not allowed here. Whomever doesn't abide by the rules is thrown over the side. Remember, don't swear."

The old man said, "But this isn't liquor."

A sailor explained to him, "When a person is seasick, everything tastes the same. Let *me* have a taste from your flagon, or whatever you call it."

The old man wouldn't give him any and lay back down with the canteen for a pillow. When we got to Hankoniemi, the old man was escorted ashore, still carrying that canteen of sea water.

I was transferred to another ship, but the others had to go through another special examination. I heard it said that I was a free passenger to a foreign country and that my papers were all in order. My name was recorded, along with where I came from and where I was going. I was told to stay with the ship and shown to my bed.

A girl of around eighteen came on board. Her name was "Viika Jirsti." This is its phonetic spelling. She was from the Turku/Pori district, and she likewise had a ticket on the White Star Line. She and I were the only Finnish passengers on the ship. We stopped in Turku, and a sailor accompanied us into town, acting as our guide. There were sixteen of us in all. It was evening and the street was illumined by lanterns. He showed us the city. We bought some raisin compote and one thing and another from an old woman in the central market square.

"You are all traveling to America and may never come back," said the sailor. "I'm sure you've all heard of the Cathedral of Turku. Well, we're near it now, and we'll be there at midnight." And we were.

The following day our ship called at a Swedish port. Before we arrived in England I was told that I would have to wait an entire week for the ship out of Liverpool.

I crossed England by rail. The coaches on the train were small, with about four people per coach. Each coach had four wheels and was fitted with two benches facing each other. People sat two to a bench. There was no water, no toilet, and the doors were locked. There were a great number of these coaches; at least fifty or sixty. They seemed to be moving fast, but, in retrospect, I believe they traveled thirty miles per hour at most. Otherwise, the light coaches wouldn't have stayed on the tracks. We went through tunnels in the mountains, some of which were quite long. We were behind locked doors about seven or eight hours. It was around midnight when our train stopped, and the doors were opened. I had to urinate, so I took my burlap bag and walked behind several rows of coaches.

When I returned, I didn't see any people. In front of me was a wide street that led to a lighted town. I started walking along the sidewalk. I saw several policemen, but they didn't harass me. I thought it best to show my ticket to a night watchman on duty.

"I need your aid," I told him.

He was steady, mild-appearing and about forty-five years old. I showed him my ticket.

He gave it back to me, took my burlap bag and said, "*Com.*"

We walked a short distance and met a woman who had three children with her, about six, four and two years old. She was also on foot but had a good deal to carry. The policeman stopped her and asked her for her ticket. I believe she was Swedish, and I understood her to be traveling to America on the Cunard Line. The policeman took some of her things on his back and carried the two-year-old on his arm. He gave me her suitcase, and we moved on. There was no traffic. It was past midnight, and the streets were empty. We came to a large boulevard and the policeman set down his load, but he still held the child. He blew on a small whistle. Soon a man came up to talk to him and then left. A little later a man showed up who wanted to see my ticket.

After I had showed it to him, he said, "*Com.*"

"No," I said in Finnish, "I want my burlap bag." It was still on the policeman's back. I went up to him and tugged at it. He pointed to the woman's suitcase I had been carrying. I gave the suitcase to the woman and again began pulling at my burlap bag. "Now, old man, I'll make you understand Finnish," and I pulled the bag off his back.

A man came to my aid and wanted to see my bag. He showed me a tag on the bag indicating the White Star Line. They laughed, and I got my bag back and went with him. It turned out that he was my agent.

He took me through a gate into a building, showed me the toilet and washrooms, took me to the dining room where food, which I refused, was being served, and finally took me to a room where I found a bed. I undressed and got into bed, indicating with a friendly wave that he should leave. He finally did, laughing.

In the morning it was broad daylight when I heard somebody go out. I got dressed and sat down, waiting until he came again and showed me his watch. It was nine thirty. He took me again to the toilet and washrooms, where I cleaned up. All the others had eaten already, but he found some food for me. The food was good, except for the butter, which was so rancid that I didn't want it. I tasted it and moved it aside. He laughed over that. After I had eaten, he took me to a large library. He showed me some books, but I shook my head. Then he brought me a newspaper and showed me letters of the alphabet, which I named in Finnish for him. He left and brought still more books. One was a New Testament. I took it and showed him that I could read.

He went away, leaving me there, but soon an elderly man who spoke Finnish came in and asked, "Finnish boy?"

"Yes," I responded.

"Where are you from? The district of Vaasa?"

"I am."

"Are you from Kurikka parish?"

"I am."

"Are you from the village of Mieta?"

"I am."

He suddenly grabbed hold of me. "Whose boy?"

"Isaac Polvi's," I said.

He shook his head and asked me what my father's father's name was.

"Herman Kallio," I replied.

He shook his head again.

I said, "Among the villagers he is known as Herman Kartano."

"Oh," he said, "Herman Kartano had three boys. Isaac, Herman and Samuel. Now, whose boy are you?"

"Isaac's," I said.

"Ah, I have fought with your father hundreds of times. Every time we met, we were sure to fight." He laughed.

"Were you born there?" I asked him.

"I'm a Dane, but I was there for three years staying with an instructor at Koyka, learning Finnish. I speak, write and read thirteen languages, but I am, by profession, an artist. The White Star Line often needs interpreters, so they gave me three rooms in which to do my painting. How long will you be here?"

"A week," I answered, "but I don't know for certain."

"I'll clear that up right away," he said. He wasn't gone long when he returned and asked if I would like to come to his studio for five days to be a model. "I want to paint your portrait. You'll be waiting for your ship for eight days. I'll show you whatever there is to see in Liverpool. I'll care for you the entire time. We'll come and go as we please and eat when we're hungry. You can have whatever is available in the city if you'll come to my studio for about an hour a day for five days."

I agreed, so we went to his studio. He sat me in a chair. He worked, as he said he would, about an hour a day. When he got through working, we went into the city to a Finnish restaurant where there were Finnish sailors. He also took me to a dog show where there were breeds from all parts of the world. We went to the library but didn't find any books in the Finnish language.

The entire time I was in Liverpool I didn't see a street car or anybody traveling by horse. Everybody walked. There were huge horses pulling heavy loads. These horses were seven or eight feet tall, and their weight was at least four times that of an ordinary horse. They pulled cars as wide as the street along iron rails. The cars were piled as high as they were wide, with the driver perched on top of the load. The cars carried foodstuffs and other goods needed in the city.

The artist explained that the horses never laid down. "If they did, they wouldn't be able to rise again because of their weight."

"How do they rest then?" I asked.

"Come," he said, "I'll show you."

We went into a stable, where I counted nineteen of these horses. He talked with the stable help and they went over to an old horse. These horses understood speech. A man took hold of a stout chain, one end of which was fastened to a large timber, and hooked the chain to another timber. The chain was behind the horse at a height of three-and-a-half feet. The horse was then told to rest. It glanced back, and, on seeing the chain, stepped back into it a bit, sat down into the bend of the chain, drew its forelegs back near its hind legs, closed its eyes and rested.

It was Sunday, and the old man came to get me. "We're going to eat at the Finnish restaurant again," he said. "And there's a church service in Finnish at the Finnish seamen's church. I don't know what time it starts, but they'll know at the restaurant."

We learned that the service would be held at three o-clock.

We walked a lot that day, and he showed me the city. We went to a Finnish coffee shop where we had lunch. Then we went to church. There were many Finnish sailors there, some of whom were in a drunken state, but the minister preached a proper sermon.

Then, on Monday, I got to see my portrait, and he showed me many more of his paintings. There was a portrait of a woman with two words in large letters printed below it. I asked him what the words were in Finnish. He said that he had written them there himself about six years after he did the painting.

"Perhaps you won't understand the meaning of these words yet, but if you remember them, you will understand later. In Finnish they are *elamani haaksirikko* ("the shipwreck of my life")."

"This woman was your dear friend, wasn't she?" I said.

"Absolutely," he said, "but we won't continue this discussion any further."

He showed me paintings of nature and one of his childhood home. He said he was eighteen when he painted it. "I had just returned from

Italy where I learned the fundamentals of painting. Painting is my calling. My father was one of the wealthiest men in my native land, but he had his faults. He loved wealth and his money more than people. I don't look at life from that standpoint. I see other people as my equals. He left me an inheritance, but I haven't needed to use it. I'll let it be until such time that I can't earn my own living. I don't want to live in luxury. I find joy in life when I can give a spare coin to a poorer person, and here there are a great many of them. When I feel lonely, I go among the downtrodden people and there find peace of mind."

Thus he spoke to me for a long time. He felt badly that people in every land hold the same belief: That when you have riches, you have honor.

When the day of my departure dawned, he came to get me. We went again to the Finnish restaurant where I had been so many times before. They said to me, "We know that this is your last meal here; we would like to hear from you if there is any food that you especially want. We'll try to prepare it for you."

"I don't believe you could do it," I said. "I want food that my mother used to prepare. I am lonesome for my mother and her cooking."

"What food? Name it."

"Potatoes. Either hot or cold, but boiled with the skins on. Herring. A piece of hard bread and a glass of buttermilk."

There were some sailors eating there, and they laughed, saying, "My son, go wherever you will, and the herring is sure to follow a Finn. You can't get away from it. Wherever there are a few Finns, you'll find herring."

I was brought potatoes boiled with the skins on, although they had since been removed. I was given herring and dry rye bread, but the buttermilk, I was told, was sour. "You can have some of that, too, if you wish."

"Buttermilk is not buttermilk unless it is somewhat sour," I said. So I got what I wanted. The sailors were enjoying all of this, and they laughed.

When we went out onto the street, two men who were drunk passed us. The artist said to me, "Remember what I'm going to say to you now. Don't get yourself in that condition. I'm not asking that you never touch the stuff. A person is naturally curious about its effect. But you must remember that you have already tasted it. It is a vice among people that leads to all sorts of diseases. It will take away all of your good fortune and bring you adversities and misfortunes."

He took me to a small shop that I believe was a drugstore and said,

"We'll go in and drink to your health. I'm happy to have been able to paint your portrait. It reminds me of your father's facial features, and the only memento that I have of Finland is your painting." He brought a bottle to the table. He poured lemonade into the glasses and bought a small box containing three cigars wrapped in gold-colored foil. He said, "Take these to your father and tell him 'Hardshell' sent them to him. He used to call me that name because I didn't know Finnish."

We arrived at the ship, and he came on board with me. He gave me my burlap bag, and took me to the ticket officials and announced my arrival. As we talked, a large group of many hundreds of immigrants was brought on board.

"There are all the people with whom you are traveling," he said. "You wouldn't have believed there were so many. Do you know any of them?"

"There's one Finnish girl," I said. "I've talked with her many times." Just then I spotted her, but she disappeared out of sight.

My companion and I waited for the agent. When he appeared, we said goodbye. I was most thankful to him. "You've been a good companion for me the entire time I was here."

"Now begins a new time in a world totally new to you. Remember, my good boy, avoid drunkenness wherever it is practiced. Don't take part in it, and you will succeed and prosper. Remember that!"

The ship tooted its departing signal. Soon we were out to sea and out of sight of land. We arrived in Ireland and dropped anchor. People rowed out to the ship in small boats. Several additional travelers climbed aboard on rope ladders, while their baggage was hoisted aboard with lines. They had all sorts of canes and other trinkets for sale. Mostly women were in the twenty or so rowboats.

It wasn't long before we weighed anchor and were soon far out to sea. The weather was warm. There were no seas to speak of, so the people were out on the deck. I met the Finnish girl again and we struck up a conversation. However, we noticed that the sailors were in a hurry to tie down the anchors and put everything away that was loose on deck.

After we, too, were herded below, I asked the girl, "What's coming now?"

A sailor yelled in broken Finnish, "A storm is coming, a storm is coming! Get moving!"

"I don't see anything," I said.

"It's coming," he said.

The sailors were closing the portholes below decks, but before they could secure all of them, heavy seas hit the ship broadside. Water poured in through the open portholes and through the topside grate. The ship creaked and groaned. The lights went out, and the water that had come into our quarters sloshed about from bulkhead to bulkhead. There was also some loose material tumbling about—trunks and a few tables. And it was very dark. Soon a couple of seamen came in and lashed everything down that was loose. When they went away we were left in the dark once more.

From my bunk I could hear the passengers vomiting, and the water on the lower deck sloshed to the rocking of the boat. This lasted for three days. I had been in my bunk for an entire day when a seaman brought food to us. He saw that I wasn't sick, so he took me with him to the seamen's quarters. Almost all of them knew a few words of Finnish, and one even spoke it well, though with a heavy accent. He twice brought me chocolate in a cup, saying, "Drink it." It was delicious! I stayed with the seamen and they took me to the head.

When the storm had passed, I went to check my own quarters. There were some seamen cleaning up, and when they noticed me, they swore in Finnish and pointed to the deck. "Look. That's shit."

Well, it was no wonder. The storm lasted for three days, and everyone was seasick. The deck heaved and pitched so that only the sailors could walk on it. The head was topside, and large seas washed over the ship. I was surprised that the old ship withstood the pounding, it creaked and groaned so. She was called the *Urania*.

I met the Finnish girl again. She had been very ill. A seaman brought a seat for her and told me to sit as well. He pointed to the girl and said, "Sick." She was still weak, but her strength was fast returning on deck. We sat on deck every day and I talked with her. She was in another section of the ship, though, and I didn't go there at all.

It was evening when our ship arrived in New York. It didn't dock but stayed out. I saw the girl in the evening but no more after that. I spent the entire night on deck watching the thousands of lights of the city. I thought: This is the land I've traveled to. Here I'll find my father, my mother and my new sister. What will my young life change into in this new world? I sat and meditated the entire night long and didn't even try to go to bed.

In the morning the ship began to move slowly, and I saw that it was headed for a small island. Finally it stopped at a pier for final inspection. When I had passed these inspections, they attached a tag to my lapel and said to leave it there and not try to hide it. "So long as it is visible, you will be on the right track," a man said. He then read it to me in Finnish. "This man is Isaac Polvi and is traveling to his father Isaac Polvi, Calumet,

Michigan."

After a while I was brought three rings of smoked sausage, bread, summer sausage, and I don't know what all. I put them into my burlap bag. Now someone came and took me to a barber, and, after my hair was cut, brought me back again. Another man came up to me and asked me if I knew how to read. He spread the New Testament before me and said, "Read from this." I did so, and he said, "That's good. You can read. I'll bring more." He brought many pamphlets that were mostly educational stories of men who had not succeeded when they fell into drunkenness.

Next, two official-looking men came and took me into an adjacent room. One was dressed in civilian clothes. He was a Finnish interpreter. He asked me my name, and I showed him the tag on my breast. He asked if there were other Finns on board the ship when I arrived.

"Yes," I answered, "Viika Jirsti."

"Was this a man or a woman?"

"She was a pretty eighteen-year-old girl. I first met her at Hanko-niemi. She came from the district of Turku and Pori. Has she disappeared?"

"Yes," he said.

"Listen to this," I said. "We had to wait for the ship in Liverpool for eight days. This girl told me that she found out the name of the ship she'd be sailing on. She wrote to her brother in New York. She told me that her letter would go by mailboat and be there before we arrive. She said that he'd find out when our ship would be arriving in New York, and that he would come to meet her."

"The ship arrived in the evening," he said. "Do you think that the girl was taken off the ship at night?"

"I don't think so," I replied, "as I was on the ship's deck all night. Nothing came to the ship, and nobody was taken off. If they were, I would have seen it. But listen. I saw the girl in the evening. She left me sitting on deck and went to bed. I sat there all night waiting for morning. When we got to the pier, the gangplank was lowered and some thirty or forty people went ashore ahead of me. Just as I was going indoors, I saw a boat coming to shore. I heard Finnish being spoken. It was a man's voice, but I couldn't hear any more once I was inside. The others almost pushed me in."

"So the girl has a brother in New York," he said, "and she is now on her way to meet him?"

"That's correct," I said.

"You don't know her address?"

I said no at first, but then I told them that the girl had told me either her or her brother's address. "Her brother said that the address in Finnish meant 'orphan home,' but it may have been 'children's home.' Translate that into English and you have the place."

They both thanked me, and the translator said, "We learned much more from you than we had dared hope."

Now I was taken to a flat-bottomed scow. There were some forty or fifty seated in it. The engine began to chug and the scow moved. I took my train ticket and studied it. At the same time I heard someone say, "Put your ticket back in your pocket, boy, somebody may steal it from you. You can't take your ticket out of your pocket in a place like this where anybody could snatch it out of your hand. Your journey would end here, and somebody else would travel with your ticket."

I looked at him. He was as black as tar and his skin shone. He was a well-dressed man, large and muscular. I guessed him to be a Negro even though he spoke fluent Finnish. His lips were like a smith's bellows. He was the first Negro I'd ever seen. I put the ticket back in my pocket. I kept an eye on him and realized that he was our agent and group leader. He examined my ticket finally and gave me a small slip. He looked at the tag on my jacket and handed me another slip. This one was white. He gave some a blue slip and others a white and red one.

When we got to shore, the people were separated into groups. There were eighteen white slips like mine. We were taken to a streetcar. The streets were so narrow that when the streetcar was there, nothing could pass without going onto the sidewalk. The buildings were old, two-story structures. We had gone only two blocks when we came to a cross-track where another streetcar was about to cross our street. The streets were so narrow that the drivers didn't see each other in time, nor could they stop. The collision rattled the windows and knocked both cars off the tracks. Each driver blamed the other. They were out on the street arguing, and if the police hadn't come, I'm sure they would have fought. The police arranged to get the cars back on the rails. Soon many men were there. The cars couldn't have been very heavy, because they were pushed onto the tracks by manpower.

And away we went. We changed streetcars at a place where the streets were four times wider. The buildings here appeared to be made of brick and stone. They were many-storied and much more imposing. And the streetcars moved faster. The trip was long, and I thought that they couldn't find a railroad station, but finally we stopped in front of a large, tall hotel-like building with a wide stairway in front. We were directed to at least the fourth floor, where I hoped we'd be put to bed because I was so tired after my all-night vigil aboard the ship. But what a marvel! They opened a door, and there was a train. At that height!

I went into a coach and found a good place to rest. I heard the train leave and fell asleep immediately. I don't know how long I slept before they awakened me and chased me out. Now at least the train was down on the ground and not up in the air. I saw that many trains were ready to leave. I tried to get on one, but they shoved me off. I tried a second, and a third. But they wouldn't let me in. I stopped to look around and spotted an express car. I made a new attempt to board and this time succeeded. There were a lot of people, but I found a good place to rest between a seat and the end wall. I placed my burlap bag under my head and slept immediately.

When I awoke at daylight, it was cold. The train felt like it was moving at great speed. I noticed I had been covered with a thick quilt. A soft pillow was under my head. I looked for my burlap bag, and it was in the corner. I thought: This is just like my mother's doing. I got up and folded the quilt, tossing it over the back of a seat and looking out the window. The sun shone, and I saw that we were headed west. Large herds of cattle were being driven east by men on horseback.

The conductor came and wanted to see my ticket. I felt in the inside pocket of my coat, but it was empty. I remembered the Negro's warning that my ticket would be stolen if I didn't keep it in my pocket. I remembered putting it there, but it was gone!

The conductor examined the slip on my lapel and went away, soon to return with a Finnish man who asked me if I had lost my ticket. "It seems so," I said unhappily.

"What pocket do you keep it in?" he asked. I showed it to him. He looked at it. "Take your coat off," he said. "See this unraveled seam? I believe that the ticket will be found somewhere in the lining." And indeed it was! All was well once again.

I kept an eye out to see who came to get the quilt and pillow, but when evening came, we had a different conductor. He turned two seats down, making them into a bed and indicating that I should lie there. I guessed then that it was the trainmen who had covered me.

The trains didn't run on Sunday, and so we stopped. To this day I don't know the name of the city, or where we were. It was November 3, 1894, at around eleven in the evening when the train stopped at the Nestoria depot, in the Upper Peninsula of Michigan. Merchandise and passengers were taken off. An unpainted pine box was also taken off and lifted onto the floor. The others went to a hotel for the night, and I was left alone in the waiting room. I couldn't lie down on the seats because of their armrests. It was a cold night. The door was flimsy and the threshold so worn that rats ran in and out under the door. The floor wasn't fit to sleep on, it was so cold. So I lay down on top of that box. Soon they came in and chased me off. After a while I went to lie there again, and they came and chased me away. I wondered why they wouldn't let me lie there. I didn't see what harm I could possibly do to that box if I lay on it. I got on it a third time, and this time the depot agent saw me. He went out to where people were emptying a baggage car and came back in with four men, plus a hammer and some other tools. He indicated that I should sit on a chair, and then they pulled the top off the box. Inside was a coffin, which they also opened. I nodded my head. Satisfied, they closed the coffin and nailed down the box cover. I took my coat, put it on the box and said, "It won't hurt me." They laughed and went back to work, leaving me and the body in peace.

I slept, and it was broad daylight before I awoke. Someone had come in from the hotel and was speaking in a loud voice. The depot agent was there, and I had the feeling that they were talking about me. I decided to get up, as I had had a sound sleep.

At that time, only a narrow-gauge railroad extended as far as Calumet from Nestoria, so the freight goods had to be transferred onto other cars. It was many years later when the gauge was expanded so that ordinary trains could go up the Copper Peninsula in the Upper Peninsula without changing cars.

A little after noon the "Calumet" came up the tracks. The locomotive was turned around to haul the same cars back to Calumet. When we were near the Houghton bridge, I saw a man through the window who was running down the bank waving a stop sign. The train stopped, and the man got into the coach I was on. When he saw me he asked, "Whose boy are you?" I told him. He saw the tag on my lapel, looked at it, and then, with scissors he retrieved from his pocket, cut it off. He said to me, "You won't get lost any more. Put this tag away for safe keeping." I asked him his name, and he said, "My name is Koskela, and I'm a clerk at the Raini Store in Calumet." When he got off the train at the old depot in Laurium he said, "When the train stops, it'll be the end of the line. Your long journey will end there. Perhaps you'll meet your father and mother at the station."

Fifteen minutes later, the train stopped, and everybody but me got off. I just sat there looking around when I heard a tapping on the window right next to me. I turned and saw that it was my mother, whom I had longed for all this time.

7

Mining Town

I DIDN'T TARRY long on the train and was quickly outside with my burlap bag. I put my arms around my mother's neck and wept with joy. Here was my all in everything. My mind was on all the hardship I had endured since the last time I saw her, but I never told her about it. I let her go on thinking that I had been in the village of Mieta the entire time. As for my father, eight or nine years had passed since he had left Finland, and I didn't know him.

It was election day, November 4, 1894. We were in the middle of a depression, and many were idle. Many Finns begged for their bread and for a place to spend the night. One Finn had picked up a rock and thrown it through a church window while the police were watching. Of course, they took the man to jail. He spent the night there and in the morning was taken before a judge. The judge wanted to know why he had done it. The man very candidly said, "There is no work and no food, so I want to go to jail where I can spend the night and have a meal."

The judge thought the matter over and said, "There are many of these unemployed, and if this one is taken to jail, he'll have to be fed. If we do that, there may be scores of them tomorrow, and, in a few days, there won't be an unbroken window in the entire town. Where would we put them all? We don't have enough food to feed the unemployed."

So the judge ordered a policeman to take the man out and give him a kick in the backside. This was a big man, so the policeman said that he would take the man out, but the judge himself could administer the kick. "Take him out!" the judge yelled. And the man was taken out, but they didn't kick him.

My mother and father fed a large group of men. My father's wage was only forty-five dollars a week, and since there were five of us children, mother fed the men with the understanding that when they got work, they would pay ten dollars a month board. Many paid, but there were many who didn't. Yet food was not expensive. For instance, a dollar would buy a seventeen pound bag of coffee.

After my arrival, the other boys snowballed me. I was treated badly and called "greenhorn." An Italian boy my age lived nearby. They snowballed him and called him "greenhorn," too. So I sought him out and said to him, "You greenhorn, me greenhorn." This made him laugh. He spoke Italian, and I spoke Finnish, but it wasn't long before we understood one another. His name was Mike Rossu. I visited his home, and he came to mine. Meanwhile, the other boys laughed at us and threw snowballs.

One day Mike came over. He was speaking Italian and laughing. I could see that he had something first rate in mind. He took a slingshot from his pocket and showed me how it was used. He had one for me, too, along with some stones. We collected more stones from underneath buildings where there was no snow. We practiced shooting stones at a target for a while, and then we put some in our pockets and went off to find the other boys. When they started snowballing us, we let them have it with our slingshots. And did those stones hurt!

Salmo Rautio, an old man, came to their rescue and told them that it would go badly for them if they persisted in harassing Mike and me. "They're defending themselves. All the blame is yours. If one of you gets hit in the head, it will kill you. I've seen everything and will testify to the boys' innocence. The fault is all on your heads." Needless to say, they didn't snowball us anymore.

Many men were killed in accidents in the mines every day. There were hundreds of men around the mine offices looking for work. Mike Rossu and I decided that there might be something for two boys to do, so we went to the Tamarack mine around noon one day. There wasn't any activity at the No. 2 shaft house, so we went in. The shaft was simply a vertical hole in the ground. Vapor enveloped the shaft opening, but an occasional breeze would clear it momentarily. In the mist we could see the steel cable moving, indicating that someone was ascending the shaft. We waited. A man emerged from the vapor. Then he went back in and returned with a platform on which lay the headless body of a miner. Other men appeared with another body. One carried the first man's head by the hair. Mike and I followed them. An undertaker came and sewed the man's head back onto his torso. Then the two bodies were placed in long baskets and taken away. Mike and I ran home and told everyone how two bodies were brought up from the Tamarack mine.

One of the men who was looking for work said, "This means that there is work for two men." These poor fellows were in competition for the jobs that had been held by the dead men.

A miner from North Tamarack was staying with us, and I asked him to help Mike and me find work—which he did. The mine was about three miles from our house, and every morning, no matter what the weather was like, I was on my way at four o'clock. My pay was thirty-two dollars a month. It was a big help to my mother and father. They occasionally gave me a quarter or half-dollar, which I saved. I had about eight dollars to my name at this time. Men who worked on the Mineral Range Railroad often stayed with us. They were paid only a dollar for a ten-hour day.

The mine where I worked was a five-thousand-foot vertical shaft. It was hot underground, and the men wore shoes but no socks. Men wore trousers but were bare from the waist up, except for a hardhat worn as protection against small rocks. It took the trammers about a half-hour to fill a tram car; when they emerged from the shaft, their shoes were full of sweat. In that place, everything possible was taken out of a man.

There was a so-called "small-boss" whose job it was to yell and swear at the workers. "If you can't do any better than that and load more cars per day, I don't need you at all!"

Men were free, and timbers were expensive. Since the mining company had to pay for timbers, the shoring-up of the mine's shafts and drifts was inadequate. Rock falls were frequent. Many workers offered token resistance to company policy, but they nearly always got their time slips; or they were forced to work in the most dangerous places in the mine— so that they could be sent to the surface as corpses. There were always men who were willing to take the places of the dead.

Once a small-boss said, "You have to load several cars now." The place he indicated was unstable. Falling rocks made the men reluctant to enter the area. "If you won't do what I tell you, what are you doing here?" said the boss.

I had to go there with a truck and wait while the trammers filled the cars. Suddenly a slab of rock broke loose from a tunnel roof and fell on edge, cutting a man through at the shoulder. I ran over to him and removed the rock. His heart was exposed and still beating, but not for long. I took hold of him under his arms, and his Finnish partner came to help. We dragged him clear first thing, because we knew more rocks would fall. We put him on two boards in the truck and pushed him to the shaft. The boss was there and accompanied us to the surface in the cage. We took the man out of the cage, and the boss immediately ordered us to go back down into the mine.

I showed him my clothes. I was covered with blood. "We won't go back," I said, "until after we've washed our clothes and they have dried."

The boss followed us to the changing room. "I'm shorthanded," he said, "and I have to get that spot cleaned out."

"Go in there yourself," we told him, "and take the dead man for a partner. We'll come back tomorrow evening."

"You don't need to come at all," he said.

I said, "We'll be back tomorrow evening to work. You forced the men to go into that section. You're a murderer, and I can prove it. I know what I'm talking about."

The next evening the Finn—the dead man's partner—said, "I don't know whether it pays to change clothes. There won't be any work for us."

"I'm changing," I said, "because I believe I got the boss to think things over. He knows deep down that he's responsible for that murder. There's no enforceable law if nobody says anything. If he doesn't have work for us, I'll report this so-called accident to all right-thinking people. It was a deliberate murder."

I worked there for three years and was witness to many tragic events. I felt that my young life suffered because of mine work.

Eventually I was put to work on a machine with an old Swede miner. My wage was forty dollars a month. My partner was a very stubborn man. If I suggested anything, he wouldn't listen to me. There were two occasions on which I would surely have been killed had I listened to him. He admitted as much, but he asked me not to mention it. It would cost him his job, and he had eight children.

I promised to keep quiet, but I wouldn't work with him anymore. I said, "I'll have my sister pick up my check so that I won't see anybody. I don't want to rat on you. For all I care, you can keep your job." He tried to talk me into staying, saying that there were holes to be blasted. It was around four in the morning. "I won't work in this mine another minute,"

I said. "I'm glad to get out of here alive. Twice I've been within a hair of losing my life, and you know that you're responsible. I'm going up on a car."

"But what should I tell the captain?" he asked.

"Tell him whatever you want," I replied. "I won't be back to contradict your lies."

I went to the shaft as the trammers brought a car of rock. I jumped on top of it and said, "Ring four bells."

"I'm not allowed to ring four bells unless someone is sick or injured," said a trammer.

"Ring four bells," I said. "I'm having a heart attack, and I want to die on the surface, not down here. Ring four bells!" He rang them, and, when I got to the surface, I was asked if I was sick. "My heart hurt," I said, "so I couldn't wait any longer."

"Do you want help?"

"No, I don't believe I'll need any now." I went to the dry-house to wash up and change my clothes. I took everything that belonged to me and went home.

I hardly spoke to anybody and lay around for three days. My father was in a bad mood and didn't like what he saw. I told Mother why I had left my job. "I know how to talk and I think I can get work when I want it. I haven't been out of work for a day until now. I'm going to rest for a few days. I don't believe I'm going back into the mine. But don't be concerned, I'll get work."

My mother then explained why my father was in such a bad mood. He had just purchased a house and had hoped to get help from me in order to pay for it.

"Do you and Father think that the job I quit is the only one that can earn me a living? I now know the language of the land. I'm not a greenhorn anymore. I'll show you very soon, perhaps as early as tomorrow, what I can do." And I went out.

It was afternoon when I saw hundreds of men going to the Hecla barn, which was part of the complex at the Calumet & Hecla mine. I heard that they were taking on men, but I was well-dressed in my best clothes. There was an old man there who said he wasn't taking on any more workers. I stepped forward and said, "Take on one more. Give me some stinking job no one else wants, and I'll do it. I promise that I'll never complain about it. And I'll do it well."

His name was Tomson, and he laughed heartily. "You're so young. Are you eighteen yet?"

"Not yet," I said, "but I'm not afraid of work. I've been in the mine for three years and haven't missed a day, but I had a feeling that the Tamarack mine would kill me. My father isn't happy that I quit my job. A couple of hours ago my mother explained that my father had purchased a house that he expects me to help pay for. I promised Mother that I would find work immediately. Can you give me some dirty job nobody else wants?"

The old man was amused at my proposition and said, "Come to work tomorrow morning."

When I got home Father was already there. I told my mother that she could fix a lunch for me in the morning. My father was angry and said, "Why do you joke? There are thousands of men idle and you, a mere lad, come to deceive us."

"So we won't deceive anymore," I said and went upstairs to wait for the men to go to eat. I didn't say anything when three men who didn't have work went to eat.

When Mother saw that I didn't go to the table, she called, "You come, too, Isaac."

I did as she asked, and after I had eaten I went, as was my custom, to see my old pal Mike Rossu. We both spoke English now and were the best of friends. He was working in the Hecla mine.

The next morning I dressed myself in my work clothes. After I had eaten breakfast, I noticed that my lunch had not been packed. I said, "Don't worry, I think that I'll get by without it."

I went on foot to the Hecla barns. They set me to digging post-holes. At around nine o'clock old man Tomson said, "Come to my office." He prepared some papers for me to have a physical exam. When I was through with it, I went back to his office. He looked at his watch and asked me if I had my lunch with me.

"No," I said.

"You can go to lunch now," he said. "It is ten to twelve. Be back at one."

I went home and Mother asked me where I'd been.

"At work," I answered.

"Where were you working?"

"Hecla surface work," I answered. "Give me something to eat. I'm going back. I have work for the entire summer, and the pay is forty-three dollars a month. I would have told you more about it last night, but Father was angry with me." I then told her how I had asked for work.

She laughed and said, "You father still doesn't believe that you went to work. I told him that you wouldn't have asked for a lunch, but he maintained that you are lying. I told him that I've never caught you telling a lie."

The following morning Mother had not prepared a lunch for me, and I asked her why. "Oh," she said, "I thought that you were coming home to eat lunch."

I said, "I'll gladly come home if I'm working nearby, but when I leave in the morning, I can't say where I'll be at noon. I could find myself in Lake Linden, Dollar Bay or Hubbell, so let me have twenty-five cents for a little food."

She gave it to me, and things went on in this way—although I didn't want to ask her for money every morning. Once I didn't have a lunch or any money to go to a restaurant. I was unloading a boat load of bricks in Lake Linden with some Finnish partners. I asked them for twenty-five cents so that I could buy a meal, but they said they didn't have it. I went to town thinking that I would try begging, just as I had done in the old country.

By and by I came to a house on the veranda of which sat a young, beautiful French girl. I approached her and asked, "Excuse me, may I talk to you?"

"What can I do for you?" she replied, getting up. "What do you want?"

I explained to her that I lived in Calumet and did surface work at Hecla. "I was sent here to unload a ship. I don't have a lunch or money to buy one. If you would give me a meal, I'll come back tomorrow and pay you for it."

"Sit here," she said, and went in, returning in a few moments. "Wait a bit; Mother will prepare a meal." She was friendly and pleasant. Another girl came out and asked me in to eat. The girls were both nice. When their mother told them to see that their guest had what he needed, they immediately asked me whether I would like a glass of beer.

"No," I said, "give me a cup of tea or coffee."

Their mother wanted to know how old I was.

"Not yet eighteen," I told her.

"Are you a Finn?"

"I was born in Finland," I replied, "and I came here three years ago. At first I worked in the mine, but I felt that it was dangerous to my health. So I quit mine work and found this job right away."

When I asked the girls for the time, they told me I still had fifteen minutes to get to the boat. I got up, thanked them and said, "I'll be back tomorrow to pay for the food."

"We'll have lunch ready when you come," said the girls.

But I didn't have that in mind. "I'll bring a lunch instead. I don't want to put you to any trouble."

"We want you to do it," they insisted. "We want you to come here for lunch."

So I agreed, and when I got back to the ship my partners asked me if I got any food. "I'm a good beggar," I said. "They even promised me a meal again tomorrow."

"But there aren't any Finns around here," they said with surprise.

"Do you think that only Finns are human," I said, "and people of other nationalities aren't the equals of Finns? I've found good and bad in all nationalities. I haven't found a person yet who is so bad that there isn't some good in him, or, for that matter, a person who is so good that there isn't some bad in him. There are good and bad in all of us, but we often don't see our bad side the way our fellow men see it."

They said I talked like a preacher and wanted to know my name. "Iikka," I said. "Call me Iikka."

The moment the whistle blew, the bricks began flying two-at-a-time from man to man. It wasn't awfully hard work; it was as steady as the movement of a clock. But after five hours of that, we gladly took a break. I always used to say that it was good that we had such a job. "This work is just like the movement of my late grandfather's clock. Tick-tock, tick-tock, tick-tock. Just as steady as a clock. For that five hours that the bricks are flying, I can hear my grandfather's clock ticking." I had all the Finns laughing by now. Some Frenchmen who were there wanted to know what was so funny. I explained it to them, and they were quite amused.

All the Finns knew me as Iikka. The majority of the surface workers were Finns. Tomson was the highest official and next to him was Welton. He was a dark-skinned man who spoke fluent French and English. Welton was thought of as a nasty person by the workers. The Frenchmen said that he was half French and half Indian. There were a couple of Finn small-bosses, whom I believed were much worse than Welton.

It was the last day of May, and we were at work near the barns where Tomson's office was. Tomson came directly to me and said, "Do you still stand by your word?"

"I stand behind what I promise," I answered, "and fulfill it if possible."

"Well, good," he said with a laugh. "Come to the office. I want to discuss it further." We started walking, and when we got to the office, he had me sit down. "I've been waiting for just this day," he said. "I didn't need you when I put you to work, but I couldn't let you get out of my reach. I thought about what you said about taking a stinking job that nobody else wants to do. That tickled me, and I was impressed that you told me you wanted to help your father pay for a house, and that you promised your mother that you'd find work right away. You promised that if I would give you some dirty job that other people don't want to do, you'd do it. Do you remember?"

"I remember," I said.

"Then I have just the job for you," he said laughing, "and it was just for this job that I originally hired you. Every time I met you, I couldn't help but laugh. I've always had trouble getting men for this job. My hope was to get a young man, but nobody wanted it. The pay has been raised to seventy-three dollars a month. There will always be days when it rains, but the pay is not by the day or hour but by the month. If something comes up that you can't come to work—say you're sick or have some valid reason; you must notify me so that I can send a man in your place. Your pay will still be seventy-three dollars a month, even though you've missed work—because you promised to help pay for the house. Now you have a good opportunity to do that, and I believe that you won't spend the money foolishly. The work isn't heavy, if you can just stand the smell and get the job done without getting sick."

"I can't guess what the job might be," I told him.

Old man Tomson laughed. He was highly amused. "I've had two old Italians on that job, but one of them died last fall. You're going to take his place. You know that Calumet & Hecla have many employees. They live in company houses or have houses on company property— each with its individual outhouse. Once a year the company empties the outhouse pits. This is the dirty, stinking job that I'm offering you, and if you keep your promise and take the job, I'll give you seventy-three dollars a month. If the dirty work and the smell don't bother you, you have a job."

I laughed and said, "I'll take it." I thought for a minute and then said, "Now if only I can get a fur hat from someplace, I'll have a little fun. I'm new and not known hereabouts, as I haven't been around the young people much. Since I have black hair and my face is suntanned, if I put on a fur cap, the Finnish girls will think I'm Italian. They'll talk among themselves about me, and I'll be able to hear what they have to say. I'm most happy for the wage, for which I thank you. How long will the job last?"

"Four months," he said, "but if it rains, five. I'll guarantee you your wages for five months."

I asked him if I should report for work as usual in the morning, and he said yes. This was fine with me, and so I went back to work.

The other Finns wondered what on earth I had to do with the old man. "You were there at least an hour."

"It was nothing bad," I said. "You're just too curious, though, so I won't tell you now. You'll all see where they put me in the morning. It can remain a secret until then."

We had eight or ten boarders at that time and had already moved into the house my father bought. Two of the boarders were out of work. When I got home I was amused by everything that had happened, and thinking about it I laughed.

I went to eat and one of the men asked me what I was laughing about. "Do you see something wrong somewhere?"

"No," I said, "I don't see anything bad anywhere. I'm laughing at my own good fortune. I'm the luckiest brat who has ever lived. I was given a new job and my wage was raised thirty dollars, and from here on in, I'll be on a monthly salary, not a daily wage. If it rains sometimes for a week or two, my salary will still be seventy-three dollars. I'll be at work ten hours a day but will actually only work two."

My father heard this and was beside himself. "I told you not to lie!"

"I'm not lying," I said. "The first five months my salary is seventy-three dollars, come rain or shine. I'll need a change of clothes at work, because I must change when I come in. I know I can get the clothes, but I don't know where to get a cap. It should be crazy-looking."

My father wasn't having any of it. "Stop your lying," he thundered.

I laughed and reassured him that I spoke the truth. I said, "Father, I promise you that for those five months I'll bring you seventy-three dollars each month. I won't take out a penny. If I need money, I'll come ask you for it."

Father was angry and said, "If you pay your board, I'll be satisfied."

"I can't do that and be honest, too," I continued. "I promised I'd bring every penny to my parents, and that if I needed money I'd ask them for it."

"I don't believe you," said my father.

I asked the men if they believed me, and they said they didn't know. I asked Mother if she at least believed.

"You've never lied to me, and I believe you—even if I can't understand how such a thing is possible," she said.

I got up from the table and went and put my arms around her neck. "Mother, you know that I speak the truth, and from here on I will not tell you a lie. I remember you taught me not to lie when I was a small boy, and that if I can't tell the truth I'm not to say anything. At times I've remained silent, unless I was just having fun. I'm happy that you believe me, Mother, and I'll tell you this evening how it is possible for me to get this job and salary. It's more than any of the men here with us earns. I know that everyone will laugh, you and Father included, when they learn this small secret. I'm one lucky and happy brat, as you'll soon see. I have often noted that when you have the will and desire to reach your goal, it will happen. No power on earth can stop it. A strong will and desire will sooner or later win out. I have *sisu*, intestinal fortitude, so that if at first I don't succeed, I'll try again. I've succeeded for now and I don't think there's a person on earth who would begrudge me my success. Even now I'm telling the truth. There's a little riddle for you all. Mother, don't fix a lunch for me tomorrow. I believe I'll be able to come home to eat. But give me a quarter in case I can't come home."

I went out and sat on the steps. Nobody spoke to me until a man came by, and I asked him if he knew where I might get a fur cap. He thought awhile and said, "I believe Salmo Korkeakaski has one like that." I asked him to tell Salmo that I'd buy it from him.

A little later, Salmo came over with a fur cap and asked, "What in the world are you going to do with a fur cap? It's summer."

"It goes with my official uniform," I said. "You'll find out later how important it is to me. What do you want for it?" I asked. He answered that he'd donate it to me. I went back into the house and asked Mother, "Where are my mining clothes?"

"I haven't washed them. The flannel underwear are here, too, but we've been busy moving and I've had so much work, I haven't had time to wash clothes."

"It doesn't matter if they aren't washed," I said. "I need to wear them tomorrow." Father came to the door, and I said, "What I said awhile ago is all true, but I left two words unsaid. If I had said those two words, you and the other men would have believed that I speak the truth. If you don't say those two words to the others, I'll tell you what they are. These two words precisely describe my official duty. It's a duty nobody wants, and it is the reason for such a salary. 'Emptying outhouses.' These are the two words that I left unsaid."

Mother and Father paused momentarily. Then they both laughed.

I said, "Let the men remain in the dark until they smell what work I'm doing. I don't feel the least bit bad. I'm just happy to have such a good paying job. I promised Tomson that I'd give all the money to Father."

My mother asked why I wanted the flannel underwear. "They're hot."

I explained the two-gallon bucket with its six- or seven-foot dipper-like handle. "I dip from the outhouse pit into a watertight wooden box on a wagon. Sometimes I'll get splashed. The flannel underwear will keep it from getting on my skin. In the evening when I get home, I'll go into the barn, wash up and exchange my smelly clothes for clean ones."

"But why the fur cap in the summer?"

"There are many Finnish girls, and they'll believe I'm Italian," I said, "and they'll talk among themselves in Finnish; I'll be able to hear their conversation." Mother and Father laughed, and I added, "I have an old Italian partner. When the girls are around, I'll speak Italian to Tom. I only know a little, but I know enough to make them believe that I'm an Italian and don't understand Finnish."

In the morning I went directly to the stables where the wagons were parked. There were three wagons with a box on each one, and three pairs of horses. One wagon was always with us on the job site being filled. When the driver returned with one team of horses, he took the full wagon and box, trading it for the empty one he had brought. It took one of us about a half-hour to dip a box full, while the other man sat and waited. When it was full, we had a third man who directed us. His name was Sam Millington. He was an Englishman and a pleasant old man. He showed the driver where to go. Sometimes we had to open a fence to get the box near enough to the outhouse. Sam had plenty to do. When we emptied an outhouse, Sam applied lime to kill the stench. He had to replace the fence, too, and put everything back in order. I climbed up on top of the box, and we left the stables a little before seven. All the workers had assembled, and when they saw me atop the box, they let out such a cheer that those who hadn't noticed me yet, now did so. I waved my fur cap at them.

Everybody was laughing, including old man Tomson, who called out, "So you did find a fur cap!"

Millington, seated next to me, turned to me, saying, "The men think a lot of you, so don't misunderstand them. If they didn't like you, they wouldn't have cheered." He laughed then and said, "They are honoring you for taking a job nobody else wanted. Work doesn't spoil the man, if, that is, you don't ruin yourself on this job. I hope it doesn't happen. I'll say again, there's a danger here. You're still a young man, and you could ruin your life."

"I don't understand," I said.

"You'll understand soon enough," he said. "It won't take many weeks before you catch on to my meaning."

As we began our work I asked my partner to show me what to do. "I haven't done work like this before."

Old Dominic replied, "Don't worry about it. Just watch me while I fill the first box."

He filled one, and the horses took it away. One set of wagons was always located at the next outhouse, though the first wasn't empty yet. Sam said it would make up another load. They set me to loading a box, and Sam showed me how to do it without getting myself too messed up.

The Italians living here brought a bottle of whisky to us. "Have a drink."

"I don't want firewater," I said, "I'm too young to indulge." But one of them left us three bottles of beer, half of which I drank, giving the rest to Sam. "I don't want any more."

It was ten-thirty by the time I had filled the second box. Sam asked me if I was going home for lunch, and I told him that I was. "You can go," he said, "but be here when the whistle blows at one. You've filled two boxes already, and one more will be a day's work. It's easy, but the stench and filth is what you are getting paid for, not the work itself."

There were Austrians, Germans, Poles and Rumanians living there. They all offered us beer or spirits to drink. I took beer. At first it was just a little beer; two glasses or so a day—one in the forenoon and one in the afternoon. But by the middle of the second month, I was drinking four quarts of beer a day.

It was Saturday—payday—and I was to receive my first check for seventy-three dollars. I remember well that old Dominic was filling a box while Sam Millington sat in the shade. A Pole brought us a half-case of beer saying, "Here, boys, this is yours."

I went over to Sam carrying two bottles of beer, one of which I opened and handed to him. He took it and I said, "Move over and make a little room for me. I want to talk to you." He moved and I sat down. "Sam," I said, "when I started on this job you said that there was a danger here for me, a danger that could ruin my life. Is the danger you referred to in this bottle?" I held up the bottle of beer.

"Oh, then you have noticed?" he said. "That is exactly what I was referring to. When it is offered free, it is very hard to turn down."

Old Dominic came over then and took a bottle. "Let me open it for you," I said. "I hereby vow that these bottles are the last I'm opening for you and for myself. I'm swearing off alcohol so long as I'm on this job. When I go into town now, I have an urge to go into the saloon and have a glass of beer. But I have the will and desire to quit drinking. I'll drink this one bottle, but this will be my last bottle for many years." I opened the bottle and drank, saying, "I vowed to you and I'll make the same promise to my mother also. And I will hold this promise sacred: Drunkenness must not interfere with my life."

I asked them which of them would go to get the checks, and Sam said that Dominic had promised to go at noon. I asked him to bring mine as well, but my time book was at home. Sam told me to go and get it, which I did and gave it to Dominic.

"You can go," I told Dominic. "I'll fill this box, since you have to wash up and change clothes before you go to the office. I'll fill one more box after this one. Don't worry, Sam and I will take care of everything while you're gone."

Dominic went off to get the checks, and I continued working. Every Saturday I used to take a sauna, and since Dominic knew it, he would give me the opportunity to go home to change underwear and clothes. Often I was cleaned up and home before six, but now I was home again a little before four. I gave Mother my check.

"I'm going to sauna now. Give me a little money. Plus I want to tell you something," I said.

She came to me and asked what the "something" was that I wanted to tell her.

"You've asked me on two different occasions why I'm putting on weight so fast," I began. "I want to tell you why. The reasons are, first, that my work is easy. Second, I eat well. But the third reason is one that you're not aware of, Mother, and I beg your forgiveness. I promise you, Mother, that I will mend my bad habit. So listen, but don't tell anyone else.

"When I started my new job I didn't see anything wrong when they brought us beer and spirits—as much as we wanted to drink. I haven't had anything but beer, and at first only a couple of glasses a day. But now, after being on the job six weeks, I'm having three or four quarts every day. When I go to town I feel an urge to go into the saloon for a glass of beer, but today I made a vow that I shall not continue down this path. Drinking must not interfere with my life, and I promise that it won't. Mother, forgive me for having gone so far. I'll join the temperance society and urge other boys to come along."

Mother was surprised at my confession and said, "I had no inkling that anything was wrong. It's good that you can stop just like that."

"I wanted to make a promise to you, Mother," I said, "and to keep it sacred. The evils of drunkenness must never have any effect on my fortunes, nor be a problem along my life's path. I hate a drunk, yet I myself was sinking into that evil. Forgive me, as I have the will and the desire to amend my life."

Mother forgave me and said, "I hope from the heart that you will remain steadfast in your decision."

I thanked her and went to the sauna. I didn't go out that night. I began to exhort the boys to join the Good Hope Temperance Society with me. "I have no idea how much it will cost to join, but I do know that the dues are fifty cents every three months. I don't believe it will cost more than a dollar to join." I got a couple of the boys to agree, and by Sunday night there were already six of us on our way to the Finn Hall. I hadn't been there before. When we got to the entrance, there were some men sitting there. I asked them if they were Society members.

"I am," said one.

"Has the meeting started?" I asked.

"It has," he answered.

I said to him, "Go in and announce that there are six young men out here who want to make a temperance vow and join the Society—if they will have us."

He went in, and after a short time a young man came out and took down our names. He announced that they had accepted my request, and that of the others, too. So, we accompanied him inside and made our vow of temperance and became members of the Good Hope Temperance Society. I found a great deal of pleasure there and made many an acquaintance with whom I kept company.

Meetings were held every Sunday evening, and I never missed one. Soon I was known to all, and, when it came time to elect officers, they elected me recording secretary, albeit against my will. They were asking that a young, inexperienced boy demonstrate ability, fortitude and knowledge. I was helpless. Yet, I decided not to give up, but to see it through and do my duty to the Society. There were about three hundred members, and it was my duty to take note of all that was discussed and decided upon at meetings. I wasn't that proficient a writer, but I'll never forget a man named Kalle Kaski. He was a writer—a poet and newspaperman. He heard me say that if I could only write I'd be satisfied. Kalle took a look at my writing and said that it was good.

"And you have never been to school?" he exclaimed. "I've been to grammar school, high school and all, and just look at my writing. The only people capable of reading it are those who have specifically studied it, and sometimes I must ask myself what it was I meant that I wrote yesterday. As long as you can read your own writing, all is well." He read the minutes I had written and said, "You have a good hand, except when you're in too much of a hurry." Kalle gave me fortitude and enthusiasm.

I should have mentioned my mother's brother, who left Finland many years before my mother did. Isaac, Mother's brother, was married and moved to Canada as a settler in order to farm. John, her oldest brother, was somewhere in Arizona, I had heard. But a month or two after I came over from Finland, John came over one evening, greeted Mother and said that he wanted to visit with her a bit. "I'll stay here a night and travel tomorrow. Since you know my past, read this letter and you'll know as much as I do."

Mother read the letter and then asked John, "Are you going to go?"

"I've already written to her that I will come immediately."

Mother took her brother by the hand and said, "I wish you all the luck and God's blessing."

I knew the circumstances surrounding John's love for the mistress of Antila, so I drew my own conclusions from my mother's and John's conversation. As soon as I had the chance, I asked Mother if John was going to the old country. "Has the master of Antila died, and is John going to marry the mistress of Antila?"

My mother looked at me for a long time and finally said, "How do you know to ask about such matters? Did you know that Antila had died?"

"No," I replied. He had indeed died over a year ago, and I guessed right away that it was while I was at Kauhajoki with Sanna Takamaa. I was about to tell that to my mother, but caught myself in time and didn't give away my secret. Instead I said, "I hadn't heard."

"You asked about his getting married," said Mother. "What do you know of that?"

"I know that John came to America because he couldn't bear to be in Finland when the love between himself and the mistress of Antila got too hot to handle," I said. "I read your thoughts, and John's. Was I correct that the letter was from the mistress of Antila?"

Mother said, "You are, but I don't understand how you know how to talk like this of love."

"I know no other love but love for my mother," I said, "and even that I didn't really know until you left Finland. Those two years provided a good education for me in the subject of mother love. I now know what love is, and if love between a man and a woman is greater, as I have read, then John and the mistress of Antila cannot live apart and manage."

I then asked my mother to tell me what was in the letter and she said, "Well, since you know and understand so much, I'll tell you what it really said. The letter is from the mistress of Antila, and she said that John's sister Heta got his address for her so that she was able to write to him. 'I only want you to know that my man died a year ago, so I am single and free. With all my heart I hope that you will come to me if you still feel the same as you did when you left. If you don't have enough money for passage, I'll send you some immediately. Let me know right away, as I am eagerly awaiting your reply.'"

John Polvi, my mother's brother, went back to Finland and married the mistress of Antila. Their enduring love was finally consummated. I don't know if there were any children from the union.

Nothing in particular happened at my work except that I kept my promise not to have any beer. Nothing goes into a man's mouth without the permission of the man. When I was thirsty, I drank water. I said only that I was a "water-boy," and that I was for many years.

One day Sam, Dominic and I were emptying an outhouse behind Tampa Lake. Two girls were washing clothes, and they started talking about me. I heard everything. One opined, "He is a handsome young boy. If he were given a bath in this washtub and dressed in clean clothes, he'd be fit for anybody."

One of the other girls replied, "Surely that rascal would smell even then. He's of the nationality that eats food that makes their breath smell. You know, they eat that strong stuff the Finns call *kynsi loukka* (garlic), and it smells the same as that stuff he's dipping out of the pit."

The girls were having a lot of fun, and I enjoyed listening to their conversation. I had a lunch with me that day, and I could have found some shade somewhere to eat it when lunchtime came around; but it would have put me out of hearing distance of their conversation. So I climbed under the box we had just filled.

Now Mary called to Katri, "Look! Look where that pig has gone to eat his lunch." They laughed at me and went inside. I heard their happy laughter continue indoors. It seemed that they told their mother about me, too, since she came out to have a look. When Sam, Dominic and I were finished and ready to leave, I pulled the fur cap far down on my head and said, "Girls, remember to go to the outhouse often. I'll return next summer to see what has dropped in."

I walked away, but not before I saw the girls turning beet red. I didn't get far when I heard them laughing. One of them said, "Why, that rascal is a Finn!"

Time passed, and autumn came. I was on Pine Street and saw Mary come out of a store with a big load to carry home. I said in a friendly manner, "Mary, do you intend to carry all that home by yourself? My good girl, allow me to carry them for you."

She laughed and said, "I don't even know you."

"Don't know me?" I said. "Don't say such things. Is Katri at home? I should see her, too. I'll help you carry those home, and at the same time I can hear what your sister Katri has to say." I took several packages from

Mary's arms and said, "So, Mary, you don't recognize me. It could be that Katri won't recognize me either. But I believe that when I do introduce myself to you, you will remember me . . . and perhaps too well."

When we got to her house, we went in and Mary asked Katri, "Do you know this boy? He insists that we both know him."

There was a third girl there and she said, "I know you. You're the recording secretary of the temperance society."

"True enough," I said, "but these girls know me from an entirely different kind of occupation. I have another official duty, not only that of secretary of the temperance society. One day, as I was performing my official duty, Katri opined that if she could bathe me in the washtub and attire me in clean clothes, I would be fit for anybody. Do you know me yet?"

"I don't recognize you," said Katri, puzzled.

I said, "I'm the Italian boy who came and emptied your outhouse."

The girls burst out laughing, and their mother came into the room. She laughed, too, but she also chided them for failing to conduct themselves properly.

"You needn't admonish them," I told their mother, "they haven't done anything more than I had hoped they'd do. First, I wore a fur cap to attract their attention. Next, I spoke Italian, so they would think I was an Italian, and then I went to eat my lunch under the waste-box. Anybody would laugh at that. Plus I saw that you smiled broadly when you saw me. I only did it so we'd have something to laugh about. I remember that when I started to speak Finnish the girls first turned red, then white, and then got angry, calling me a rascal. I beg your forgiveness. Come to our meeting tomorrow evening and join the temperance society. There are a lot of young people there, boys as well as girls. If you don't want to join right away, I'll present you as guests. There's nothing bad there for young people. It's really a youth meeting place. I have made many acquaintances and good friends there. In times of need, a good friend is worth all the world's gold."

The third girl was already a member of the society and she said, "I promise to see that these girls come to the Finnish Hall tomorrow evening."

I started to leave but their mother said, "Well, you don't have to leave just like that—without first having coffee and telling us about yourself." So it was late when I left for home.

I made quite a few visits of this sort. I was always looking for new members for the temperance society—boys and girls. In my capacity as an official of the temperance society, I did a lot of this important work.

8

Walking in Step

B Y THE END of October all of the outhouses had been emptied. Throughout the fall the surface work force at the Calumet & Hecla mine decreased day by day. I expected Welton to lay me off, but it was December before he came to me and said that he had orders to dismiss all the summer workers. "But I hesitate to do that in your case, and I'm not sure what I should do."

"If I'm surplus labor around here, lay me off," I told him. "I'm sure I'll be able to find work. Besides, I don't like surface work in the winter. Lay me off and I'll gladly go. Tell Tomson I'm thankful to him for giving me a good-paying job that enabled me to help my parents. If it happens that I don't find work, I can always come back to see if it's possible to get back on."

He agreed to that, and the next day I went to the Hecla smithy where my father and brother worked. I walked into the office and told the boss, a Mr. Morrison, who I was. "I've been doing surface work," I said, "and I'd like a job here in the smithy, as I've been laid off."

"I can't take anybody on now," Morrison said, "but come back in May. I can give you work then."

"Good," I said. "I'll see you then." I went home, and while we were eating I told my parents the news.

"And do you plan to stay idle all winter, plus eat?" my father said.

"This is the first day that I've been idle," I said to him, "and I've given you all my earnings. Even when I got my first check, I gave every penny to Mother."

"Pay your board," my father said. "I don't want anything more."

I had reached eighteen, the age of majority, so I said, "Fine. I'll do just as you request. I'll pay my board, no more and no less, just like the others. And I'll pay for the meal I just ate." With that I got up from the table and went downstairs. My father continued his ranting, but I didn't answer. I had a great deal on my mind now and couldn't think clearly, so I didn't say anything to anyone.

One of the boarders came to me and as a friendly gesture said, "Your father hasn't done right by you."

I told him not to talk to me. "Let me resolve this matter in my own way. And don't speak badly to me about my father. I don't want to hear it. I forgive him for everything, and I'll survive this. It's no big deal." But I continued thinking about it until I went to bed, and then I couldn't sleep. I tried to figure out what I had done wrong. I had given all my earnings to my father and mother during three years in the mine. Every payday they gave me a quarter or fifty cents, and I saved even that. This past summer when I had earned more than Father, I had given them that, too. I hadn't spent over three dollars the entire time. I took ten cents each week for a sauna, plus I paid some membership dues to the temperance society.

There was only one conclusion I could reach; Father is so greedy for money that he can never get enough of it. I will try to find work immediately: But must I go back into the mines? I simply don't understand Father. He said, "Pay your board. I don't want any more than that from you." All summer I have paid it four times over. The other men paid eighteen dollars, while I brought in seventy-three dollars every month. This was my first idle day, and even so I gave Mother sixty-six dollars. I don't see any sense in what he said, so now I'll get a job, pay my board and nothing more.

I finally fell asleep, and, in the morning, when I was half-awake, my mother came to me. She knew the state I was in and tried to soothe me. But I asked her not to be concerned about me. "The world is open before me and I know that I won't starve to death. I'll get work, but I'll do just as Father wants. I'll pay my board and pocket the rest, so that when I'm not working I can still pay my board. All summer I brought home seventy-three dollars a month, but he yells at me to pay my board. Even so, I forgive Father all this because he doesn't know any better. Yesterday I gave you all my money, and by evening he was yelling at me to pay my board. He doesn't want any more than that from me, but he acts as though I owed him board."

I could tell that Mother felt bad so I said, "I don't blame you, Mother, but I assure you that I'll support myself and do what Father wants me to do. I'll pay just as much board as the other men."

She urged me to come and eat breakfast, but I said, "No, I'll come for lunch."

When the morning had passed and lunch was ready, I took a place at the table and ate. Afterwards, I put on my coat, and Mother wanted to know where I was going. "Mother," I said, "I don't know where exactly, but it's nowhere bad. I have to find a job, but I don't know where. There are many unemployed, but I'm not going to work in the mine again. I'll find a job though, even if I have to dig it from the inside of a rock. I'll earn enough to pay my board until I get work in the blacksmith shop and can draw a check there."

"If you leave, you should have a little money with you," Mother said.

"I don't want any money from you," I replied. "Money or no money, I won't be in need. I'll find a job, and then I'll have money. People say a young man is all money, and I'm exactly that."

I left on foot towards town and hadn't gone far when I met someone driving a buggy. As I tried to let them pass, the horse stopped, and I saw that it was an acquaintance of mine. He told me he was working in the Arcadia mine and needed a partner. I didn't hesitate. "You have one," I said. So I climbed up and sat next to him, and we drove off.

It was December 17, 1897. The trip was long, and we had much to discuss. The weather turned terrible, and it was late by the time we reached our destination. He put the horse away and said, "We still have to get to work, and I don't know how things will work out."

We went to the mine opening to see the captain and were met by somebody bringing up a dead man who had been caught in a dynamite blast. He was a Finn. I believe his name was Savela. The captain told us to come with him to the dryhouse. He got some clothes and a lunch for me so that we could go underground. Then we went down, and I once again found myself working in a mine.

In the morning when we came up, I told my partner I needed money to buy a postcard. He gave me one, and I wrote to Mother that I was working in a mine and not to worry about me. This was a new copper mine and wasn't very deep as yet. I remembered that I had promised myself that I wouldn't go into a mine again, but I thought that I could endure the smoke and smell for one more winter. And everything went well. I worked there until April and thought I would quit, but a major storm came up, so I decided to continue on for a while.

On April 22nd I injured my back and was forced to stay at my boarding house for a few days. On the 25th I got a ride back to Calumet. My mother noticed that I moved around with difficulty and inquired if I had hurt myself. I told her it wasn't serious. "I'm already much better, and in a week I'll be completely well. It's just a sprain."

Three days later I went back to the temperance society and got my secretary job back. Two people had occupied the position in my place while I was away. It was the first of May when I went to the boss at the blacksmith shop to inquire about the job.

The boss looked at me and said, "You're Isaac Polvi's son."

"Yes," I said.

"Where have you been all winter?"

I explained, and then said, "I hurt my back on the 22nd and came home."

"I noticed that you don't walk as well as you did in the fall," he said. "Stay home for a week or two. You must go through a physical examination for this job, and I'm afraid that right now you wouldn't pass it. When your back is well, come and I'll give you work."

I was satisfied as I didn't really want to work yet. On the 16th of May, a Saturday, I knew that I was to receive my severance pay from the mine. So I took a horse from the livery stable and drove to the Arcadia. I got in line and handed in my timebook. The paymaster said I had to go to Hancock to get it from such and such shop. I tried to argue with him but was told to get out of the way.

I walked into the office and asked for the head clerk. There were several men there. "Which one of you is he?" I demanded.

One of them spoke up. "You have to go to that store, because you owe them money."

"That's not true," I said.

"Well," he countered, "if you aren't in debt, you can get your pay there."

I told him, "I work for the company here, and I'll get my pay here."

"There must be someone with the same name," he said.

I said, "I know there isn't another name like mine in the entire country, or anywhere for that matter, and you'll pay me my wages."

He told me to have a seat, and he got on the telephone. He came back with the name Isaac N. Talvi.

"My name is Isaac N. Polvi," I said.

"Wait here," he said, "and I'll bring you your check."

"You tell them that I'll wait," I said, "but if you aren't back within the hour, they can pay me a dollar, and a dollar for every additional hour besides. And I'll get it from you if I have to sell your hide." He laughed and passed my message on to them. Soon I got my money, and I didn't say another thing to them.

When I drove into the yard at home, my Sister Hilma was there. I sent her in to fetch Akseli. I gave Akseli a little money and instructed him to take the horse to the livery and pay the charges. I went into the house and Mother told me to eat. Some boarders were getting up from the table, and they paid Mother the eighteen dollars for their board and up-keep.

"I'll pay as well," I said.

"That would be a good idea," my father said, "—now, while you still have the money."

I didn't reply to this.

While I was eating, a surface worker from Hecla whom I knew well told me that a man was leaving immediately for the old country and that he wanted to send money to his mother. "But the bank is already closed, and he can't get his money out. He's leaving this evening and needs to borrow some money until such time as I can get into the bank."

"How much does he want?" I asked Nels.

"He'd like to have a hundred dollars," he replied, "but if he got fifty, he thinks he could get fifty more from somewhere else."

I pulled a wad of money out of my pocket, took out five twenties and said, "Here, Nels, you don't need to pay it back right away. Leave your money in the bank and pay me as you see fit, a little at a time." I crammed the larger wad of money back into my pocket. Nels took the hundred dollars, thanked me and went back home. Everyone remained silent.

This house of ours was a large building divided into two residences. The other half was owned by Antti Marjamaa. He had a wife and three boys, and they lived there separated from us by only a thin wall. Antti had a hotel building in Hancock. He had gone to collect the rent a week earlier and hadn't returned.

His wife, Tiina, came to our side of the house and said, "Antti is over there drinking. Go there, Isaac, and get him home. Take a policeman to help you. I'll pay any costs. I can't find another person as reliable as you are, and I'll pay you a wage. Take the train in the morning, and bring that bum home on the evening train. Here's ten dollars so you won't need to spend your own money."

"Antti will be home tomorrow evening, I promise you that," I said.

The next morning I was in Hancock and met a policeman on the street. I asked him if he had any pressing business at the moment. He said no, and I told him about my mission. He laughed and said he had seen two men from Calumet who had been drinking there for a week.

"One of them," he said, "is a dark-complected man who stands in front of the saloon and calls in Finnish, 'Come here, all you poor and sinful, here is a man from Calumet who will buy you a drink.' I'm told that the other man pays the man doing the calling." He laughed again. "The man doing the buying is small and red-bearded. He appears to have money."

I said, "The red-bearded one is the man I must get on the evening train, if I have to hire all the town's officials to do it."

"You don't have to hire anybody," he replied. "I'll help you. You were right to explain it to me before proceeding on your own."

There were sixteen Finn saloons in Hancock. I looked for Antti but couldn't find him. I saw the policeman again and asked him for advice. "I have to find him and get him home."

"Come with me," he said. "I believe you'll find him over here."

We went into another saloon, and there was Antti. I took him home after the policeman told him that if he wouldn't obey, he'd make him.

In the latter part of May I went to work in the smithy. I worked there for sixteen years. My pay was only forty-three dollars a month, but I wasn't attached to money so I didn't care—just so long as I was healthy and earned enough for my livelihood. I was known among the Finns, including the younger generation, and was welcome everywhere.

In the evening on Memorial Day when I was twenty I went to town, as I knew that there would be a lot of people about. As I neared town I met a good friend of mine who was accompanied by two girls. I stopped them and said, "You appear to have two. What do you say I see how firmly they're attached to you."

"Fine," he said. "What doesn't stay, falls."

"Annu," I said to one of the girls, "come here. We'll walk in step— two as one."

She moved next to me and said, "Let's."

I said to the other girl, "You come, too. I promise to find you a boyfriend for the evening." And both girls went with me to town. We had traveled about a block when I saw a boy standing on the other side of the street. I called him over and said, "Here is a young man I know to be a decent and well-behaved boy." I turned to Katri and said, "Here, Konstu, is a young girl, decent and pure, and I hope that you two will learn to walk in step together and come to know one another. I'll do the same with Annu." And from that time on we were always together.

As our friendship grew the girls began to put pressure on us to rent a team of horses and drive to the lake shore. I said, "Konstu and I must discuss it first among ourselves."

"I can't make that decision," said Konstu, "it's up to Iikka."

But the girls were determined and said, "You should make up your minds whether or not you'll get the horses."

I told Konstu to take Katri home and then come back and wait for me so that we could discuss it. Konstu agreed, and we met again later. "What do you think?" I asked him.

"I like Katri very much," he answered, "and we should get the horses and take that trip to the beach. . . ." He noticed that I was laughing. "What are you laughing at?"

"Let's do it," I said, "but let's make it a trip we'll never forget. We must get some old workhorses that can't run, and a wagon that is barely holding together. If those girls will come with us, we'll know that they really like us. And if they won't come, then it'll be best if we don't keep company with them anymore."

"That's a good plan," he said. "We'll only tell the girls that we'll get the horses. The girls can decide whether we'll go or not."

It was a Sunday evening, and we saw the girls once again at the temperance society meeting. When we left for home, we told them that we had decided to hire the horses, give them a ride to the beach and otherwise make the trip so enjoyable that we'd never forget it. "You must decide when we'll make the trip; on Sunday, or a weekday, by day or by night." The girls decided that the trip should be on the following Sunday and that we should pick them up on Coleman Street with the horses.

Pekka Lahti had a livery stable on Pine Street, and he arranged the rental of horses and rigs for trips to the beach. When he rented both horses and rig, the cost was something like six or eight dollars for the day. Konstu and I went to talk to Pekka on Monday evening. Pekka was an older man, but into fun and games.

I explained to him that we wanted horses for a beach trip on Sunday. "We came to let you know in plenty of time to get them ready. They should be ready Sunday morning at seven-thirty, but I don't believe you have the horses we want," I said, "so you'll have to get them from some farmer. They must be horses that won't run, but plod along slowly. The rig must have a top in case it rains, but the rig has to be old and so worn out that it barely stays together. I don't care how big it is, just so it has room for the four of us. Remember now, it can't be sharp-looking—just barely drivable. If you have an old one, use that. We want it to attract everybody's attention."

Pekka laughed and said, "I understand. All is well. Just come ahead and I'll arrange everything just so." He laughed again. "Just like you want it."

On Sunday we went to the livery, and Pekka had the rig ready. He had torn the seats out of an old four-seater, placed a bench on each side and patched the top with an old oil-cloth. One rear wheel was from an old, heavy-duty work wagon. One front wheel was painted red, and the other, with the paint peeling off, was a smaller size.

"Good," I said.

"That's not all," said Pekka. He had made a birch-bark horn. "Blow a blast on it now and then so that people will notice you."

"Thank you, Pekka," I said. "I'll be doing the driving myself, so rest assured that these horses won't be jerked about by the reins, nor whipped and pushed. But I don't know when we'll get back."

We climbed onto the wagon and pulled out of the livery stable. A lot of people were always on Pine Street and they yelled and cheered us on as we passed through an open area near the ballpark. The girls came to greet us, and, using the expression common in the Finnish countryside to halt horses, I said, "*Truuuuuu. . . .*"

The girls saw us and tried to say something, but they couldn't. They just grabbed hold of one another and laughed and laughed. Konstu asked if they weren't coming along for a ride and they said, "We certainly are. What's good enough for you is good enough for us." They were so tickled, they could only laugh.

I blew a blast on the birch-bark horn. "That was the signal that we are about to leave on our trip," I said.

After a while they said that it was a magnificent undertaking. "We didn't expect anything like this." And they laughed all over again.

When we returned to Pine Street, I blasted away on the birch-bark horn. The crowd laughed and cheered us on. The horses moved like tortoises. Even Pekka had come out to see us. He had a bag of oats he put into the wagon. "Here boys," he said, "I don't want the horses to go hungry."

We got to the beach and unhitched the horses before going to see what food the girls had prepared. There were a good many people at the lake shore that day. Many were temperance society members, but there were many who didn't know us. It was a day never to be forgotten.

Time passed all too quickly.

When Konstu and I went to hitch the horses to the wagon, we found our rig, but it reminded us more of a hut of leaves like we used to make in Finland on Midsummer's Day. This, too, was Midsummer's Day. There were flowers all over the wagon as well. I don't know where they came from. Even the horses were decorated. Our good friends had done it, and they all came to see us leave for town. Again I tooted our departure on the birch-bark horn, and we heard cheers and well-wishes from everyone assembled. We all enjoyed the scene immensely. Our horses moved forward slowly, and everyone passed us by, yelling and laughing. They were full of fun.

It was late that evening when we got back to Pine Street. Pekka asked how things went.

The girls laughed. "This was all so splendid. We wouldn't have enjoyed it more if we had had one of your finest rigs and best horses. Everything went well for us."

I was late for my duties as secretary of the temperance society, and the question of my whereabouts came up. Somebody explained our trip to the entire society, with a little embellishment added here and there, and the result that the trip was talked about all summer. The girls didn't ask again for a buggy ride, but they didn't hold it against us either. We were good friends. Konstu, Katri, Annu and I. Always together, we knew each other's affairs.

It was the early part of August in the year 1900. At the temperance society meeting I asked if there was anyone present who wanted to become a citizen. "I've decided to take out the first papers, and if I could get a few boys to go with me, we could hire a horse and rig together to save on expenses. I have decided to stay over here, and it is best to become a citizen." Three volunteered, and so there were four of us. Some others went for their second papers.

I walked into the clerk's office and asked for him. A woman there who was the clerk's secretary asked, "What can I do for you?"

I said, "Help me to become a citizen. I came to this country in 1894 when I was fifteen years old."

She asked me many questions and said, "If you will swear that you were not yet eighteen when you came, and that you were twenty-one prior to the November elections, you'll become a citizen immediately after the district judge questions and accepts you. Is there anybody in the courthouse who knows you?"

"I think there is," I replied.

She wrote on a piece of paper and told me to go straight to the judge and place it before him. "If there isn't a vacant seat, find a place nearby to stand."

I remember I paid the clerk only three dollars. I gave the papers to the judge and found a seat nearby. When they finished with other matters the judge asked, "Is there anyone who knows this young man?" Six men stood up, but the judge said, "I need only two. You, Ospren. . . ." I looked to see who that could be and learned that it was an old Scotsman I had known for many years as David. Sakria Silvala was the other witness. They both said they knew me to be a good man and qualified to be a citizen. The judge asked me questions that were easy to answer, and so I became a citizen of the country on the thirteenth of August, 1900.

Time passed, and Katri and Konstu got married. They had their own home, and we went to see them occasionally; but they really weren't with us anymore. We had lost our long-time friends after being together evenings and every Sunday for a year and a half. And now there were only two of us—Annu and I.

My father bought the other half of the building from Antti Marjamaa. He repaired the entire twelve-room structure and set it on a stone foundation. My brother got married and came to live there for a time. I don't know why, but my father never liked me, and our relationship was never a good one. Once he asked me to leave home and live elsewhere. I never talked with him, regardless of what he said to provoke me, but this time I said, "It won't look good if I move in with the neighbors, and I won't leave home."

He listened, and, having got that much out of me, he opened up himself. It was another provocation, however, so I said, "Let's call a thirty-day truce. I'll decide what to do and then let you know." I didn't want to live anywhere else and said as much to my mother, who told me not to be concerned with what my father had said.

This had happened on my birthday, the eleventh of September. I had just turned twenty-three. Annu worked at a store and was through at eight p.m. I went to meet her but didn't have much to say. She asked what was bothering me. "There's going to be a change in my life," I told her. "I'll either leave my job and go to work elsewhere, or, if I had the money, I'd get married and establish my own home. If I had three hundred dollars, it would buy enough furniture to get by on. My wage is small—only forty-four dollars a month—but two can get along on that . . . if they're not particular about their diet, that is."

She looked at me a long time and finally asked, "Whom do you plan to marry?"

"The person with whom I've kept company these past three years," I replied.

"You haven't asked *me*," she said then.

"I know without asking. You once said that what suits me suits you. And if you suit me, then I suit you. Is the matter settled?" I asked. "I want only a yes or no answer. In three years you should have come to realize whether you would answer in the affirmative or the negative."

"The affirmative," she said, and so we made a life-long union.

We discussed it again the following evening and I said, "With the wage I get, we can't buy furniture and keep the house warm, too. We'll have to postpone the wedding."

She said, "We're talking about setting up a home for both of us, so we'll do it together, as we both have an equal need for it. Perhaps we can buy the furniture together, and then live on your earnings. Maybe the future has possibilities. Let's hope so."

"I only have a hundred-fifty dollars," I told her.

"I have the same amount," she said, "and that makes three hundred, so let's set up a joint home. Matters clear up by talking them over."

I said, "Let's think over what we've discussed, and tomorrow evening we'll continue, if necessary. Matters must not be spoiled by too much haste. We have kept company and have been good friends, but I have yet to buy you even a small gift. But now I will. Understand me, this gift is in no way an engagement, nor is it binding. You are free to do whatever you wish with it."

I gave her a fine gold watch and said, "Tomorrow evening I'll come to see you again."

The following evening we decided to order the furniture from Sears & Roebuck, because we could get it cheaper there. But then the question arose: Where should we live?

"I'll take care of that," I told her.

A few days later, I learned that one of my father's flats would be vacant in October, and I told Annu about it. "Maybe he won't rent it to us, but I'll ask anyway, and then we'll know. But he never gives me a straight answer."

It was Saturday evening before I got around to asking him. "Will the flat be vacant next month as I've heard?"

"What of it?" Father said.

I laughed and asked Mother to answer my question.

"It will be available on the fifteenth," she said. "The people are moving to the Iron Range."

"Have you rented the flat to anybody yet?"

"Not yet."

I asked how much they charged for rent, and she said seven dollars.

"Mother and Father," I asked, "will you rent this flat to me?"

"What would you do with a flat?" my father asked.

"Answer my question," I said.

"Why not rent it to him?" my mother asked. Then, turning to me, she said, "For my part, I'll say yes. You can depend on that."

I counted out seven dollars on the table and said, "I'm paying the rent from the fifteenth of next month to the fifteenth of November." Then I went out.

Time passed quickly, and it was soon October sixth. We went to the home of an acquaintance of ours and ordered our furniture. My father's flat was vacant, and he asked if I wanted any repairs done to the rooms. I told him no. And I told Mother, "If any goods are brought there for me, unlock the door for the deliverymen and lock it again after they leave."

I didn't offer any further explanation. I also asked the timekeeper at work to notify the freight company to deliver everything to that address and to leave the bill there for me. The furniture soon came, and when it was Sunday, I picked Annu up, and we went over to open the crates and put everything in order. I asked my mother to come over, and I introduced my girl to her.

"When are you planning to get married?" she asked.

"We haven't yet decided," I said.

We were at my parent's home for the rest of the day. Mother asked us to eat, but I didn't see Father. We finally got married on the twenty-ninth day of November 1902, and we began to share the good and the bad together.

Isaac and Annu Polvi, a wedding portrait, 1902.

9

Father and Son

THE BILLS were piling up by the time a son, John, was born to us in September of the following year. An acquaintance of mine who was a businessman in the city asked me how things were going with us. I said they would go really well, except that my wages were only forty-four dollars a month. "I must find work that pays more, but I don't want to go back into the mines, and I don't know where else to look."

A couple of days later this same man and another came over to visit Annu and me. They said they had a job for me and knew that I could do it well. "We'll pay you ninety dollars a month and provide you with a four-room, heated house, rent free. It's a place of business, and you would take care of the entire operation. You can hire yourself a helper; we'll pay him a reasonable wage. Don't give us your answer now; we'll return in thirty days. Tell us then.

"And now we'll tell you what the job is. We businessmen own a saloon together, but the men who run it are alcoholics. If we could get you to take over this operation, your salary would begin to increase rapidly. You have thirty days to think it over."

They got up and left the house. I sat down and thought, recalling my past. As my wife walked by, I hoped she'd make some kind of comment, but she didn't say anything. Finally I asked her, "What do you think of this?"

"I won't say anything about it," she replied. "You have to make your own decision. I'm confident that it will be the right one. You have thirty days. Think about it, and then do what you think is best."

Ten days passed, and I didn't say anything to anyone about the whole matter, although it was always on my mind. I thought about having done temperance work for so many years, urging others to join the ranks of the temperate: Should I now sell them alcoholic drinks, and for no other reason than to make more money? No, I decided. Absolutely not. I must do otherwise. So, I thought, I now have a job I like, but with my wage I cannot support a wife and child. But I had an idea: I'll go talk to the head official.

I saw him sitting in the office. I dropped the hammer from my hand and walked over to him. As he turned to see who had come in, I said, "I want to let you know that I'm married. We have one child, and my wage is forty-four dollars. When I have paid my club dues and rent, I have thirty-five dollars left for food. The question becomes: With what do we buy clothing? I haven't even been able to buy work clothes. I want a higher wage." When he didn't answer me, I said, "It would be best if you think about it."

I turned and went back to work.

A couple of hours later he came to the shop to see me. "I'll raise your wage to fifty dollars," he said.

I didn't say anything. It was as though I had heard nothing. I was thinking: I've done this work for six years. He knows where I stand—what I have to provide for, and how much food and clothing one can buy for fifty dollars.

Tomorrow is the last day of the month. Instead of coming to work, I'll go and inquire about a new job. I don't need to tell him what I'm thinking. He's not stupid. Fifty dollars a month! If he had said at least fifty-five, I would have been satisfied. This is hell. I won't run a saloon, even though it seems that this is my last day on the job. Of course, he can see that I'm not satisfied. I don't believe he expects me to be at work tomorrow.

Another three hours passed, and once again the official returned to the shop. He tugged at my sleeve to get me away from the others. He said, "I've checked your record and see that in three years you've been off work only five hours, and you've put in a lot of overtime. Your record is good; there is none better. So I'll give you fifty-five dollars a month. I expect that you'll continue to work overtime as you have up to now, so your pay should be between seventy and seventy-five dollars per month. What do you say now?"

"That sounds better," I said.

We were paid time-and-a-half for overtime, and I recall that in one month I worked forty-four days and spent almost all my time at work. Lunch was brought to us on the company, and we slept by turns on company time. No person can work night and day without resting, but we were the only ones who knew the job. Nobody else was qualified.

I remember one time I got word to come home immediately because my wife was "sick." The furnaceman with whom I worked asked what I thought it might be. "I believe she is about to give birth," I said.

"Go and see," he said, "and come back as soon as everything is fine. You'll get paid for your time away, but come back. You can't sleep at home."

We had given our cookstove to my brother-in-law when their house burned, taking away everything they had, including their clothing. We had a cookstove in the cellar but not in the kitchen. When I got home my wife said, "Get a stove, get a servant girl, get a midwife and get a doctor here." When I laughed, Annu said, "Don't laugh. Move fast!"

We had previously decided to get an iron cookstove, so I said, "Well, now, all the things you ordered will soon begin to arrive."

I hopped on my bicycle and went to a store on Pine Street. There was a woman there whom I didn't know. I said to her, "You are probably familiar with the telephone. Will you help me?" There I was in dirty clothes, hands and face covered with oil.

"What do you want me to do?" she asked.

"Look up the number of the midwife. Call her and tell her to go to my house." I gave her the address, and the midwife promised to go there right away. I also asked her to call a certain Dr. Rice, and I told him to go there, too. Then I went to the hardware store. They didn't know me there, as it was a new establishment. I went in a big hurry and said, "Take that range and set it up at this address. And build a fire in it. You'll find wood in the cellar. Then take the kettles from the stove in the basement and set water to boil in the kitchen just as soon as you can. I'll pay for all of it."

The clerk said, "I don't know you."

There was a man named Kotila there who came over and said, "No, but I do. I will pay if he doesn't do as he has promised. Just do as he tells you."

Now where would I get the girl? I went to talk to a woman I knew, and she just laughed. "I have a girl visiting here," she said, calling her.

The girl immediately agreed to come. When I got home, the midwife and doctor were already there and performing their respective functions. I waited there a short while, and then the stove and the girl arrived. The child—a son whom we called William—had been born as well. And all of this happened within the short space of three hours.

"I must go to work," I said to everyone, "and I don't know when I'll return. If all doesn't go well, let me know."

I was on that particular work stint for three solid days. Needless to say, Annu was angry, but she was well on her way to recovering physically.

"Annu," I said, "you should be happy that you have my type of man. Just think about all the things that I accomplished the other day when I got home. I produced a stove, a doctor, a midwife, a girl and a baby boy in a matter of three hours."

Annu said, "And you produced the boy, did you?"

"That's exactly right," I retorted, "I produced him, so now you must nurse him." She laughed, and so the others did, too.

By this time we were already living in a home that we had purchased. When I wasn't at work, I would sell books to my acquaintances and earn a little money that way. We didn't have the money when we found the house, and it cost fifteen hundred dollars. But an acquaintance of mine gave me the money on a five-year contract. We paid it off in that five years. Buying that house was something I had desired and had the will to do, once again confirming what I've always believed.

The basement of my house had a wooden floor that smelled rank because soapy water had seeped under it. I decided to put in a concrete floor and asked a contractor how much it would cost. He said ninety dollars. I asked another who charged seventy-five dollars, and a third wanted sixty-five. When I saw my friend Joupperi, who also worked for the mining company, he said, "That job won't cost you twenty dollars if you can buy the cement, rock and sand from the company. You take the wood floor out of the basement yourself, and I will come over some Sunday and lay the concrete for you, if you can get a few men to help me."

I got the cement from the mining company, but I had to get the rock and stamp sand through a mining company railroad official named Sairls. I went to see him about it, but he said, "You don't need any sand or rock. See a contractor; they'll do it for you. I won't give you anything."

I went back to my boss' office and explained what had happened. He asked me when I had seen Sairls, and I said, "I just came from talking to him."

He laughed and said, "Go back right now and tell him that you want that rock and the sand. Tell him I told him to give it to you. He'll give it to you all right."

When I got back to Sairls' office, he said, "You have a lot of nerve coming right back. Do you think I'll give it to you now?"

"I don't *think* you will," I said, "I *know* you will. Morisson told me to tell you to give me everything I need."

He suddenly became very polite. "Oh, oh," he said, "that's a horse of a different color."

I got what I needed, and Sairls even provided company horses to haul the load for me. I didn't have to pay for anything. I was amused to learn that a boss had a boss.

There was an incident that happened about this same time that I shouldn't fail to mention. The Calumet & Hecla Mining Company decided that there were too many dogs running around all over, and so notice was given that anybody who had a dog must buy a license for it. Any dog found without a license would be shot on sight. But the grace period for the purchase of licenses passed, and dogs were still running around without licenses. The Hecla railroad had a Finn employee—I've forgotten his name—who was known as an accurate marksman. Sairls ordered him to kill all the unlicensed dogs.

The Finn told him that he didn't want this kind of job. "All the people will curse me, at least those whose dogs I kill."

Sairls' reply was, "So why didn't they buy a license? I'm ordering you to do the job. I'm the boss, and you work for me, and I pay you. I'll even provide the rifle. And if you don't do it, I'll give you your time."

The Finn saw that he had no choice, so he just laughed and said, "Well, don't give me my time quite yet. I'll start my assigned duty tomorrow morning, but I'll use my own gun so I can be sure that every bullet goes where I aim."

Sairls had two small dogs, and our Finn thought he'd check to see if they had licenses. They didn't, so the Finn shot them both.

Sairls cursed the man and said, "You crazy Finnlander, why did you kill my dogs?"

"Why didn't they have licenses?" the man replied. "Your dogs aren't any better than any other dogs. Why haven't you bought them?"

Sairls swore again. "I don't want a man as crazy as you. You can go to hell. I won't ever forgive you for what you've done."

The marksman now walked away, but he went straight to some newspaper reporters and told them the entire story. Others were asked to write to the paper about this and state their opinions as to whether the

Finn had done wrong by shooting Sairls' dogs. The story tickled the public's fancy, and Sairls was roundly condemned in every paper. As it turned out, the Finn soon got back his original job, so the dog hunt ended right there, and no more were killed.

In 1910 a daughter, Elma, was born to us, and we now had two boys and a girl. We were successful, and I made a good living. We were never sick, but my father was ill with diabetes. During his illness, we watched him waste away from a robust two-hundred-forty pounds down to one-hundred-twenty-five. I felt sorry for him and often went to talk with him. Then in 1914 came the copper miners' strike. I joined the union, and the union gave us strikers some relief; but I decided not to take it, thinking that I would go somewhere else to find work. My sister lived in Ishpeming, so I went there; but there were many unemployed there, too, and I didn't want to go into the mines. West of Ishpeming was the American Mine. A train went there every day, so I thought I would go there to see about a job.

I told the surface boss who I was, where I was from and that I was looking for work. A Swede—he was a pleasant fellow to talk to—said he didn't have work for me. I started to walk away, but then he laughed and said, "Let me tell you about a job I can give you that pays more than the other surface workers get. I've had many men on that job, but nobody stays over three or four days."

"What's wrong with the work? Is it so hard that no one can do it?" I asked.

"There's a man there whom they don't like," he said.

"And why not?" I asked.

"Well, he has the strength of a horse and is a little peculiar," he said. "There was a murder committed here, and he was accused. They put him in prison, but he was released for lack of evidence. Everyone is afraid of him, and right now he's doing the work of two people."

"Is he getting the pay of two men?" I asked.

"No," he replied.

"In that case, let me go and help him."

You can go there first thing in the morning," he said. "We'll lend you work clothes. This is a quota job; when you haul enough coal to last until tomorrow morning, you can go home. If there are steam pipes to repair in the boiler room, you must repair them." I was familiar with this kind of work.

It was ten in the morning when he gave me the clothes. I said, "Take me to the job site," so we walked to a large coal pile from where railroad tracks led up into the boiler room. A small sheet metal car was being lowered by steel cable.

The man with the strength of a horse came over to see us. "I've brought you a helper," said the surface boss.

He took one quick glance at me, grabbed a shovel and began shoveling coal into the car.

"Give me a shovel, too," I said.

"Pete," said the boss, "you know where the shovels are kept. Go get him one."

I took Pete's shovel and started shoveling coal into the car. Pete returned with the other shovel and said to the surface boss, "Now you've finally brought me a man to do this job."

Soon the car was full. "What now?" I asked.

"Come with me," said Pete, "I'll show you." We climbed a scaffold, and he showed me how to start a small engine up there. The engine raised the car up, opened and closed it, and then lowered it down again. "I'm glad I finally got a man who can work," he said. "I've been down here six months, and I've had to fill the cars alone. The type of men he brought me, it didn't really matter whether they had a shovel or not. In a couple of hours we'll have loaded enough coal, and we can go home."

We accomplished the task quickly, and by twelve o'clock he said, "We're ready to go home, but after working together all morning, we still don't know one another. Let me introduce myself. My name is Peter Ossi. I'm French. My parents immigrated to Canada. I live here on a small piece of land with my wife and child. Now, who're you?"

I volunteered the same kind of information. He got up and shook my hand. "Are there any Finns here?" I asked him.

"I know of a family by the name of Anderson who has a boarding house," he said. "I'll take you there."

I returned the borrowed clothes, and we went to the Anderson place. Pete went in with me. I asked for a place to stay, and they obliged me. I said to Pete, "I have a place here, so I'll see you again on the job at seven tomorrow morning."

"Come outside with me a moment," he said. "I want to tell you something more about myself." We stepped out of the house, and he continued, "All the people around here know me. I haven't done anything bad to anybody, so I beg you not to listen to their lies. I'll explain what I mean, perhaps as early as tomorrow."

When I went back inside, the woman asked me if I would need lunch. "Yes," I said.

"Will you be working here?" she asked.

"I'm starting tomorrow morning."

"Where, the mine?"

"No," I replied, "I've already been to work. We're hauling coal into the boiler room. The man who brought me here is my partner."

"Do you know with whom you are working?"

"Don't say anything about it to me," I told her. "Let me get to know him myself. Now I'll just tell you who I am. It's better this way." So I went ahead and introduced myself and asked them where I could buy some work clothes.

The woman was incredulous and said, "You were at work already. Where did you get the clothes you wore?"

"They were loaned to me," I answered her.

The woman said, "I have a lot of clothes, so I don't believe you'll have to buy anything now. Tell me what you need, and I'll let you have it for small change. I've never thrown anything away. I'm a widow. My husband was killed in the mine only four months ago, and I have three small children. We have between ten and twelve men who are working both the day and night shifts. Are you on days?"

"Yes," I said, "and I won't take a lunch. I'll come here at noon, as far as I can tell now. I may be late at times, but it doesn't matter if my food is cold. I'll eat what's given to me and be satisfied."

I got my clothes, and the woman said that I didn't have to pay for them until my board came due after I received my pay. "Whatever you need, just ask me," she said. "I have underwear in all sizes which you can have for next to nothing. I've washed and mended them. I don't waste anything. I've learned that time finds a need for everything."

I had been working for eight days when a Finn came up to me and asked me how I liked my work partner. I said, "If all people were like him, this world would be a good place to live in." He didn't say anything and went away.

One day, Peter and I were working together and were almost through when a heavy rain began. Not wanting to get wet, we decided to wait for it to pass. So, we struck up a conversation.

He spoke openly about the incident for which people were condemning him. "It was at the 'Dog House'—*koira torppa* as the Finns call it—where the murder took place. I was sober, and I saw a man lying outside. I thought nothing of it, since I had often seen a man lying drunk in that very place. I went in, bought a drink and then left. The following day I was jailed and charged with murder. They kept me in prison for thirty days but couldn't prove me guilty. Yet, all the people still believe that I am. Hasn't the word come to you that I'm a murderer?"

"I had already heard that before I saw you," I said, "but I don't pay much attention to stories. I've seen and experienced enough not to believe everything I hear. The best thing for you is to not use liquor. If you hadn't gone in that place to have a drink, you would have been spared the torment of these accusations. Now, Pete, I ask you, do you believe that I'm your trusted friend? Do you trust that I want everything good to come to you all your life? All people have problems, but they are easy to overcome with a strong will and desire. Do you believe what I am telling you?"

"Yes," he said simply, "I believe."

I took him by the hand and said, "Dear friend, promise me that henceforth you will not drink and that you won't frequent places where drinking is done. Do you promise?" He made a vow, and I said to him, "If you keep your promise sacred and don't break it, in a short time you will have the good will of the people, and fortune will follow you. I'm sure your wife will be pleased with you, and you'll be much more successful. Drinking brings with it bad things and nothing good."

When the rain had passed, we went back to work. When we were through, he turned to me and said, "Now begins my new life. You have spoken the truth—nothing but the truth—and I am going to follow your advice about no more liquor. I believe everything that you have told me, and I won't break my vow."

Several days passed. The weather was hot, and the sun blazed with full intensity into our work place. We unloaded the car and lowered it down, and then we went into the boiler room and drank ice water. We went back to work, and I don't really know what happened next; but I found myself in a shed with some surface workers around me. At the same time, my partner Pete Ossi came in with the company doctor.

The doctor said, "He drank cold water, right?"

"Yes," said Ossi.

"He hasn't had any alcohol has he?" asked the doctor.

"Absolutely not. I don't believe he's ever used it."

The doctor took me by the hand and asked, "Do you have cramping in your stomach?"

"A little," I answered.

He gave me a pill and said, "The ice-cold water did it. There's no sign of sun-stroke. You'll be okay in a while."

Ossi asked the doctor if he had time to take me to the Anderson boarding house. "We have our work almost done, and I can finish it alone. First I want to be sure that he's in good hands."

"You go instead," answered the doctor. "Take my horse and buggy. I have things to do here. Drive the horse to the stable, and they'll take care of it there. Then come back and finish your work."

Ossi was as strong as a bear. He took me in his arms and put me on the seat next to him in the buggy. We drove to Anderson's, where he carried me inside and sat me on a chair. I was much better already, but I didn't want anything to eat. I just sat in the rocker. Later my boss came to inquire about my condition, and we talked for a short time.

The doctor came, too, and felt my pulse and said, "The danger is now past. You can begin moving about slowly. It was good that you had a partner who immediately carried you out of the hot sun and into the shade. He's like a bear."

My boss and the doctor both laughed. "How do you like him?" they asked.

I told them that I didn't believe there was a better man anywhere. "I haven't observed in him even the slightest fault," I said.

"He has one bad fault," said the doctor, "He's an alcoholic."

I told them that Ossi had made a temperance pledge to me. "I don't believe that he will drink again."

"It's true," said the boss. "He hasn't drunk since you came, and you're the only man he's ever liked for a partner."

Peter Ossi now came in and asked me how I was. I told him I was fine. "Why haven't you washed and changed then?" he asked. "Did you have to call the doctor again?" The doctor said no. "But you said you'd be back, and that you were very concerned about his condition," Peter said to the doctor.

The doctor said, "I was passing this way and stopped by to see him, and he's O.K. I'll see him again tomorrow. But I'm warning you, boys, don't drink ice-cold water when you're too hot." And with that my visitors left.

We worked every day, Sundays included. Time passed and Friday came. Peter said, "I don't live more than a mile from here, and I'd like you to visit my place. Tomorrow morning when you leave for work, tell them at the boarding house not to expect you back before Sunday at eleven or twelve for lunch. And don't say anything else. I've spoken of you to my wife, and she told me to bring you over to our place on Saturday. We have much to discuss, and if you agree, we can get better acquainted with each other. I can say beforehand that you won't regret it if you come, and that you'll come again."

On Saturday we finished our work around eleven and went to the Ossi home. He introduced me to his wife, and she asked if I was the Finn who had made a teetotaler out of him.

"I don't believe he was that much of a drinker," I said.

"Is that so?" said Mrs. Ossi. "He was the biggest drunk I ever knew. The man drank a quart of whiskey every thirty-six hours, and sometimes a quart wouldn't last twenty-four."

Pete walked over to the cupboard and took out a bottle. He showed it to me. "I made the temperance pledge to you. This bottle was waiting here for me, but since you showed me so clearly what evil it brought me, and nothing good, I vowed not to drink, and I will keep my promise. Let this bottle wait. It has more time than I have. I won't waste my time or money on that kind of thing."

"Pete," his wife began, "have you spoken. . . ." She stopped in mid-sentence.

"You talk," Pete told her.

They were French, but now they both began to speak fluent Finnish. I was astonished. We had always spoken English. I had been working with him for six weeks, and during that entire time I hadn't heard him speak more than two words of Finnish, namely, *koira torppa*, or "dog house."

They explained that they were born in Canada where they lived in Finnish settlements as children. "We children spoke nothing but Finnish. In school we spoke English, but as soon as we were outside we spoke Finnish again. We associated with each other at the homes of the Finnish children."

Mrs. Ossi said she had learned Finnish from the *Aapinen*, which is the name given the ABC book, right along with the other children. "And I knew how to recite the Lord's Prayer and the benediction in Finnish. But we haven't let it be known that we know Finnish."

It turned out that when Pete Ossi was a prisoner awaiting trial, his wife had gone into one of the stores to shop. "There I heard the Finns condemn Pete. When he was freed, I wanted to return to the store to see if they had changed their minds. I was sure that I would hear some comforting words, but tears came to my eyes when, on seeing me, they said, 'And to think they let that murderer go free.' I also heard them say that nobody wanted to work with that murderer. But when you came to work with him, Isaac, a Finn asked you how you liked your partner; and you simply said that if all people were like him, this world would be a good place to live in. He told me about this, and we laughed. It was a good feeling to know that there was somebody who didn't accept others' opinions but thinks for himself and reflects on the merits of the case."

I stayed until Sunday, and the entire time I was there we spoke Finnish exclusively. During my stay, I found out that the old abandoned Sampi Iron Mine was only seven miles away along the railroad tracks,

and that there were some people living there who had been there when
the mine was still operating.

"There's no work there now," said Pete, "and that entire place belongs to the few remaining families who are too old to work any more."

I inquired about who lived there. "Are they Finns?"

The Ossis didn't know for sure, but they said they thought so, because there were so many Finns in the region at the time that the Sampi
mine was worked entirely with Finnish manpower.

I told them how I would like to visit the place, because my father
came to this country and went to work in the Sampi mine with the partner
with whom he had traveled from Finland. "Then Father wrote that his
partner died in a mining accident. 'Every day men die there,' he wrote,
'so I am going to look for surface work—I don't want to get killed.' Then
about a year passed before we heard anything of him again. He wrote
to say that he had been ill with intestinal fever—which almost killed
him—but he was well again. He has said nothing about that entire year.
His letter came from Portage Entry. The Sampi Iron Mine has always
been on my mind, and I'd like to visit it since it's so near. But we won't
have time, because we have to be at work every day."

Pete said, "We can arrange to come in to work an hour early, or even
two hours early. We two strong men can do that work in no time. Plus
on Sunday they don't burn as much coal. Tomorrow is Sunday, so when
we load the bins real full and come in at five on Monday, in a couple of
hours—by seven—we'll be through. You can go then, and I'll tell the
boss that we've filled the bins and that we have somewhere to go, but
we'll be back to work Tuesday morning. Everything will be okay."

Sunday morning before work I asked the Ossis if I could tell the
Finns that they spoke Finnish. They looked at one another, and I said,
"I don't want to divulge your secret without your permission, but I'll
gladly intercede on your behalf against their opinions and let them know
what a difficult position you're in. I just want to tell them that whenever they see either of you, they pass judgement on Pete, even though
he has been cleared of all blame. I'll tell them that you both speak Finnish as well as they do, and to stop and think what they have done and
are doing."

They gave their permission, so on Sunday I finished my work in
time to have lunch at the boarding house. All the men were seated at the
dinner table and one said, "Tell us now, Isaac, about your trip. Confess
your sins. Where have you been all this time?"

I said, "Gladly. I've been at Pete Ossi's home."

"Oh, we know that. Yesterday, being payday, you were out drinking with that murderer."

I pleaded with them, "I beg you not to call him a murderer. He was under questioning for thirty days, and they didn't find any evidence against him, so he was cleared. Yet you continue to call him 'murderer.' Those two, Pete Ossi and his wife, speak Finnish as fluently as I do, and every time you see either of them, you immediately begin calling Pete a murderer. Think of what you've done . . . and continue doing. Pete could make trouble for you because of your false accusations, but he and Mrs. Ossi forgive you."

One man insisted, "You're lying. When you got your pay, you went drinking with him."

"Look at my paycheck," I replied. "Every cent is there. Now I'll pay my board and for these clothes as well. I beg to inform you that I don't drink, and that I've never had money for liquor. Pete doesn't drink anymore either. I respect these people, and when you see them, speak Finnish to them. Ask their forgiveness, because you've destroyed their peace of mind by speaking badly of them. Mrs. Ossi also speaks Finnish. I was at their home from noon on Saturday until Sunday morning. We had much to talk about, and the whole conversation was in Finnish. They were born in Canada in a Finnish settlement where they were always with the Finnish children. They even understand our religion. Ossi's wife recited the Lord's Prayer and the benediction from memory in Finnish. In God's name, stop calling him a murderer! I don't believe that he is."

Mrs. Anderson then told us that she had been in the store when Mrs. Ossi came in after Pete Ossi was freed. "Some Finns came in and began talking about how they had turned loose a murderer. I clearly saw tears in that woman's eyes. She didn't say anything or buy anything, and then she left the store. I said to somebody, 'I wonder if she understands Finnish.' I believe everything you've said, Isaac. It remains so vivid in my mind—that I suspected that she understood everything."

I got them all to think about it, and soon all the Finns knew the facts and began speaking Finnish to them and treating them differently.

On Monday morning by eight o'clock I was already walking along the tracks leading to the Sampi Iron Mine. The road climbed a hill, and I took it. I found a street with old log houses on either side fronted by thirty-foot French poplars. The houses were low and dilapidated. On some the roofs were in tact, but on others the roofs had fallen in, and a few were in the process of collapsing. I didn't see a sign of life in any of the houses, and I said to myself that this is a ghost town. But suddenly I saw a man far off in the distance. I called to him, and he stopped. I waved my hand at him and started toward him at a fast pace. He waited for me, and when I got closer, I noticed that he was an old man with a full beard.

"Are you a Finn?" I asked.

"Right you are," he replied. "My name is Anderson."

"My name is Isaac Polvi," I said.

He turned off the street and said, "Come with me, I'll show you something." He went into a place where there was a shaft opening. The earth had caved in around it, but you could see the first level below. "There," he said, "where you can see the first level . . . that is where your father was killed."

"You're mistaken," I told him. "My father is still living."

"Oh, so you are Isaac Polvi's son from the village of Kurikka. I knew him as well. Come over to my home now, and we'll soon solve a matter that my wife and I have often thought and talked about." I followed the old man to a big house made of logs hewn and fitted with dog-neck corners. When we opened the door he said, "Mari, here is Isaac Polvi's son from Kurikka. Do you remember him?"

"Why wouldn't I remember him?" she replied. "His partner, Kalle Perakorpi, was killed, and he didn't go back to work in the mine. Is he living? What do you know of him?"

"He is alive," I told them, "but he has diabetes and is slowly wasting away." I told them how Father had written us when Kalle died and said that he wasn't going back into the mine to work. He didn't want to be killed and decided instead to look for surface work. "We didn't hear from him for at least a year. Then we got a letter saying that he had been ill with intestinal fever, which almost killed him, but he was now well again and working. However, we haven't been able to get him to tell us anything about that period, like where he was when he got sick. He mailed the letter from Portage Entry."

They looked at each other for a moment, and finally Mr. Anderson said, "I don't understand how he got away from there."

"Got away from where?" I asked. "Tell me."

"Yes," Anderson said, "we'll explain everything. But, Mari, find some food for our guest, and we'll eat at the same time."

We sat at the table to eat, and the food tasted good. I had been in a hurry that morning and didn't have time to eat right. None of us said anything until Mari brought *viilia*. I asked her if they had a cow, and she said yes.

When we left the table Mr. Anderson said, "You are a welcome visitor. We were sure that your father had died long ago, but just yesterday Mari said that we'd soon hear something of Isaac Polvi. Although we didn't believe him to be alive, he has been on my mind. I didn't place any significance on having thought about another Isaac.

"Well, this is what happened. Your father went to work on the railroad that was being built between Nestoria and Duluth. Someone took the contract and began hiring the needed men. But none ever came back, and they always needed more men. A train went out to the work-site twice a week pushing ahead of it a freight car loaded with food and other necessities, and any men they were able to get. According to my figures, there should have been hundreds of men working on the railroad, but those who took the food there by train said there were no men there. Finally, the word leaked out that the men were dying of intestinal fever. The orders were that nobody was to be brought back, dead or alive, but that more men should be collected to work there. When somebody died he was carried out, but nobody knows where.

"The contractor making the roadbed for the tracks cut down hills and filled in the low spots to make a level grade. The bodies of the men made good fill. Say a man worked there three, four or five months. He wouldn't need any money there in the woods, so he hadn't been paid. Now, about three years later, holes were being dug for power poles, and they found the bones of men. When I heard that, I said, 'Well, they didn't place them all under the tracks. Some have been laid alongside.'"

Mr. Anderson continued, "Your father went there, and he surely became ill with typhoid. But I don't understand how he got away from there."

We talked on like this for a long time, and I finally tried to leave, but Anderson said, "It won't take you long to walk to the American Mine. Stay here for supper. I'll accompany you to the railroad tracks so you won't get lost. If you do get lost here in our town, there's nobody from whom to get directions."

It was late when I left, and I thought deeply about everything I had heard and seen. The Andersons had run a boarding house when this mine was in operation. The old man had shown me a large register containing the names of all the men who had stayed there, plus the names and addresses of their wives in Finland. My mother's name was there, too, and where she could be found.

I worked at the American Mine until the end of November, when I got very homesick and went home. I came to regret this move many times. Had I stayed where I was, I would have avoided much trouble. The strike in the copper country had turned vicious. Gun-hounds beat, jailed and killed strikers. Nobody's life was safe. When you went out, you didn't know whether you'd come back, or if you'd be jailed—or possibly even killed. We strikers didn't have the protection of the law.[*]

When I went home I visited my parents and met my mother outside. I told her to prepare herself to hear my discussion with Father about the period between the time he left the Sampi Iron Mine and a year later when he finally wrote home again. "He has never mentioned where he was for that year, but I have found his tracks, and we will now follow them."

Mother laughed and said, "It will soon be thirty years since that time. I don't believe you'll get him to tell you anything."

"I believe that I can," I countered, "as I know so much already."

My mother remained in the kitchen to sit and listen. My father had grown much thinner, his flesh wasted away from diabetes. He was seated on the sofa. I greeted him and told him where I had been.

"Where is the American Mine?" he asked.

"About seven miles east of the old Sampi Iron Mine," I told him. "I was there, too, and there are only two or three old couples left there. All the buildings I saw were built out of large, round pine logs. I even ate two meals in your old boarding house."

"How do you know it was my old boarding house?" he asked.

I said, "Oh, Mr. Anderson and his wife Mari still live there. They showed me a register, which contained the names of all the men who had stayed there, plus the names and addresses of their wives. I found Mother's name in there, and also that of Kalle Perakorpi, who was marked "Deceased." After he died you left to go to work on the railroad that was being built between Nestoria and Duluth. Mr. and Mrs. Anderson said they thought you died there. Tell me about that time. I won't say how I came to know so much about it. Tell me, did the men have camps there?"

"There were only canvas tents," he said, "and often when I awoke in the morning, my hair would be frozen to the wall of the tent."

"What caused all the men to get intestinal fever?"

"The water was taken from just anywhere—even from melted snow."

---

[*]Polvi's feelings were further expressed when he wrote: "At that time strikers were called 'socialists,' whereas now a person who stands up for his rights is a 'communist.' I have followed in newspapers and on the radio the news of strikes in foreign countries. It is always reported that 'communists' called the strike. The 'communists' are blacklisted, and, if in some country the people overthrow the government, the radio announces that Stalin's hand is in the game. The people of China fought for years and years for their freedom, and they finally won it. Yet, even without a single Russian and with no Russian arms, Stalin was said to be behind it. Even now the peace-loving Chinese people are being bombed and killed by American aircraft. Why? Because they won't allow themselves to be exploited anymore. They are now 'communists' because they defend themselves."

"Did men die from it?"

"Yes."

"Where were the bodies placed?"

"Don't ask."

"Did you see them being shipped out?"

"I didn't, but I don't believe that anybody else did either. At least during the winter, I believe that they were covered up in the road bed. I only know that when a man died, he was wrapped in a blanket and placed in a railroad car. Where the body went from there, nobody knew."

"Were you paid a wage?" I asked him.

"The agreement was for one dollar a day and keep, but the food was poor. In the fall it was spoiled. The living conditions were of the most miserable sort. I know that some men ran away, but I doubt if they were ever heard from again. It was a wasteland."

"Is it true that the train men had orders not to bring anybody out of there, dead or alive?" I continued.

"At least that was the way it was told."

"How long did you work there?"

He thought a moment and said, "For three or four months."

"Did you work Sundays?" I asked.

"We worked every day."

"Were there many men there?" I continued.

My father answered, "When I first got there, there were maybe sixty or seventy of us, but some became ill and then died. More men were brought in every week, but still our numbers decreased. There were only forty when I got away."

"How did you manage to get away?"

"Listen," he said, his eyes shining, "I'll tell you how. As you know, some had become ill and died of the fever. One morning I felt very sick. I couldn't get out of bed and thought: Now my turn has come. The others went to work, and I was left there to think about it. Just then I heard the train coming and remembered that the fireman on that engine spoke Finnish. I tried to rise but couldn't, so I crawled to the engine and asked the fireman to take me away from there. I told him, 'I have the intestinal fever and will die within three days, and then they'll bury me in that railroad bed. Take me with you so that I can get some help and get well.' But he said, 'We don't have permission to take anybody out.'

"I pleaded, 'Nobody will see me.'

"He turned to speak with his partner for a moment and then asked me if I had any money. I answered that I had been working there for almost four months, but we hadn't been paid anything yet. They continued to talk among themselves and then, looking around and not seeing anybody, they took me by the hand and told me to lie down on the coal-pile. 'We'll take you to Nestoria,' said the fireman. 'Then we'll buy you a ticket to Houghton. There are people there who will help you.'

"When we arrived in Nestoria, they got me on a train that soon left. I was very sick when the train pulled into Houghton. People tried to talk to me, but I couldn't understand them. Some time passed before a fisherman named Nelimarkka came by and asked me who I was. I told him and then said, 'I believe I have intestinal fever. I'll die if I don't get help. I have no money, no friends and no relations in the entire country. There's nobody I can turn to.'

"The man said, 'Hold on, you don't have to die right now. Are you able to walk?' I told him I couldn't, so he commanded me to wait and then left. He returned with a doctor, who examined me thoroughly and prescribed medication, which was then purchased for me.

"Some men came and took me to the fisherman's boat. This fisherman, Nelimarkka, explained that he was taking me to his home in Portage Entry. 'We'll take care of you. You don't have to die. I will say, though, that it will be a long time before you're well, but I promise to help you to the best of my ability.'

"As I recall, he explained that after three months I could begin to learn to walk and move about again. It was a long time before I was back to my old self. Nelimarkka even got a lawyer and forced the railroad company to pay my wages, but even at that I didn't get to keep much of it. Nelimarkka found work for me at a quarry so that I could begin making a living again."

And that was my father's story, told to me as my mother sat in the kitchen, listening attentively.

I prefer not to write any more about the strike, but I cannot leave the subject without commenting on the practice of blacklisting workers. I was among those blacklisted, and in the middle of all this I went to Hancock to see a friend of mine.

"The blacklisters don't have a clear conscience," he said. "They are afraid of evil spirits, even though they are leaders in the church."

"How do you know this?" I asked.

He said, "Last week my son and a neighbor boy went fishing. They caught a big sackful of bass, plus two pike. They were on their way home when one said, 'We should divide these fish.' My son replied, 'Let's go into the cemetery to do it; there's too much traffic here.' So they tossed the two pike into the grass near the gate and went further into the cemetery and began to divvy up their catch. 'I'll take this one for myself and give this to you.' And so on. Well, the parish clerk was taking the black-list to the company officials. As he passed by the cemetery, he heard all this and went to get the minister. 'Come quickly, evil spirits are in the cemetery dividing the souls of the people.' They arrived at the cemetery gate and heard one boy say, 'I'll take this one for myself and give that one to you.' Then the other boy asked, 'What about those two there by the gate?' The first boy answered, 'You fry one, and I'll fry the other.' That's when the minister and the clerk decided they'd heard enough. They took off at a run, leaving the blacklist undelivered."

The Good Hope Temperence Society, 1900. Isaac Polvi is sitting in the front row facing the camera, third from the right, wearing a black hat and bow tie. Annu, in a white hat and blouse, is looking over his left shoulder.

The Polvis: An Immigrant Family in Calumet, Michigan, 1900. Back row, left to right: Isaac (the author), Viktori, Hilma, Selma, and Anni. Front row, left to right: Isaac Polvi (the author's father) Helmi, Lempe, Anna Soffia (the author's mother) and Ruth (Helmi, Lempe and Ruth were born in the United States).

10

The Road
Home

B Y THIS time I already had the start of a cabin. I left my home in
Calumet to go there on the fourth of March, 1915, taking food
with me from Ewen, which is located in the western part of the
Upper Peninsula. I had no bed or mattress and only one thick quilt. The
snow was still hard, and on top of the snow was what we called in Finnish *kuoleman kouraa*, or "fist of death," the dried fiddlehead ferns that
are abundant in the area. I gathered some into sacks and slept on them.

The weather was still very cold, but spring came early that year. It
was just too bad that there was nobody with whom I could communi-
cate. I did all kinds of work, and when I had been there alone for a few
weeks, I sometimes caught myself talking to some object, such as my axe
or my shovel. My food supply was nearly depleted, but the melting
snows had left water everywhere, and I didn't feel like wading through
it to replenish my supplies, as it took a day to wade to town and back
through the woods.

Early one morning I heard a commotion outside and went out to
investigate. I found a horse there chewing dried grass. I had some oats
left over from the previous fall, so I called the horse and fed it. Naturally,

the horse liked the oats, so I grabbed a rope, fashioned it into a bridle, got on its back and rode to town. I went to Greeno's stable, and he was pleased that I had returned his horse to him. I could have used it on the return trip, as I had a great deal to carry.

I was there alone and continued to work hard. I washed and changed my underwear, and I mended my other clothes with loose stitches when they tore. I didn't shave or get a haircut and was beginning to look more like an animal of the forest than a human being.

By September I had been away from home for six months. My rubber boots were worn out, and my toes were sticking through. My clothes were in tatters, my hair was long, and my beard stuck out like the quills on a porcupine that's been attacked. Since I had injured my hand and couldn't do any more work, I decided to go home even though I was low on money. I had $1.20, but a ticket to Calumet by train cost $3.00. If I sent for money from Annu, it would take about a week, so I decided to walk from the cabin to McKeever, as it would cost only eighty cents from there to Houghton. I can certainly walk the twenty-six miles, I thought.

I took an empty fifty-pound flour sack and put in it a ten-pound chunk of dried venison, some butter in a coffee cup and a loaf of bread. Then I started to walk. I walked first to the village of Baltimore where two brothers lived who I knew were either Russians or Poles. I found one of them, and he drew me a map of Holt's logging railroad. The men were loggers and had many logging camps, but all these camps had been shut down two years earlier. I knew of the camp near Military Road, and this is where I wanted to go.

A heavy thunderstorm came up while I was traveling. When I got to the camp I saw that a forest fire had burned down the buildings, although one equipment shed was left standing. Someone had cut the hay around it with a scythe and had stored the hay in the shed. I set out to look for the way to the Military Road, but darkness, fallen trees and hay as high as my head made it impossible to find. I knew it had to be only half a mile away, but in the darkness and rain I knew I would get lost, so I decided it would be better to spend the night in the equipment shed. I opened my bag and ate heartily as the thunder rumbled, lightning flashed and the rain came down. I got soaked, but the weather was warm. I stretched out on the hay and was content.

Then I heard something moving about in the hay. I took out my water-proof matchbox to find out what my buddy in the hay looked like. I don't generally get frightened, but this time I jumped up and ran out the door, for next to me was a large snake. I considered my next move, since I surely wouldn't spend the night with a snake. I back-tracked about a mile and saw a railroad bed from which the rails and ties had been removed. I knew it led across Military Road, so I took it and began walking. Long, thick poles had been hewed and then put down along the railroad bed. On these poles ties had been laid. These were good for walking on in the dark, with occasional flashes of lightning showing the way. I moved slowly and often had to wait for a lightning flash. At one point, a pole on which I was walking seemed to sway unnaturally, so I stopped and waited for the lightning. When it flashed, I saw that I stood on the end of a timber overhanging a deep ravine. To my left was a small lake, and there was nothing ahead on which I could walk. I backed up and got on solid ground and then crossed over to the other side where I found the timbers again. I forged ahead and was soon on the Military Road.

Military Road was a very old army road. It was quite straight but in bad condition. I started walking toward the Ontonagon River. The rain and lightning had stopped. It was very dark indeed. Suddenly, directly ahead of me against the backdrop of the sky, I saw something that looked like a tall man. In the language of the land, and very politely, I said, "Good evening." When I received no answer, I said, "Out of my way!" It moved aside, and a bell tinkled as it did so. I realized then that it was a horse, so I continued on to the river.

Coyotes howled all around me, and so I had a match ready to strike if they got too close. But a coyote won't show itself if you are moving. One time many years later, I was in the woods during a harsh winter. I heard coyotes nearby. I remembered what I'd been told, so I stopped walking. I stood there in my tracks while the coyotes ran around me in a circle, slowly making the ring smaller by degrees. There were eight of them, and they were very hungry and excited. I shot one, and they all disappeared.

Now I waded across the river. Deer were blowing on the other side. When I got to the railroad, I paused. It was six miles to McKeever but only one mile to Rockland. I was already tired from having walked about twenty miles, so I decided to walk to Rockland. If I was right about ticket prices, that seven miles from Rockland to McKeever shouldn't cost much. I continued walking to the cut through the mountain where the railroad turned. I saw a fire ahead. I knew that there wasn't a house there. When I got closer, I saw four men gathered around a bonfire.

They called to me to stop. "Who are you?"

"A man," I answered, "who are you?"

They answered, "We are four tramps, but who the hell are you?"

I walked toward them and said that I wasn't any better than they.

"I'm just another tramp, I guess." When they saw me clearly, they laughed and then asked me what I had in the sack. I told them.

"Give it here," one said. "Do you have any tobacco?"

"A five-cent package of Peerless," I answered.

And again, "Give it to me."

"Here it is," I said, handing it over.

"Do you have any more?"

"Only a dollar-twenty."

"Let's have it."

"O.K.," I said, "but first I want to tell you how badly I need it." So I quickly explained the purpose of my trip.

Still, he said, "Give it here."

I extended my hand toward him, but one of the other men grabbed this one's arm and said, "This cannot happen. He has given us his food and tobacco. He needs the money. He'd give us his coat to keep the money. This kind of treatment will bring shame on all tramps; besides, there would be only thirty cents for each of us."

Another tramp agreed with this man. "It can't happen," he said.

The fourth man said, "Just put your money back into your pocket. You can keep your money. Ah, but our brother is soaked through to the skin."

So they prepared a seat for me and took my coat and set it out to dry by the fire. I opened my bag and pulled out the chunk of dried meat.

One man said, "Look, how beautiful!" He cut a piece, tasted it and said, "Boys, we have never had food this good." Then to me he said, "You eat some, too."

"You go ahead," I answered, "I've already eaten." As they ate, they complimented me on my lunch, and I inquired about the train that came through from Ontonagon to McKeever.

"The depot in Rockland is still open," said one, "and they lock it up only after the train leaves for Ontonagon. Go to the depot to find out, and then come back here." So I left.

When I got to the station nobody was around, though the depot was open and electric lights shone. There were notices all over the walls: "No Smoking," "Don't Spit on the Floor," "Don't Use Profane Language." But there was one sign that caught my eye: "When This Room Is Open, It Is Open To All." Saying to myself, the room is open to me, too, I sat down.

Just then an automobile drove up to the other side of the depot, and four young men came in. One walked up to the ticket window and rapped on it sharply. It was opened.

Another of the youths came over to me and said, "Who the hell are you? Get out!"

"By what authority do you order me out?" I said.

A woman who came in just then said, "It would be best if you left."

"Listen, my good woman," I said, "you are an employee of the railroad, and it is your responsibility to see that the rules are adhered to. This man just broke the rules."

"We'll put you out of here," the man said.

I got up and crossed the room, quickly closing the distance between myself and the other men. I caught a glimpse of my reflection in a mirror and was convinced that none of them would lay a hand on me. "Listen to me," I said, "I've met your kind before, and I don't fear you. If you so much as touch me, I'll defend myself in my own way. If something happens to you it will not be my fault. Later, when I change out of this uniform and get into another, I'm certain that my voice will be heard further than yours." I sat back down. It was quiet for a moment, and nobody said a word. I heard somebody come down the stairs from the second floor. The woman slammed the ticket window shut. The four young men went outside, and the train pulled into the station.

A man came down and turned off one light and said to me, "We are now closing the depot."

"What time will the train to McKeever be in?" I asked.

"At four forty-five in the morning," he replied.

I went out and the four men were there, but they went away as soon as they saw me. They thought I got on the train, but I started walking back toward the tramps. It occurred to me, though, that the tramps hadn't seen my watch yet, and if they did see it, I'd lose that, too. So I decided not to go back to them and went instead to the roadside and lay under a tree. It was midnight. I was tired, so I slept a little; but before long I woke up cold. I found some dried grass and brush and made a small fire to warm myself.

At three-thirty I started walking again, going past the depot and getting on the train. I was charged forty cents for the seven-mile trip, which would leave me six cents short for a ticket from McKeever to Houghton. But I thought I could get around that. When the conductor came to ask for my ticket, I took out my eighty cents and said, "I'm six cents short of what I need. I can't ask you to trust me for it, but I'll give you my watch to hold if you'll give me a ticket to Houghton. I'll redeem my watch later."

The conductor saw the Odd Fellows emblem on my watch fob and made the lodge's sign of recognition with his hands, which I answered.

He asked which lodge I was with and where, and I said it was the Hecla Lodge in Calumet, Michigan.

"Where in the world are you coming from?" he asked.

He stopped to chat with me for a while, and I told of being in the woods for six months; and that now I was on my way home to Calumet where I lived with my wife and three children. He asked if I had street-car fare, and I said no; but that I had friends in Hancock and could get what I needed there. I told him of my trip, and people on the train stared at us as we laughed about it. He wouldn't take my watch, and I promised to pay in Houghton.

After arriving in Houghton, I walked across to the Hancock side of those twin towns and went to Mrs. Juntunen's house. I knocked on the door and was invited in.

Mrs. Juntunen looked up and said, "Be seated. What does the visitor want?"

"A hot cup of coffee and a quarter," I replied.

"We get many visitors like this these days," she said. Her daughter Manda stuck her head in the room and said, "Mother, look closely. Don't you know him?" And she laughed.

Mrs. Juntunen looked me over from head to toe and then said, "I've never seen him before." Manda laughed and asked if she didn't recognize Isaac Polvi. "Well, yes . . . so it is! I recognized the voice, but I didn't think it could be him."

I told about being in the woods alone for six months and now being on my way home. She gave me a cup of coffee and offered me food, but I said, "Give me another cup of coffee and the twenty-five cents so that I can get home."

"Oh, so you were serious about that quarter," she said. "You can certainly have it."

I left by streetcar and saw some acquaintances, but I didn't bother them. When I arrived home, I knocked loudly on the door and pushed it open. My youngest son saw me when I stepped inside, and the boy ran out past me and called into the cellar, "Mother, a tramp just went into the bedroom. Go look!"

I was standing there when Annu came in. "You rascal," she said, "why didn't you clean up a little? I didn't expect to see you looking like this." We had the upstairs rented out to a fellow named August, and she now called to him to bring a pair of scissors and a razor. "Come down and cut the hair of my visitor while I find him some clean clothes."

I was happy to be home again with my loved ones, but it wasn't long before I went to Detroit. I arrived in that city one evening and told some of my friends that I intended to ask for work the next morning at a factory where they made automobile tires. When I got to the factory gates there were hundreds of job-seekers. I thought to myself, there goes another wasted dream of employment. Nevertheless, I stopped to watch.

Soon the employment officer came around and asked if there were any carpenters. "I need one."

"I'm a carpenter," said an old man.

The agent looked at him and said, "You're too old."

The man replied, "I'm sixty, but may God be my judge, if I remain healthy, I'll be good for another sixty years."

"Go inside," he said. The employment officer had a slip of paper in his hand. He looked at it and asked, "Is there a man here named Isaac N. Polvi?"

I was far back in the crowd and thought I had heard wrong. Near him stood another man who said, "Spell out the surname. Who knows, we may be pronouncing it incorrectly."

He spelled it out and I yelled, "Hey, that's my name—Polvi."

When I got up to him he asked, "Are you from the Upper Peninsula?"

"Yes," I said.

"What kind of work have you done there?"

"I worked for sixteen years in a blacksmith shop," I told him.

The man next to him said, "This is the man we're looking for. Go inside."

I passed a thorough physical examination and was shown how to get to my work place and out again. The factory was on three shifts. My shift started at ten-thirty in the evening, and I was through at six-thirty in the morning. The pay was fifty cents an hour.

I didn't understand how all this had come about. I knew only that it must have been the work of some friend of mine. I thought I'd walk around a bit, and just then I heard a familiar voice calling my name. I turned around and saw an old friend of mine from Calumet, Jacob Lustic, whom I had known for twenty years.

"I see you got work," he said. "In the evening when I left for work, I heard that you were coming here. I told my boss about you, and he said he'd hire a man like you immediately. He gave your name to the employment officer. You weren't yet there when I came through, so I went away for a while and saw you just now." Needless to say, I thanked him for his help.

Room and board was six dollars per week at that time, and I had many other needs for money. In the morning I went right to bed and slept until one or two o'clock in the afternoon. Then I often walked the streets. One day, a car stopped, and a man called to me. "Come here, I want to talk to you." He said he needed help in his moving business. They had trucks but were short of men. "If you have the time, come out and help us; we'll pay you seventy-five cents an hour."

"I have the time every day," I said, "from two until evening."

So I worked three hours for him that day and earned my tobacco money. When I was through, he paid me and asked me where I worked, which I explained. He told me that he needed help quite often, and he asked if he could pick me up again. I agreed, and he took my name, address and the times I'd be available after two p.m. He said he'd come to get me for work, then bring me back; he wanted me after two-thirty every day except Sunday. "If I'm not here to get you, then I don't need you. Now, jump in the car, and I'll take you home."

I earned tens of dollars from him, and this was basically what my stay in Detroit was like. I was there about nine months that time, and I had been there before for maybe six months. But I didn't much like it there. When it was spring, I thought it would be a good time to go build on my own nest again. I went back home, and, after a few days, went to my home in the woods.

In the interim, a neighbor had moved in. He had already been building a house at the time that I bought the land, but his family lived in Ewen, and he worked at the sawmill. My cabin wasn't in any condition to live in. The floor was rough lumber, and the wind blew in through cracks in the walls. None of the work that had to be done was completed. The efforts of one man didn't go far.

One evening I stretched out on the sacks of ferns. I thought about the homesickness I had suffered my last time at the cabin. I slept a little, and in the morning my mind was clear. I had made a decision.

I had breakfast early and went over to talk to my new neighbor. I said, "You have horses, so will you haul my furniture and my four cows here from the depot in Ewen? I've decided that it would be better to move here with my family, and I'm going to get them right now. I don't know how soon I can get a railroad car, but if I get one right away, I'll be here in a week." He agreed to help. So I left for Calumet and got home the same evening.

We came to the cabin in 1917, arriving, I believe, on May 23rd. I had a cow barn, but it had neither windows nor doors. There was a lot of work to be done, and I used to say, "It's great that I have plenty of work. Now I don't need to beg for a job from anybody."

Sometimes it seemed impossible, but my wife and I saw the humor in all our adversities. When the family first moved into the cabin, I remember our youngest children cried, "Father, Mother, let's go home from here."

But I told them, "Children, this is now our home, and we will make it so good that we won't ever want to leave it. And if we do sometimes have to leave it, we will want to hurry back because there'll never be a better place than this home."

I recall one time when we were picking berries in the fall. There were a lot of raspberries that year. My little daughter went alone to pick some, but soon she came running back crying. "There were a lot of berries on a bush," she said, "and I heard somebody on the other side of it. So I moved the branches aside and saw a bear eating berries. The bear looked at me, and I looked at the bear. The bear left, and I left, too."

I reassured her. "You don't need to fear a bear, except when she has cubs. Then run from her. When she doesn't have cubs, and there are berries in the woods, she's afraid of you. It's just an accident when you see one at all."

"Yes," she said, "that's true. It was afraid, and it left so fast that the hill shook."

"I feel sorry for the bear," I said, "it was so badly frightened, poor thing."

Elma agreed. "Yes, it was frightened. It left first."

That same fall, on November fourteenth, 1917, my father died of sugar diabetes. Years had passed, and then my mother stayed with us during one entire summer. I had done my day's work and saw my mother sitting alone some distance from the house. I went to sit next to her but didn't say anything.

My mother said, "What now?"

I said to her, "Mother, you are keeping something from me, and whenever I ask you about it, you evade the question, and it is left unanswered."

"Ask the question now," she said, "I'll answer any question you ask."

"Good," I said. "Am I your son?"

She was surprised. "How can you ask a question like that? Certainly I am your mother."

"I'm a little bit suspicious," I said, "as I am the smallest of all, smaller even than my three sisters. And I am darker than they are. Furthermore, whenever I've asked you where I was born, you have left my question unanswered. I remember well when my sister Anni was born."

She stopped me and said, "Why do you say things that are untrue? Anni is two-and-a-half years younger than you are. You can't possibly remember that."

"But I do, Mother," I said, "and I can remember further back than that even. Listen to me now. Try to remember, and think about what I am saying. I remember when you weaned me from your breast. You smeared tar on the nipple, but that didn't bother me. So you fixed up a black horn that was somewhat flat, and you put milk into it. It had a lid that you closed before you gave it to me to suck on. Where in the world did you get it? Was it the same one that was used later as a shepherd's horn? I have never seen one like it since. Where did you get it?"

My mother took my hand in both of hers and said, "Now I believe every word that you are saying. You've just proved to me that you do indeed remember. I can't doubt you now, yet it seems impossible. You weren't but two years old. Russian pack peddlers brought that horn from Karelia."

"Was it the same horn that the herdboys had?" I asked.

"Yes," she answered, "your father later made a shepherd's horn out of it."

"Well, Mother, I remember that far back, but however hard I try, I can't recollect where I first saw the light of day. I don't have the power to remember where I was born. Why don't you want to tell me?"

She said somberly, "We promised each other that we wouldn't tell you, and that we wouldn't recall it for anybody. But your father is dead now, so I'll tell you. This is what happened."

We had gotten up and were standing, but now we sat down again.

She began by asking me, "Do you remember those burned-over fields on the Polvi bog? Your father made more fields and dug a deep ditch through the bog. It was far enough from the house that he had to carry a lunch. I wanted to go there to see it, since I hadn't been there before. The weather was quite warm, and I dressed accordingly, wearing hardly any clothes. When we came to the bog, your father made a seat from the dry hummocks in the ditch and said, 'You sit there and watch while I make the ditch.'

"I sat there for a while and then said to him that I didn't feel well. Since the wind was blowing quite strongly up on the hummock, he told me to come down to the bottom of the ditch where I'd be sheltered. And he then arranged a spot for me. It was easy getting down. In fact it was almost like going down a stairway. But the minute I got down there, you were born."

She cried then, and I said, "Mother, why do you cry about that now? I turned out to be a strong and healthy man."

"Yes," she replied, "but I haven't told you all yet. Your father had on clothing of coarse cloth, and I hardly had anything on. Nothing in which to wrap a newborn baby. We tried to clean you with bog-moss. The distance home was about three or four miles, and I carried you in the hem of my skirt as we traveled slowly along. Then a frightful thunderstorm came up, and it rained by the skyfull. Lightning flashed and thunder rolled. We were afraid that you would drown in the water that ran off me and into my skirt hem . . . every so often we'd check . . . I'll never forget it."

I said to Mother, "Could that have anything to do with the fact that I don't fear thunder? The bigger the thunderstorm, the better I like and enjoy it."

"The same question has always been on my mind," she said. "When I've seen how you've always been free of fear, I've always admired your bravery."

My mother died at age seventy-three and my father at age sixty-four. May they rest in peace.

Isaac and Annu Polvi on their farm, 1948.

Epilogue

W E HAD A herd of cattle, sixteen of which were milch cows. I was good to them and treated them well, as I knew that if you treat an animal well, it will treat its keeper in kind. I had pasture land, and if the wind blew in the right direction and they heard my voice, I had only to call, and here they came. The pasture land was about two hundred twenty-five acres, and when the wind was from the wrong direction, I had to go out there and call them. This had to be done morning and night.

One evening, there was an east wind and I said, "The cows have gone as far east as possible and can't hear my voice." I had a young dog, and it came with me as I walked at least a mile before the cows heard my voice. The cows went past me, and I walked behind them. Ahead was a small ridge. Suddenly the cows turned and came charging back toward me. I was afraid I'd be trampled into the ground, and so I flailed with my staff until they turned northward. At the same time, I noticed that my dog had tracked something to the ridge, but it came back to me whining for protection. Again I swung the staff and told it to go, and it, too, went northward after the cows. I said, "Let me also see what's behind that hill."

When I got to the top of the ridge, I saw a large black bear accompanied by three small cubs. She got up on her hind feet. Then I turned northward, too, going as fast as I could, for I knew that this was not a good time to be messing with that old lady.

I have a vivid recollection of the morning of June 6th, 1932. My wise old dog and I had to get the cows, because the wind was from the east and it had just rained. Suddenly, I heard the dog give a startled bark. I knew that it had discovered something it wanted me to see. I went to look, and there was a newborn fawn lying in a puddle of water. It was shivering, so I moved it to a dryer place. I told the dog not to harm it. "Let it be," I said.

As I started to walk away, my hand went into my trouser pocket and came out with a small ring that had been on a watch chain, and which I had carried around with me for a long time. It was a snap-ring of some kind that could be opened and closed. I turned and put the ring on the ear of the newborn fawn. A piece of red wool yarn was ravelling from my sock, so I removed it and tied it to the ring, leaving it there. That same evening I went back to check on it and found the fawn with its mother. The doe ran, but the fawn, by now able to gain its feet, did not leave. I saw them often after that, and even the doe didn't much fear the dog and me.

Time passed, and it was hunting season. There were many deer hunters in the woods, having gone out early. But I wasn't able to go, as I had too much work to do with my cattle. I went out a few times at midday but thought I'd let others hunt now, and I'd hunt later when the hunters had their bucks and had left for home.

When I finally had time to hunt, I took my gun and went into the woods about a mile-and-a-half east. The snow had been melting but had frozen overnight, which made poor hunting snow. It was noisy underfoot, and my steps could be heard far away. I knew I wouldn't see a deer, so I thought I might just as well head home.

But at that moment I came upon the tracks of a wounded deer. They were several days old, and nobody had followed them. The tracks, moreover, went north, and I'd never seen that a wounded deer would head north. They always went south. There were big forests there, and a river where they threw their pursuers off the track. So why did this one head north?

I examined the tracks, but the thaw had enlarged them to the extent that I couldn't really determine whether the deer was a buck or a doe. It also appeared to be headed toward my house. I wanted to know what the deer had in mind when it headed north, so I followed the tracks. It had been badly wounded. I could see where it had dragged itself along with its front feet, and I was amazed to find that it hadn't stopped to rest, even though nobody was chasing it. It maintained a heading of due north in spite of having encountered numerous obstacles. My curiosity increased.

I went on following its tracks and eventually arrived at the far side of our cow pasture, where the deer had dragged itself under the fence and gone inside, continuing on. Finally I saw where it lay dead. It was the summer fawn I had found in the puddle of water. And then I realized that I was at the very spot where the dog and I had found it. I thought of the gold earring with the strand of red wool yarn and bent down and turned its head. There was the ring, but the yarn was gone.

I said, "Now I understand why you tried to get here. Here you could be in peace. Here you didn't need to fear anything. Even the dog didn't harass you at this place. Here is where you were born, where you first saw the light of day, and this is the playground of your childhood. Because of the freedom you had here, and for the joy of your youth, you wanted to come here to die."

I can't put my thoughts into words, but I can only say that I wouldn't have shot a deer now even if I had seen one before me. I went home, put up my gun and said, "It is very wrong to shoot thinking deer." And I didn't go deer hunting again that year.

I shall bring my narrative to a close now. My hand grows tired.

Isaac N. Polvi
Ewen, Michigan